Centerville Library
Washington-Centerville Public Library
Centerville, Ohio

DISCARD

W9-AFT-885

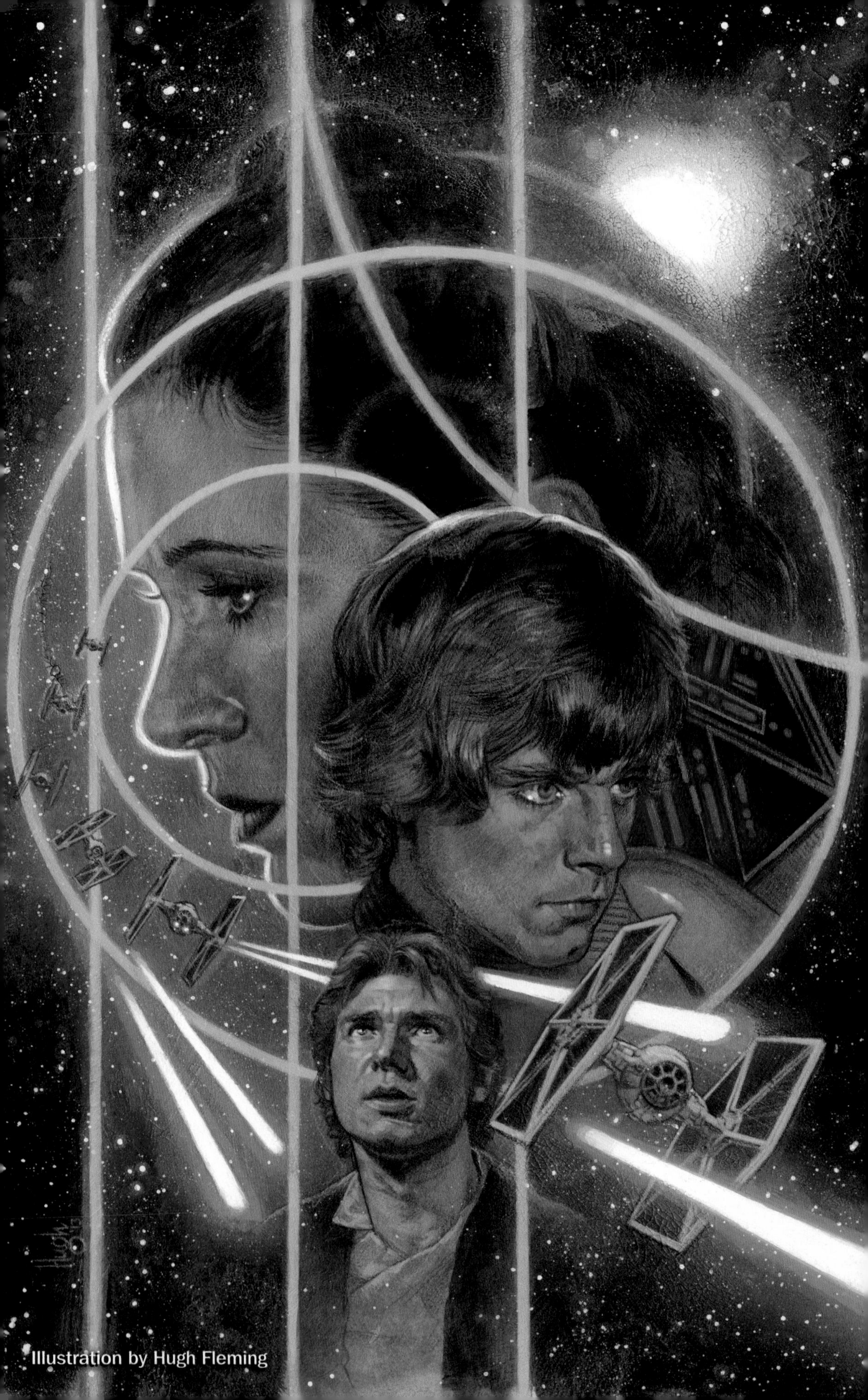

Illustration by Hugh Fleming

THE REBELLION

FROM THE BATTLE OF YAVIN TO FIVE YEARS AFTER

Open resistance begins to spread across the galaxy in protest of the Empire's tyranny. Rebel groups unite, and the Galactic Civil War begins. This era starts with the Rebel victory that secured the Death Star plans, and ends a year after the death of the Emperor high over the forest moon of Endor. This is the era in which the events in *A New Hope*, *The Empire Strikes Back*, and *Return of the Jedi* take place.

The events in this story take place shortly after the events in *Star Wars: Episode IV—A New Hope*.

STAR WARS

VOLUME TWO | FROM THE RUINS OF ALDERAAN

Script	Pencils, pages 7–72	Inks, pages 7–72	Art, pages 73–138
BRIAN WOOD	**RYAN KELLY**	**DAN PARSONS**	**CARLOS D'ANDA**

Colors	Lettering
GABE ELTAEB	**MICHAEL HEISLER**

Front Cover Art
HUGH FLEMING

President and Publisher
MIKE RICHARDSON

Collection Designer
JIMMY PRESLER

Editor
RANDY STRADLEY

Assistant Editor
FREDDYE LINS

NEIL HANKERSON . . . . Executive Vice President
TOM WEDDLE . . . . Chief Financial Officer
RANDY STRADLEY . . . . Vice President of Publishing
MICHAEL MARTENS . . . . Vice President of Book Trade Sales
ANITA NELSON . . . . Vice President of Business Affairs
SCOTT ALLIE . . . . Editor in Chief
MATT PARKINSON . . . . Vice President of Marketing
DAVID SCROGGY . . . . Vice President of Product Development
DALE LaFOUNTAIN . . . . Vice President of Information Technology
DARLENE VOGEL . . . . Senior Director of Print, Design, and Production
KEN LIZZI . . . . General Counsel
DAVEY ESTRADA . . . . Editorial Director
CHRIS WARNER . . . . Senior Books Editor
DIANA SCHUTZ . . . . Executive Editor
CARY GRAZZINI . . . . Director of Print and Development
LIA RIBACCHI . . . . Art Director
CARA NIECE . . . . Director of Scheduling
TIM WIESCH . . . . Director of International Licensing
MARK BERNARDI . . . . Director of Digital Publishing

Special thanks to Jennifer Heddle, Leland Chee, Troy Alders, Carol Roeder, Jann Moorhead, and David Anderman at Lucas Licensing.

STAR WARS® VOLUME 2: FROM THE RUINS OF ALDERAAN
Star Wars © 2013, 2014 Lucasfilm Ltd. & ™. All rights reserved. Used under authorization. Text and illustrations for Star Wars are © 2013, 2014 Lucasfilm Ltd. Dark Horse Books® and the Dark Horse logo are registered trademarks of Dark Horse Comics, Inc. All rights reserved. No portion of this publication may be reproduced or transmitted, in any form or by any means, without the express written permission of Dark Horse Comics, Inc. Names, characters, places, and incidents featured in this publication either are the product of the author's imagination or are used fictitiously. Any resemblance to actual persons (living or dead), events, institutions, or locales, without satiric intent, is coincidental.

This volume collects issues #7–#12 of the Dark Horse comic-book series Star Wars.

Published by Dark Horse Books
A division of Dark Horse Comics, Inc.
10956 SE Main Street
Milwaukie, OR 97222

DarkHorse.com StarWars.com

International Licensing: (503) 905-2377
To find a comics shop in your area, call the Comic Shop Locator Service toll-free at 1-888-266-4226

First edition: April 2014
ISBN 978-1-61655-311-1

10 9 8 7 6 5 4 3 2 1
Printed in China

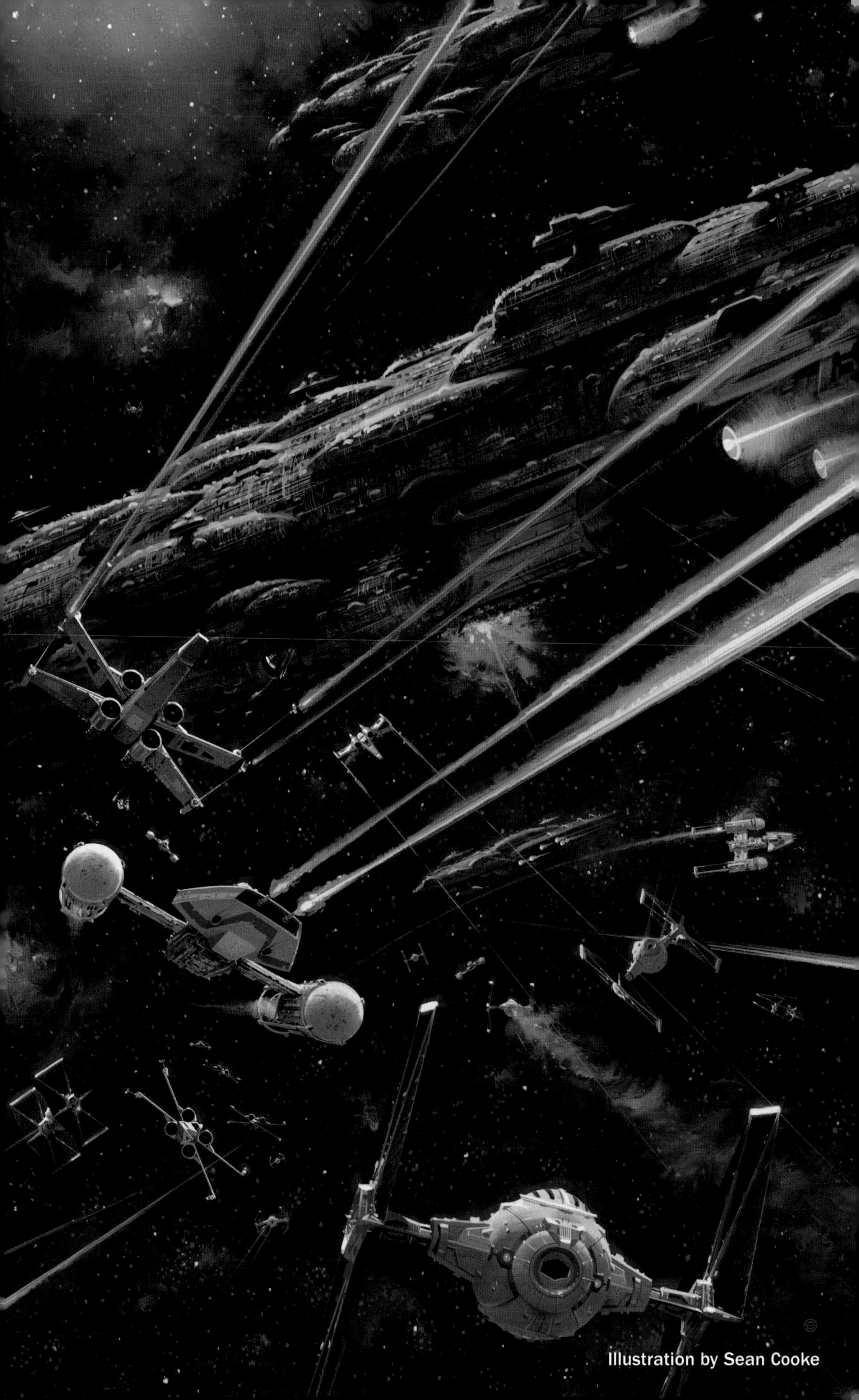
Illustration by Sean Cooke

FROM THE RUINS OF ALDERAAN

Having been ambushed by Imperial forces, Princess Leia and her companions were rescued by the timely arrival of Luke Skywalker and fellow X-wing pilot Prithi—after Luke was alerted to their plight by the ghost of Obi-Wan Kenobi. Even still, Leia barely escaped with her life.

On Coruscant, Han Solo and Chewbacca are one step ahead of the Empire and their bounty hunters Boba Fett and Bossk, having found help from an unexpected quarter.

Meanwhile, in his efforts to return to the Emperor's good graces, Darth Vader has enlisted the aid of fellow Force sensitive Birra Seah, putting her in charge of aspects of the construction of the second Death Star and promoting her to the rank of acting Moff . . .

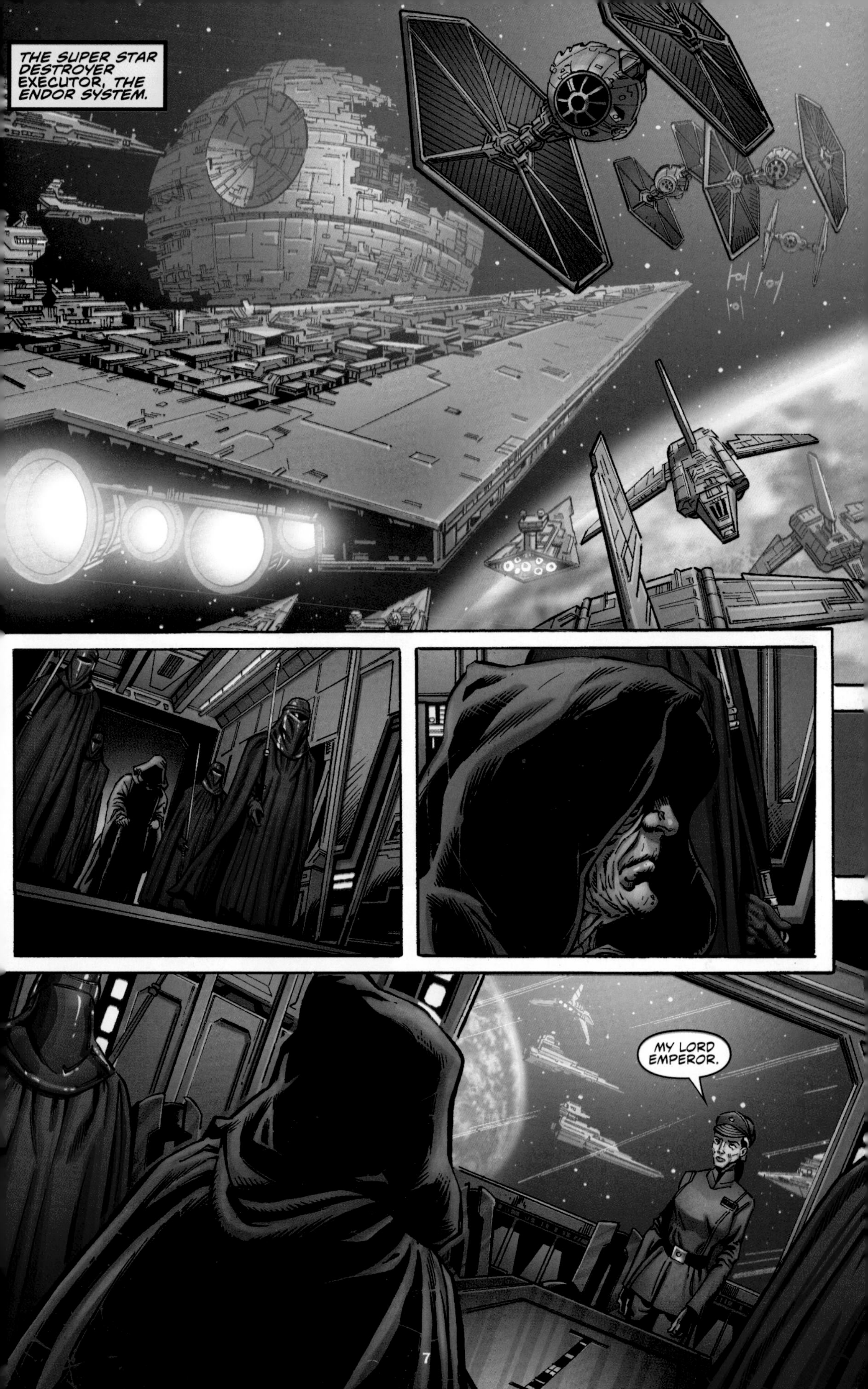
THE SUPER STAR DESTROYER EXECUTOR, THE ENDOR SYSTEM.
MY LORD EMPEROR.

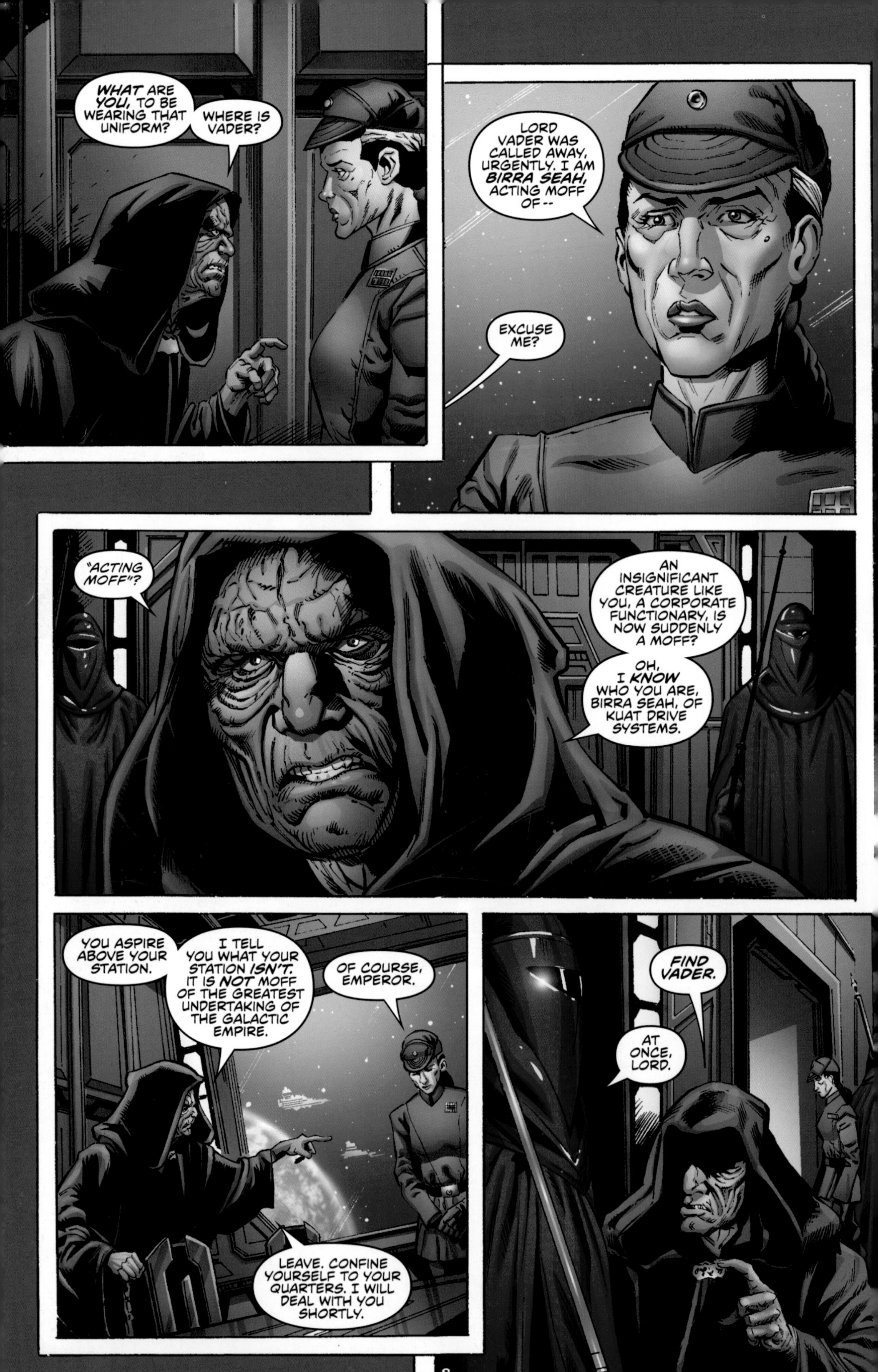

WHAT ARE YOU, TO BE WEARING THAT UNIFORM?
WHERE IS VADER?
LORD VADER WAS CALLED AWAY, URGENTLY. I AM BIRRA SEAH, ACTING MOFF OF --
EXCUSE ME?
"ACTING MOFF"?
AN INSIGNIFICANT CREATURE LIKE YOU, A CORPORATE FUNCTIONARY, IS NOW SUDDENLY A MOFF?
OH, I KNOW WHO YOU ARE, BIRRA SEAH, OF KUAT DRIVE SYSTEMS.
YOU ASPIRE ABOVE YOUR STATION.
I TELL YOU WHAT YOUR STATION ISN'T. IT IS NOT MOFF OF THE GREATEST UNDERTAKING OF THE GALACTIC EMPIRE.
OF COURSE, EMPEROR.
LEAVE. CONFINE YOURSELF TO YOUR QUARTERS. I WILL DEAL WITH YOU SHORTLY.
FIND VADER.
AT ONCE, LORD.

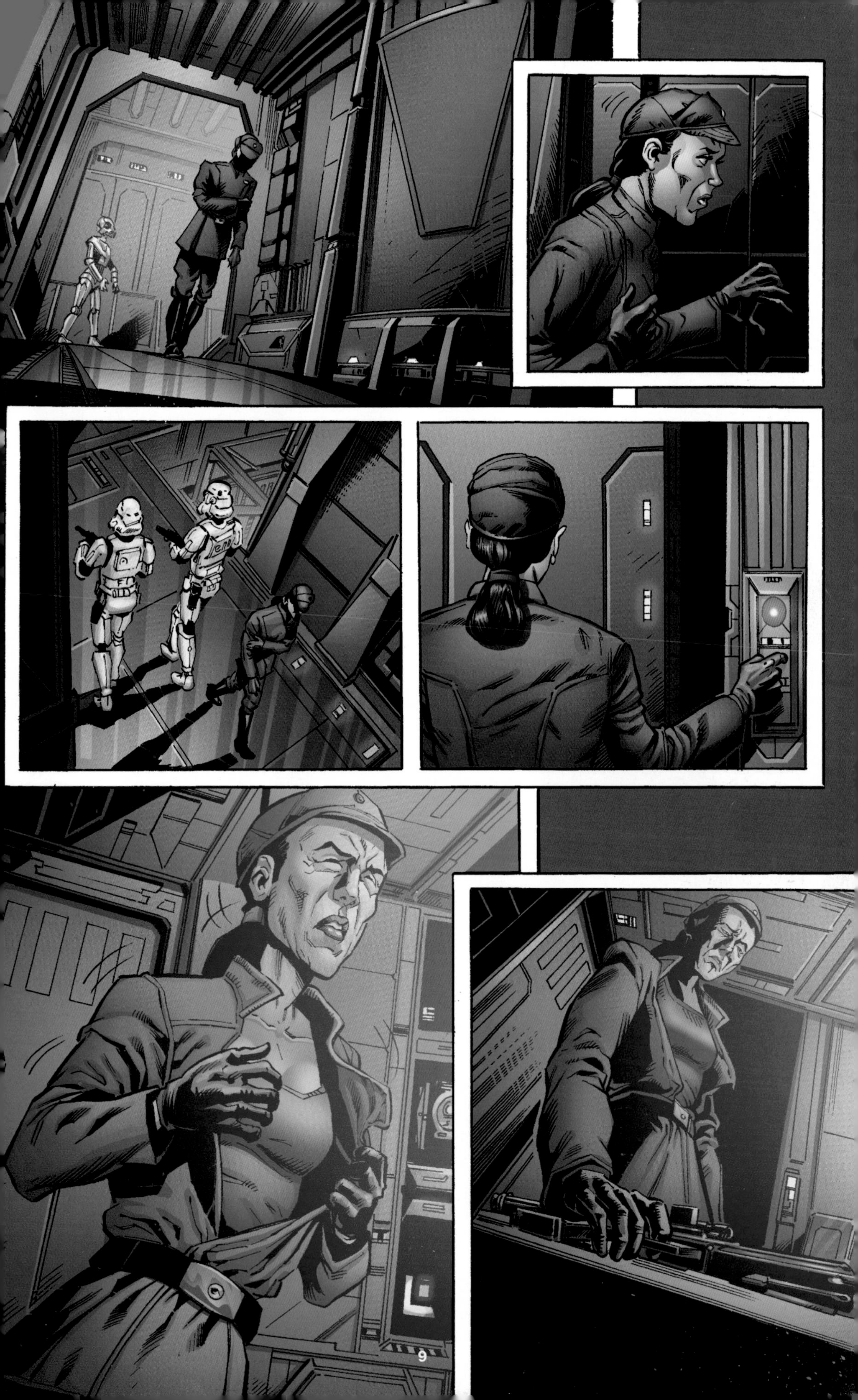

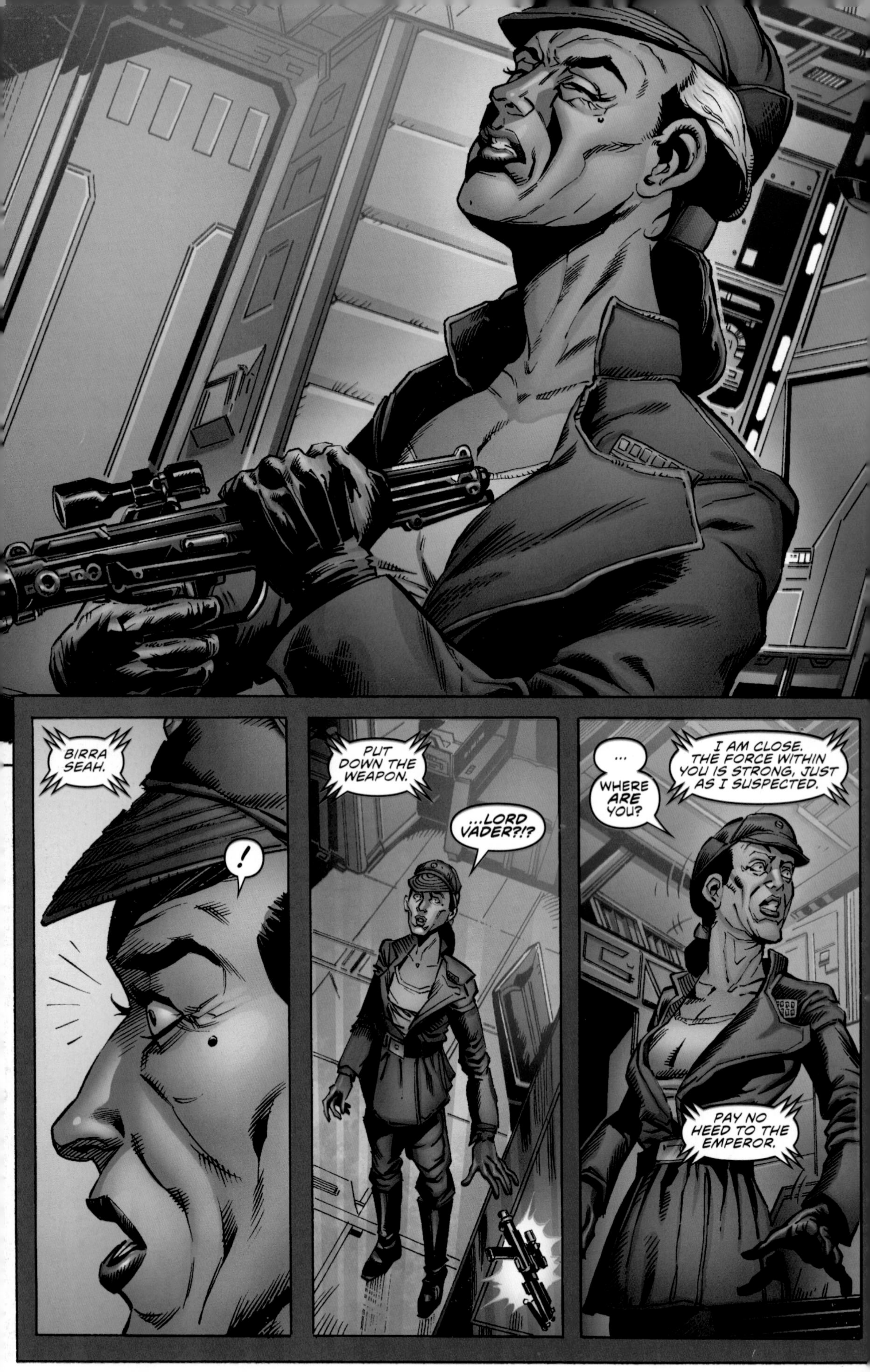
BIRRA SEAH.
!
PUT DOWN THE WEAPON.
...LORD VADER?!?
...
WHERE ARE YOU?
I AM CLOSE. THE FORCE WITHIN YOU IS STRONG, JUST AS I SUSPECTED.
PAY NO HEED TO THE EMPEROR.

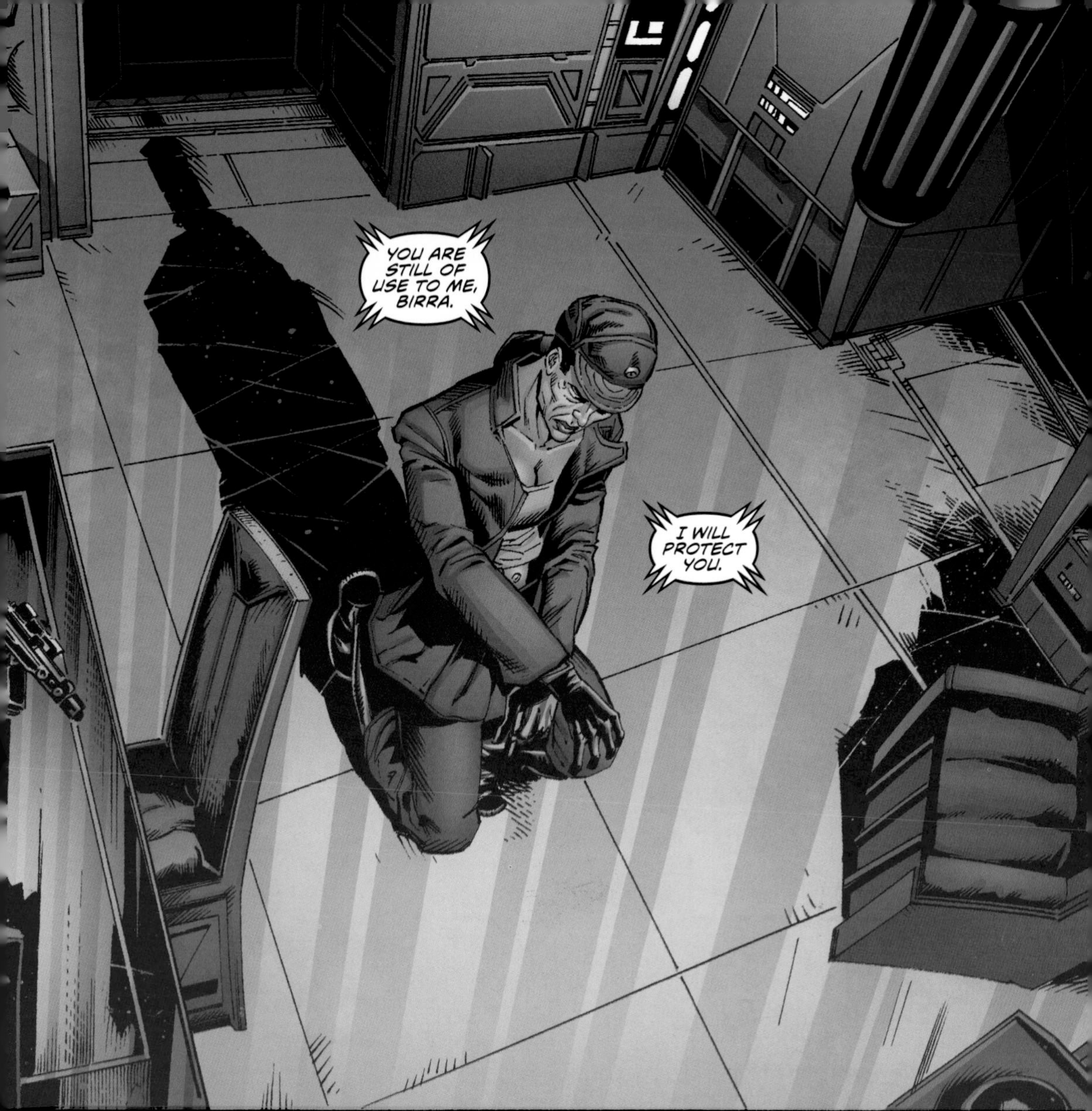
YOU ARE STILL OF USE TO ME, BIRRA.
I WILL PROTECT YOU.

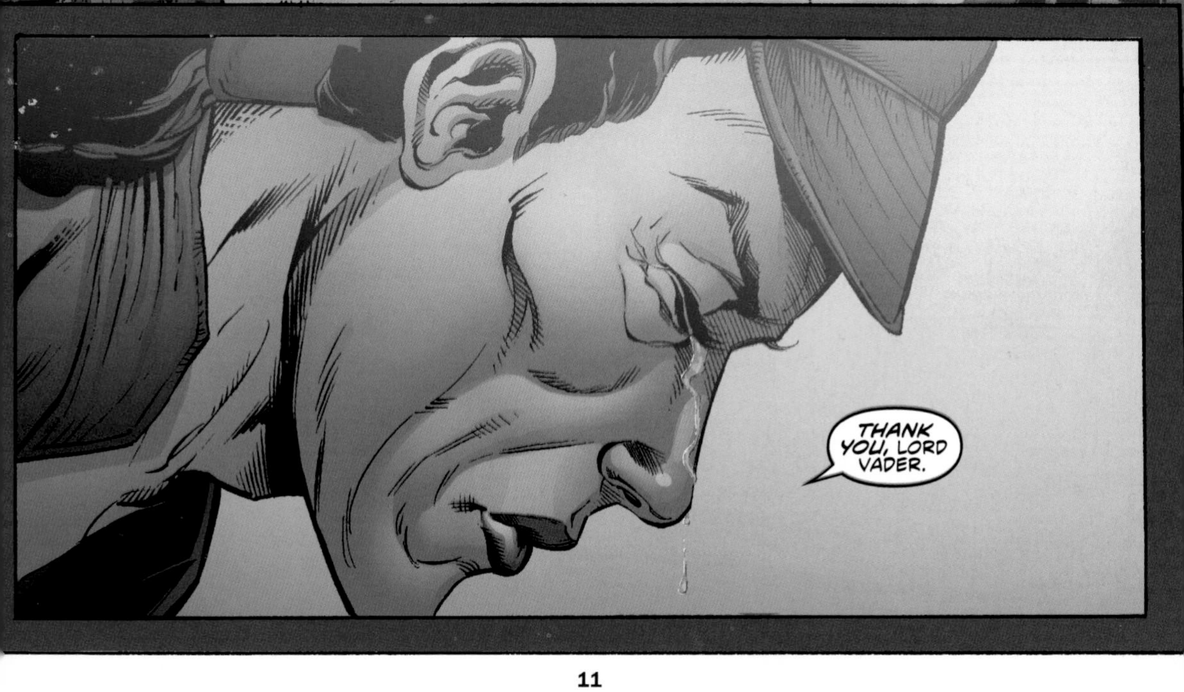
THANK YOU, LORD VADER.

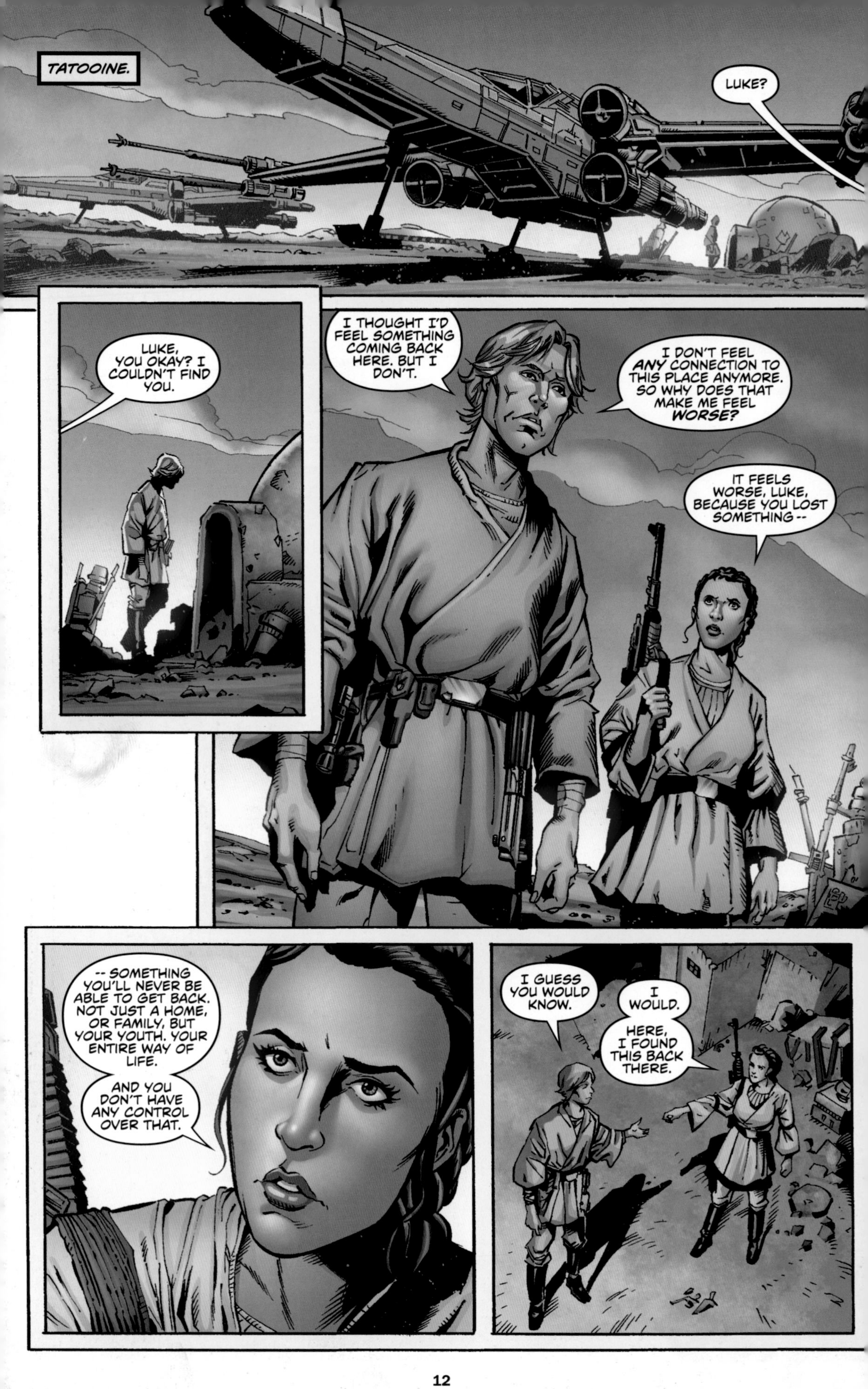
TATOOINE.
LUKE?
LUKE, YOU OKAY? I COULDN'T FIND YOU.
I THOUGHT I'D FEEL SOMETHING COMING BACK HERE. BUT I DON'T.
I DON'T FEEL ANY CONNECTION TO THIS PLACE ANYMORE. SO WHY DOES THAT MAKE ME FEEL WORSE?
IT FEELS WORSE, LUKE, BECAUSE YOU LOST SOMETHING--
--SOMETHING YOU'LL NEVER BE ABLE TO GET BACK. NOT JUST A HOME, OR FAMILY, BUT YOUR YOUTH. YOUR ENTIRE WAY OF LIFE.
AND YOU DON'T HAVE ANY CONTROL OVER THAT.
I GUESS YOU WOULD KNOW.
I WOULD.
HERE, I FOUND THIS BACK THERE.

IT'S AUNT BERU. WHEN SHE WAS OUR AGE, I GUESS.

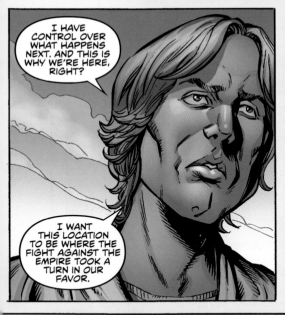

I HAVE CONTROL OVER WHAT HAPPENS NEXT. AND THIS IS WHY WE'RE HERE, RIGHT?

I WANT THIS LOCATION TO BE WHERE THE FIGHT AGAINST THE EMPIRE TOOK A TURN IN OUR FAVOR.

IT WILL BE. I PROMISE.

LET'S DO WHAT WE CAME HERE FOR, AND THEN WE'LL TALK ABOUT THE EMPIRE.

OWEN LARS AND BERU WHITESUN.

THEY'RE AT PEACE NOW, LUKE. YOU'RE A GOOD SON TO COME BACK AND DO THIS.

I'M NOT. I WASN'T.

I COULDN'T WAIT TO BE RID OF THEM, LEIA. I HATED MY UNCLE FOR TRYING TO HOLD ON TO ME.

MY AUNT UNDERSTOOD ME BETTER, BUT SHE WAS JUST AS AFRAID TO SEE ME FOLLOW IN BIGGS'S FOOTSTEPS AS HE WAS.

I'M SORRY, UNCLE OWEN, AUNT BERU.

YOU DESERVED A MORE GRATEFUL SON.

LUKE...

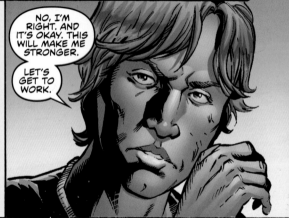

NO, I'M RIGHT. AND IT'S OKAY. THIS WILL MAKE ME STRONGER.

LET'S GET TO WORK.

YOU KNOW SOME OF THIS ALREADY, SO BEAR WITH ME. I'M STARTING AT THE BEGINNING.

THE FORMATION OF THE STEALTH SQUADRON WAS NOT ONLY TO SCOUT FOR A NEW HOME PLANET FOR THE ALLIANCE. WE HAVE A SPY WITHIN THE FLEET, SOMEONE MOST LIKELY WITHIN THE COUNCIL...

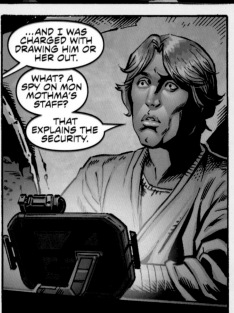

...AND I WAS CHARGED WITH DRAWING HIM OR HER OUT.

WHAT? A SPY ON MON MOTHMA'S STAFF?

THAT EXPLAINS THE SECURITY.

THE ENCRYPTION SURROUNDING OUR X-WING NAVIGATIONAL PLOTS WAS DESIGNED IN A SPECIFIC WAY WITH CONTROLLED LEAKS TO PINPOINT AT *WHAT TIMES* AND FROM *WHERE* IN THE DATA CORE IT WAS BEING ACCESSED.

BUT TO DATE, *ALL* WE'VE BEEN ABLE TO DETERMINE IS THAT LEAKS ARE HAPPENING, AND AT A VERY HIGH LEVEL OF CLEARANCE.

BUT NO ACTUAL SUSPECTS.

...

AND IN THE MEANTIME, THIS IMPERIAL OFFICER, *BIRCHER*, IS ONE STEP AHEAD OF US AT ALL TIMES.

MAYBE WE NEED TO HIT THIS FROM A DIFFERENT ANGLE.

15

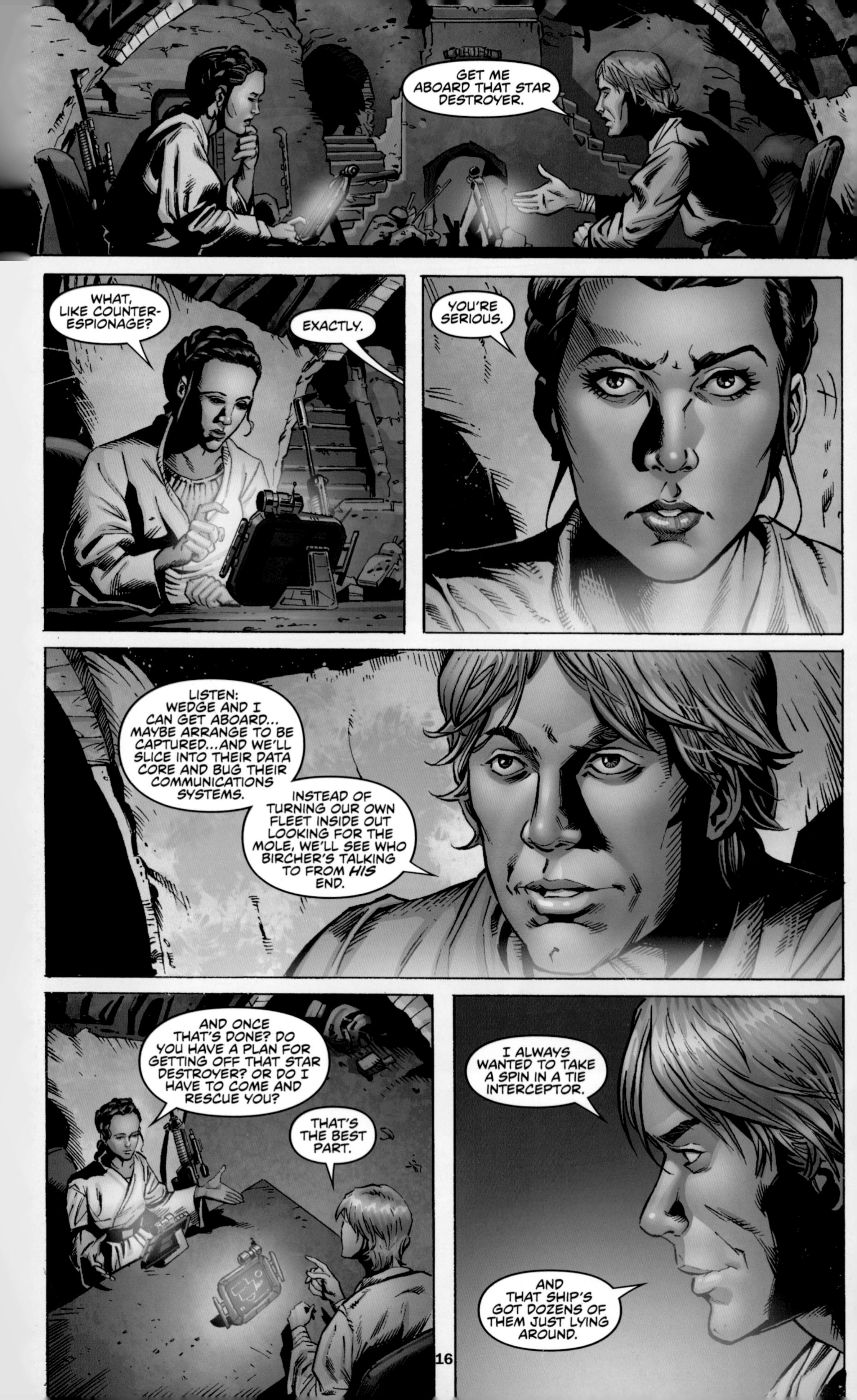
GET ME ABOARD THAT STAR DESTROYER.
WHAT, LIKE COUNTER-ESPIONAGE?
EXACTLY.
YOU'RE SERIOUS.
LISTEN: WEDGE AND I CAN GET ABOARD... MAYBE ARRANGE TO BE CAPTURED...AND WE'LL SLICE INTO THEIR DATA CORE AND BUG THEIR COMMUNICATIONS SYSTEMS.
INSTEAD OF TURNING OUR OWN FLEET INSIDE OUT LOOKING FOR THE MOLE, WE'LL SEE WHO BIRCHER'S TALKING TO FROM *HIS* END.
AND ONCE THAT'S DONE? DO YOU HAVE A PLAN FOR GETTING OFF THAT STAR DESTROYER? OR DO I HAVE TO COME AND RESCUE YOU?
THAT'S THE BEST PART.
I ALWAYS WANTED TO TAKE A SPIN IN A TIE INTERCEPTOR.
AND THAT SHIP'S GOT DOZENS OF THEM JUST LYING AROUND.

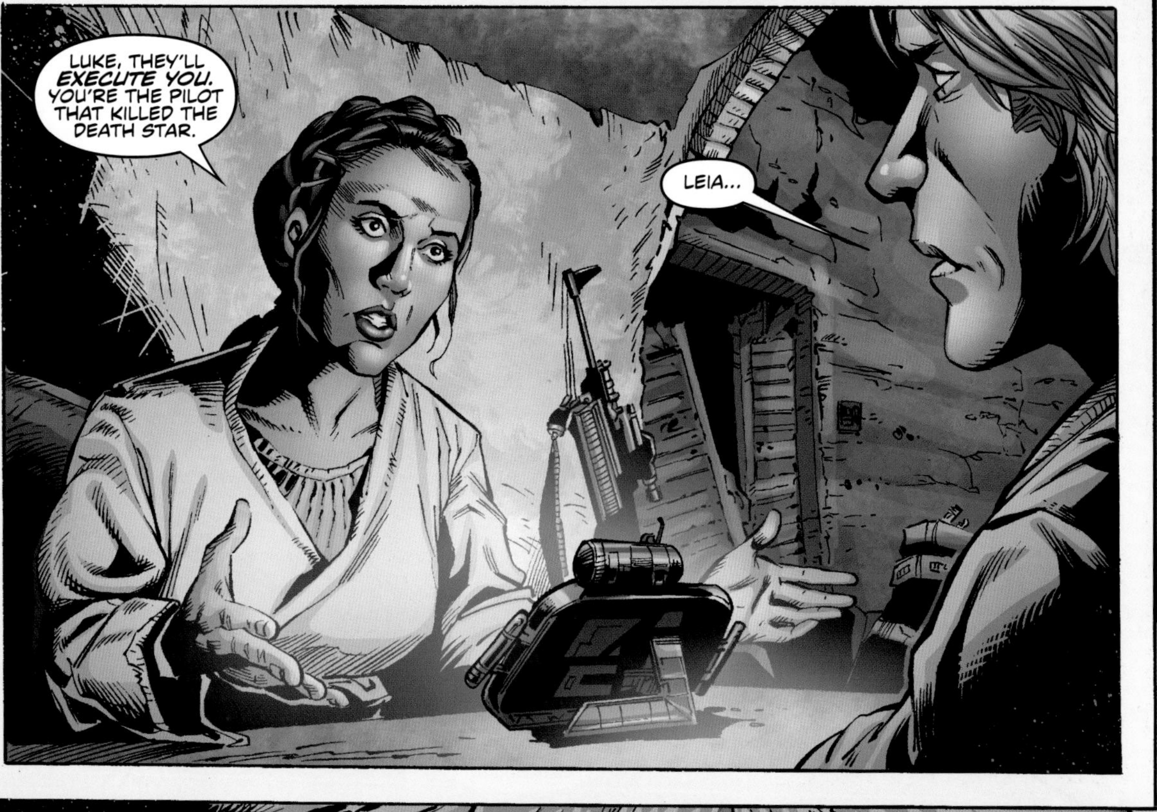
LUKE, THEY'LL *EXECUTE YOU.* YOU'RE THE PILOT THAT KILLED THE DEATH STAR.
LEIA...

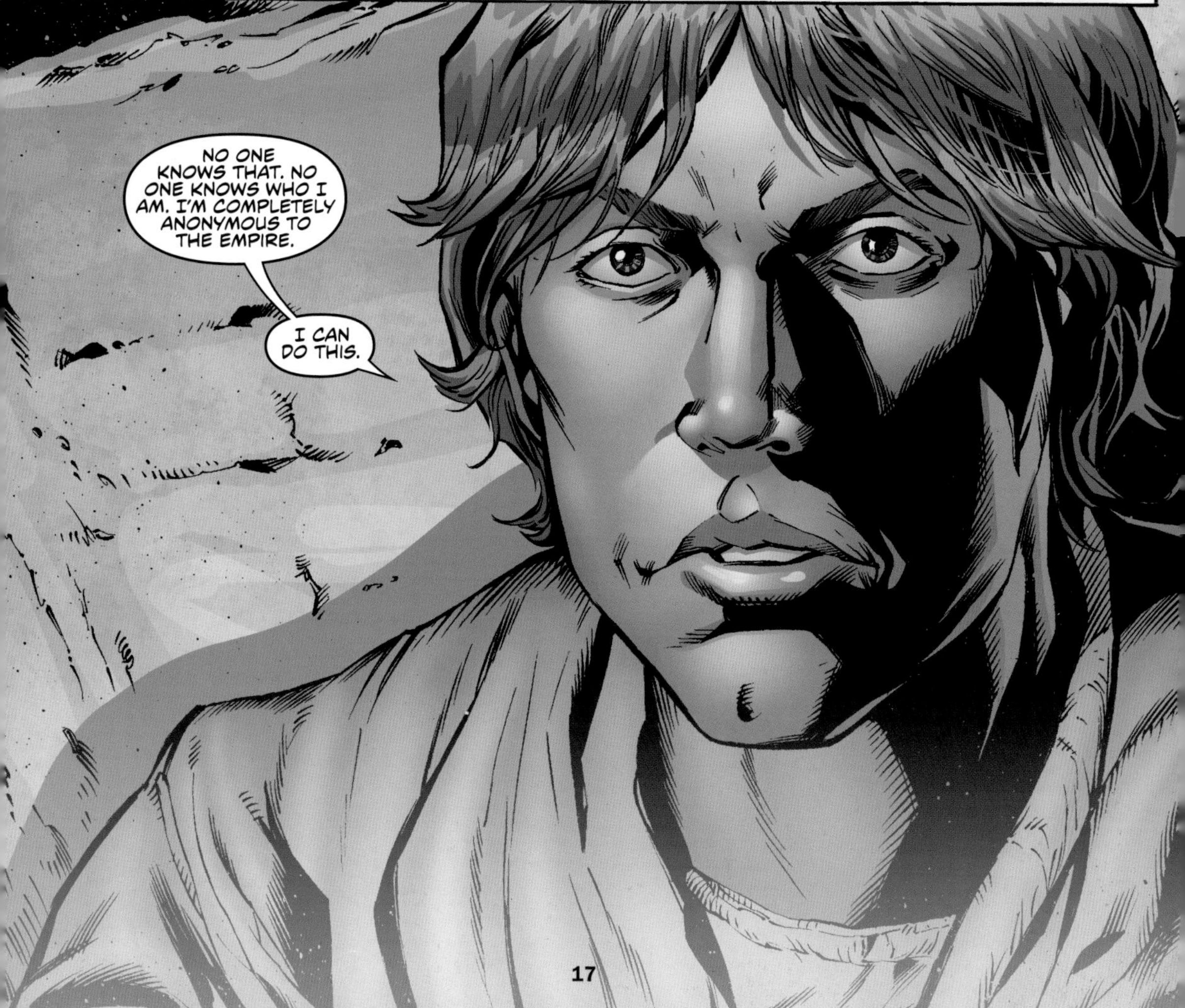
NO ONE KNOWS THAT. NO ONE KNOWS WHO I AM. I'M COMPLETELY ANONYMOUS TO THE EMPIRE.
I CAN DO THIS.

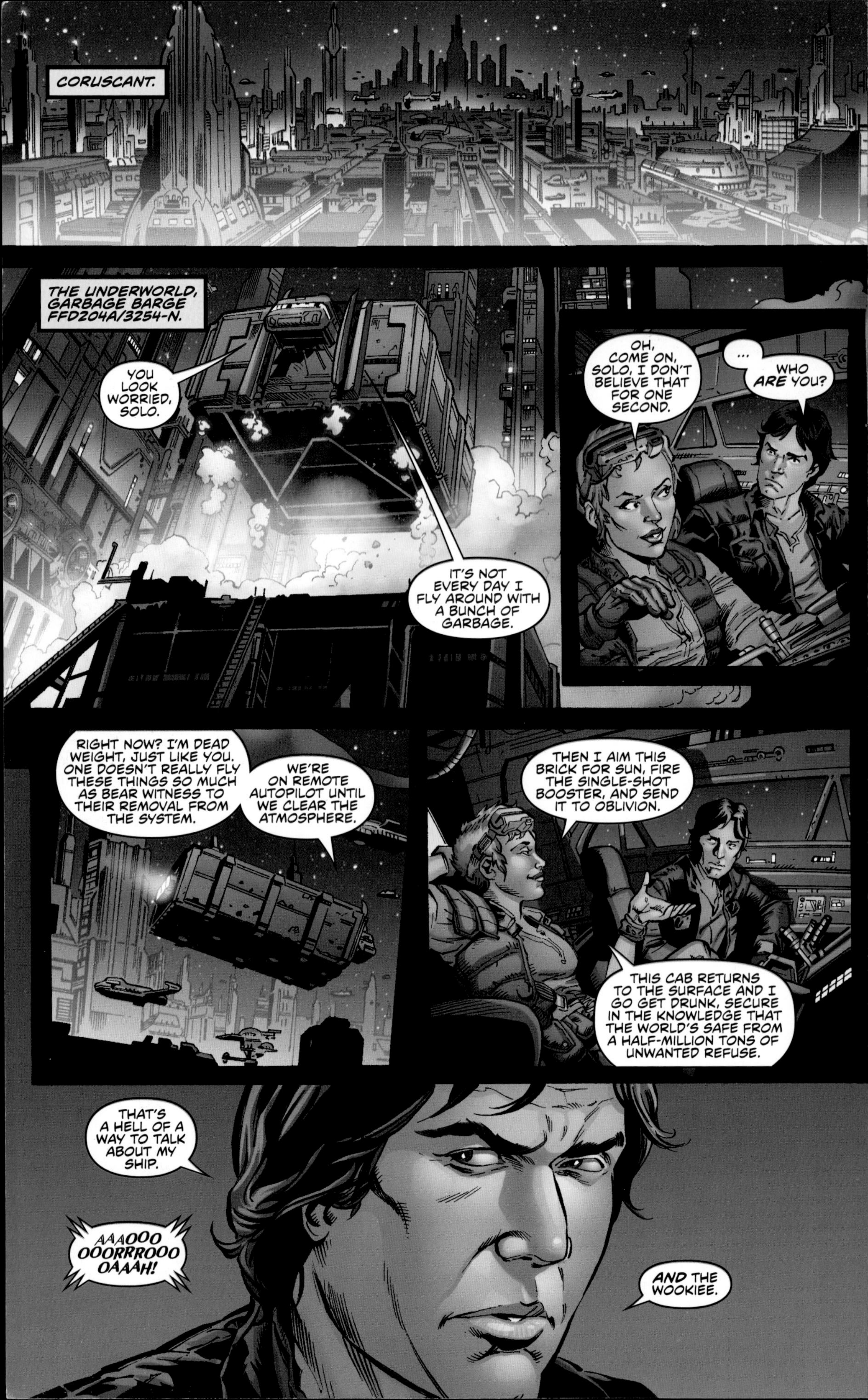
CORUSCANT.
THE UNDERWORLD, GARBAGE BARGE FFD204A/3254-N.
YOU LOOK WORRIED, SOLO.
IT'S NOT EVERY DAY I FLY AROUND WITH A BUNCH OF GARBAGE.
OH, COME ON, SOLO, I DON'T BELIEVE THAT FOR ONE SECOND.
...
WHO ARE YOU?
RIGHT NOW? I'M DEAD WEIGHT, JUST LIKE YOU. ONE DOESN'T REALLY FLY THESE THINGS SO MUCH AS BEAR WITNESS TO THEIR REMOVAL FROM THE SYSTEM.
WE'RE ON REMOTE AUTOPILOT UNTIL WE CLEAR THE ATMOSPHERE.
THEN I AIM THIS BRICK FOR SUN, FIRE THE SINGLE-SHOT BOOSTER, AND SEND IT TO OBLIVION.
THIS CAB RETURNS TO THE SURFACE AND I GO GET DRUNK, SECURE IN THE KNOWLEDGE THAT THE WORLD'S SAFE FROM A HALF-MILLION TONS OF UNWANTED REFUSE.
THAT'S A HELL OF A WAY TO TALK ABOUT MY SHIP.
AAAOOO OOORRROOO OAAAH!
AND THE WOOKIEE.

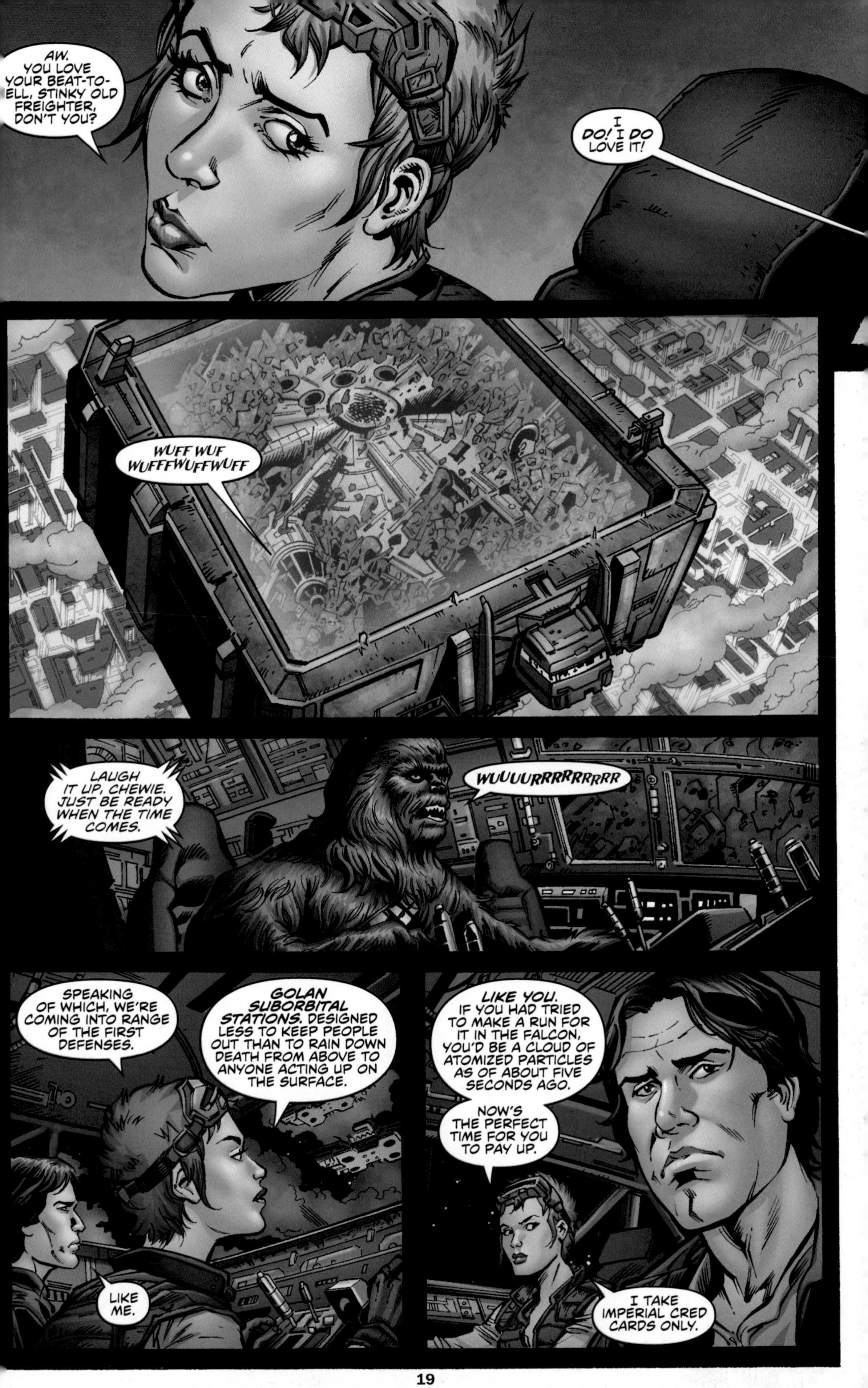
AW. YOU LOVE YOUR BEAT-TO-ELL, STINKY OLD FREIGHTER, DON'T YOU?
I DO! I DO LOVE IT!
WUFF WUF WUFFFWUFFWUFF
LAUGH IT UP, CHEWIE. JUST BE READY WHEN THE TIME COMES.
WUUUURRRRRRRR
SPEAKING OF WHICH, WE'RE COMING INTO RANGE OF THE FIRST DEFENSES.
GOLAN SUBORBITAL STATIONS. DESIGNED LESS TO KEEP PEOPLE OUT THAN TO RAIN DOWN DEATH FROM ABOVE TO ANYONE ACTING UP ON THE SURFACE.
LIKE ME.
LIKE YOU. IF YOU HAD TRIED TO MAKE A RUN FOR IT IN THE FALCON, YOU'D BE A CLOUD OF ATOMIZED PARTICLES AS OF ABOUT FIVE SECONDS AGO.
NOW'S THE PERFECT TIME FOR YOU TO PAY UP.
I TAKE IMPERIAL CRED CARDS ONLY.

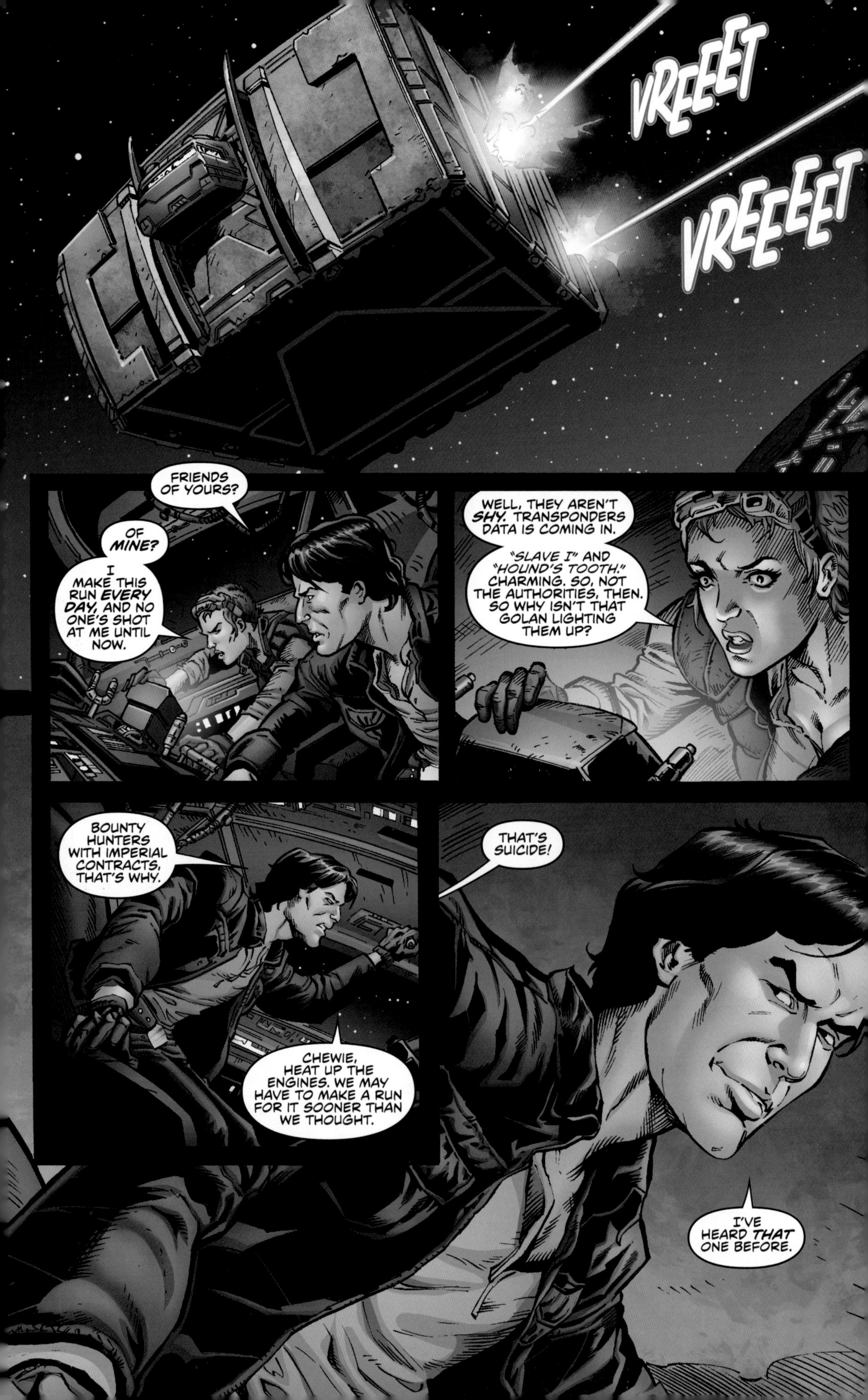
VREEEET
VREEEET
FRIENDS OF YOURS?
OF MINE?
I MAKE THIS RUN EVERY DAY, AND NO ONE'S SHOT AT ME UNTIL NOW.
WELL, THEY AREN'T SHY. TRANSPONDERS DATA IS COMING IN.
"SLAVE I" AND "HOUND'S TOOTH." CHARMING. SO, NOT THE AUTHORITIES, THEN. SO WHY ISN'T THAT GOLAN LIGHTING THEM UP?
BOUNTY HUNTERS WITH IMPERIAL CONTRACTS, THAT'S WHY.
CHEWIE, HEAT UP THE ENGINES. WE MAY HAVE TO MAKE A RUN FOR IT SOONER THAN WE THOUGHT.
THAT'S SUICIDE!
I'VE HEARD THAT ONE BEFORE.

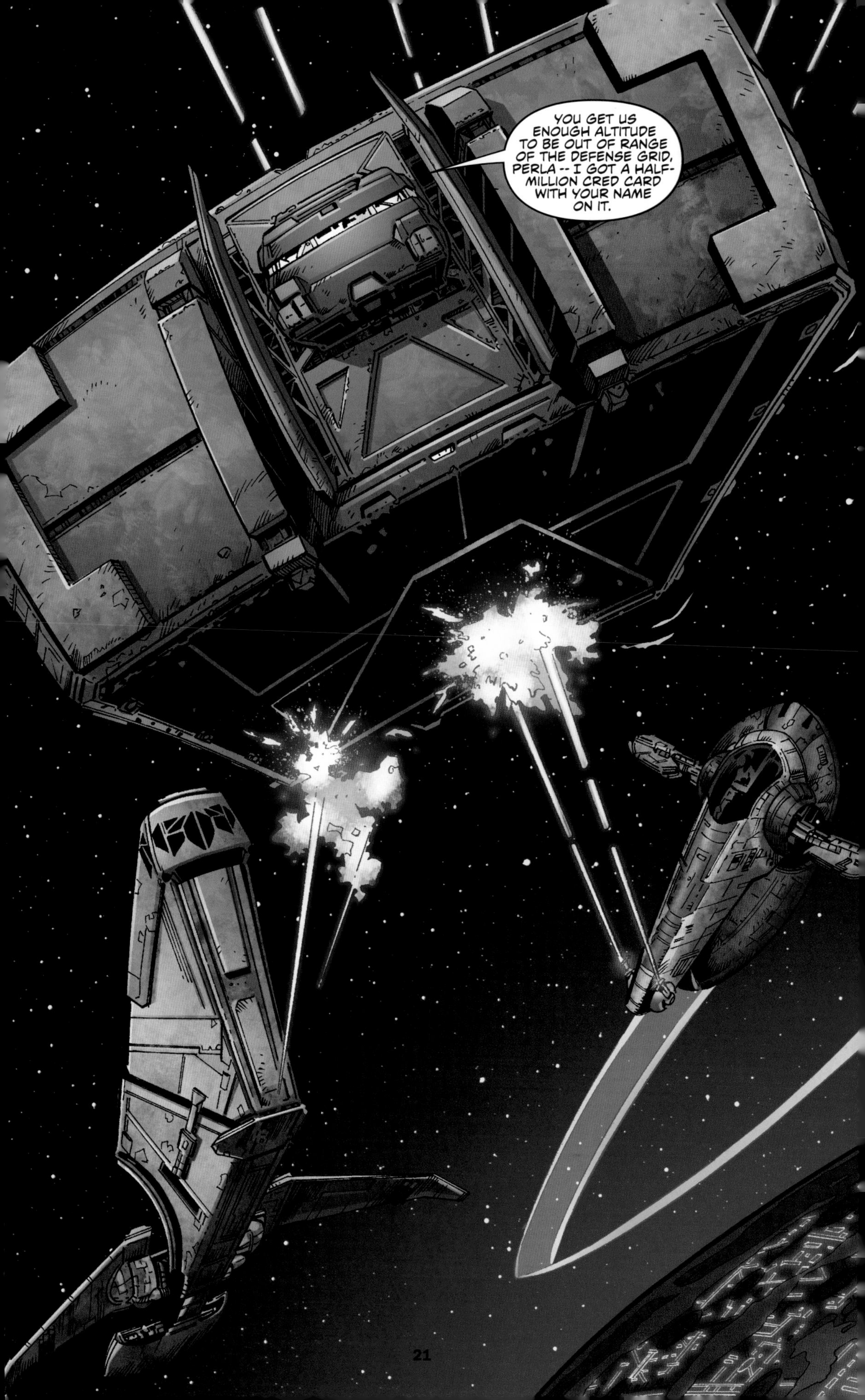
YOU GET US ENOUGH ALTITUDE TO BE OUT OF RANGE OF THE DEFENSE GRID, PERLA -- I GOT A HALF-MILLION CRED CARD WITH YOUR NAME ON IT.

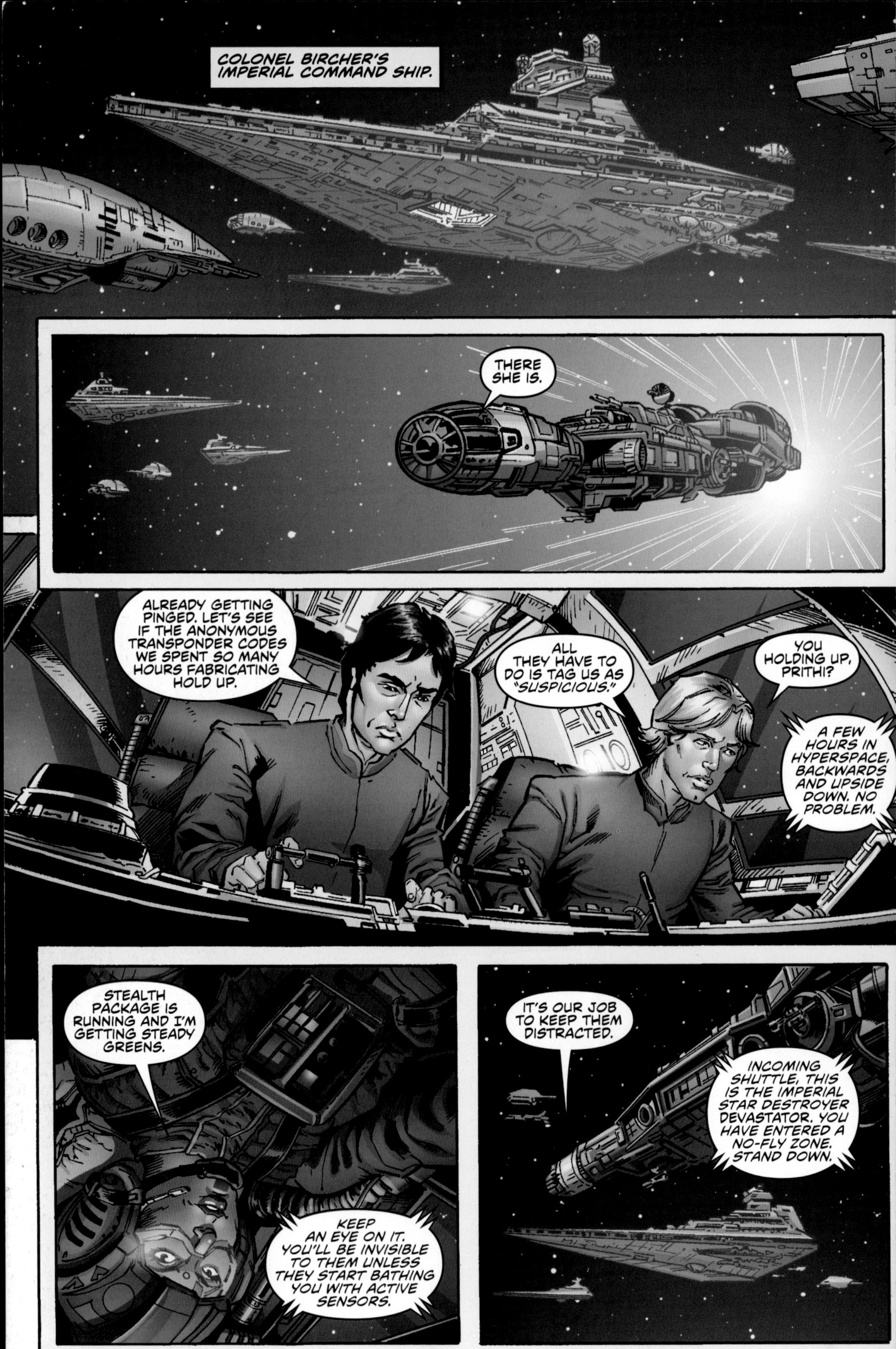
COLONEL BIRCHER'S IMPERIAL COMMAND SHIP.
THERE SHE IS.
ALREADY GETTING PINGED. LET'S SEE IF THE ANONYMOUS TRANSPONDER CODES WE SPENT SO MANY HOURS FABRICATING HOLD UP.
ALL THEY HAVE TO DO IS TAG US AS "SUSPICIOUS."
YOU HOLDING UP, PRITHI?
A FEW HOURS IN HYPERSPACE, BACKWARDS AND UPSIDE DOWN. NO PROBLEM.
STEALTH PACKAGE IS RUNNING AND I'M GETTING STEADY GREENS.
KEEP AN EYE ON IT. YOU'LL BE INVISIBLE TO THEM UNLESS THEY START BATHING YOU WITH ACTIVE SENSORS.
IT'S OUR JOB TO KEEP THEM DISTRACTED.
INCOMING SHUTTLE, THIS IS THE IMPERIAL STAR DESTROYER DEVASTATOR. YOU HAVE ENTERED A NO-FLY ZONE. STAND DOWN.

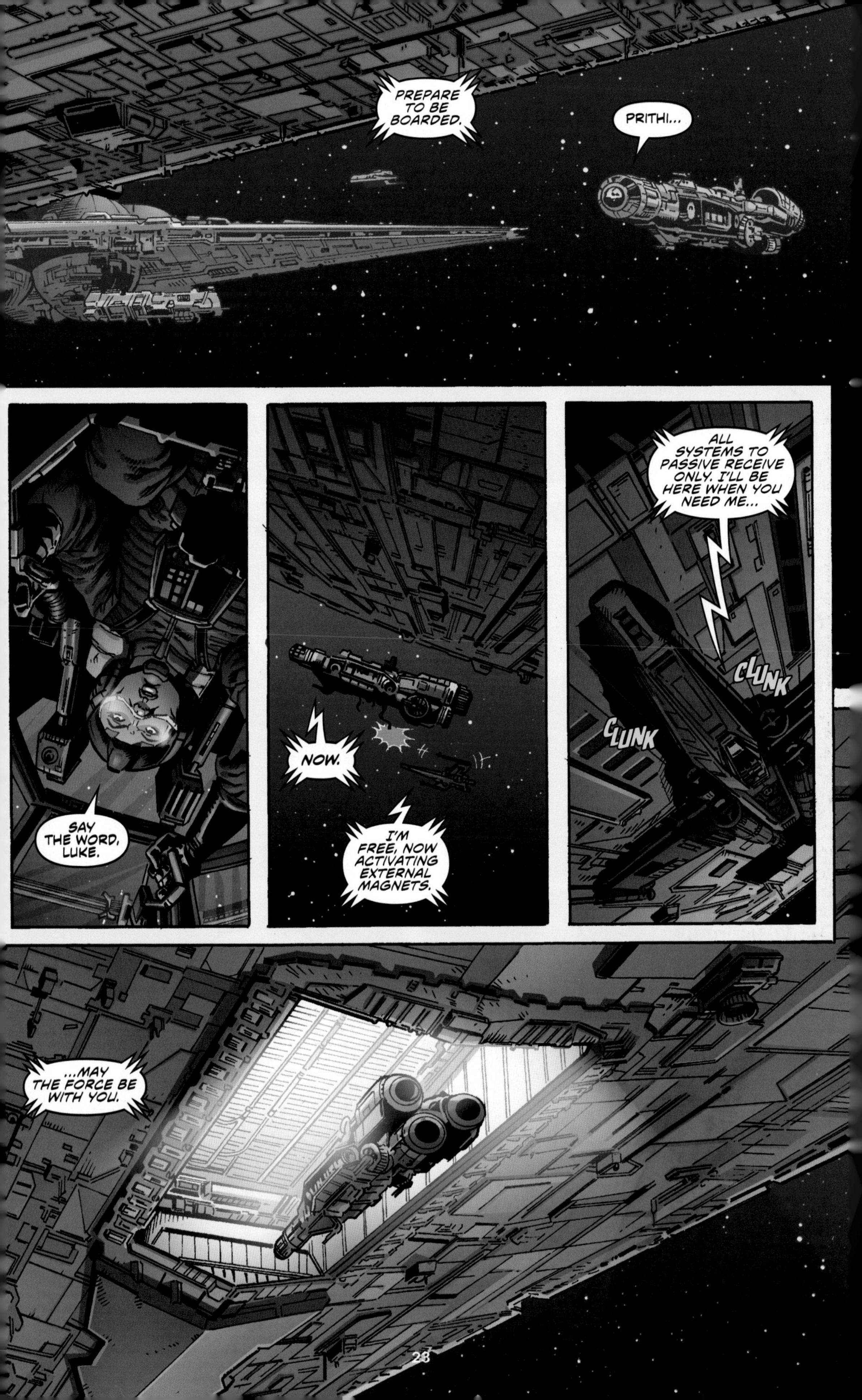
PREPARE TO BE BOARDED.
PRITHI...
SAY THE WORD, LUKE.
NOW.
I'M FREE, NOW ACTIVATING EXTERNAL MAGNETS.
ALL SYSTEMS TO PASSIVE RECEIVE ONLY. I'LL BE HERE WHEN YOU NEED ME...
CLUNK
CLUNK
...MAY THE FORCE BE WITH YOU.

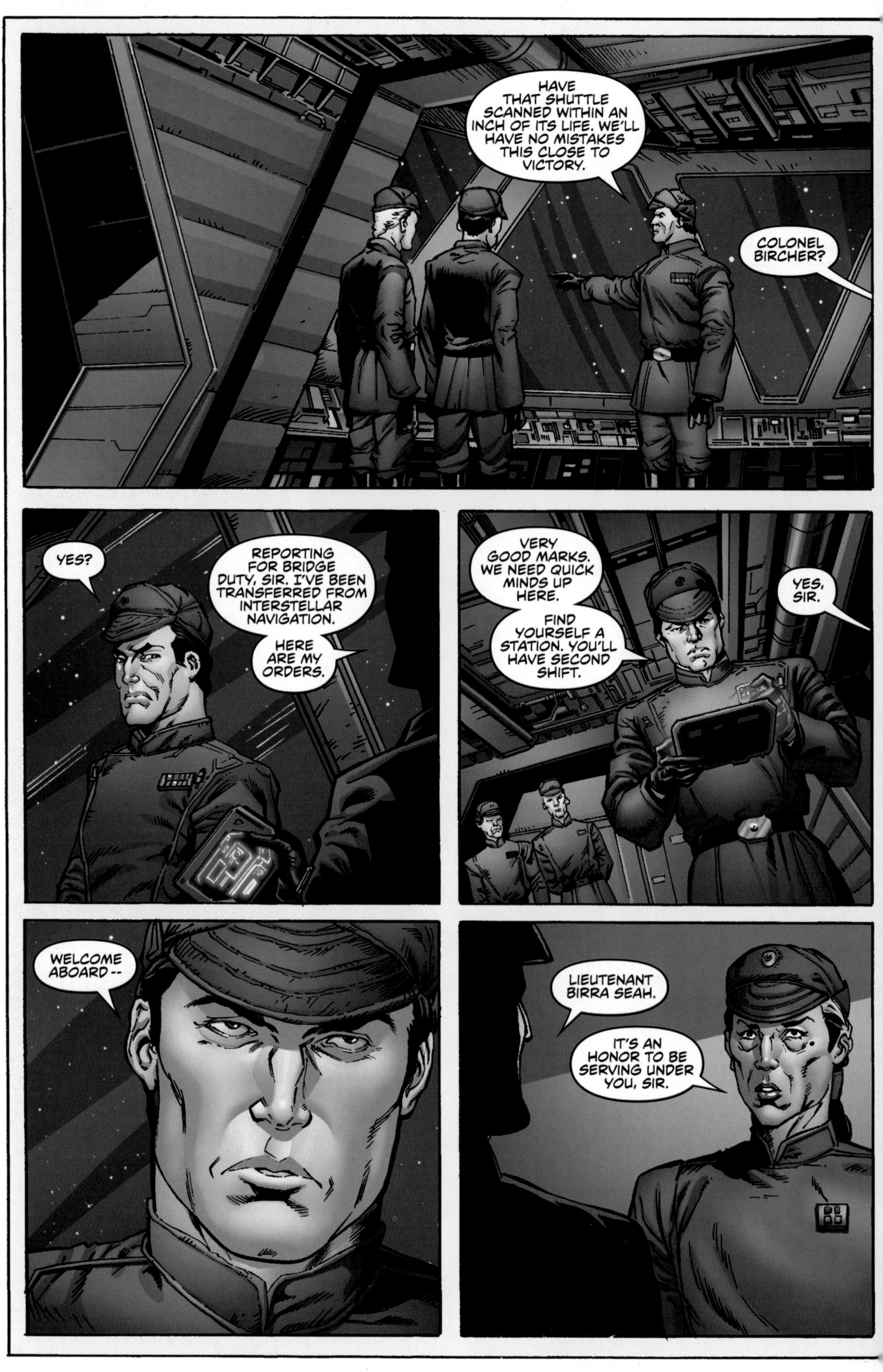
HAVE THAT SHUTTLE SCANNED WITHIN AN INCH OF ITS LIFE. WE'LL HAVE NO MISTAKES THIS CLOSE TO VICTORY.
COLONEL BIRCHER?
YES?
REPORTING FOR BRIDGE DUTY, SIR. I'VE BEEN TRANSFERRED FROM INTERSTELLAR NAVIGATION.
HERE ARE MY ORDERS.
VERY GOOD MARKS. WE NEED QUICK MINDS UP HERE.
FIND YOURSELF A STATION. YOU'LL HAVE SECOND SHIFT.
YES, SIR.
WELCOME ABOARD --
LIEUTENANT BIRRA SEAH.
IT'S AN HONOR TO BE SERVING UNDER YOU, SIR.

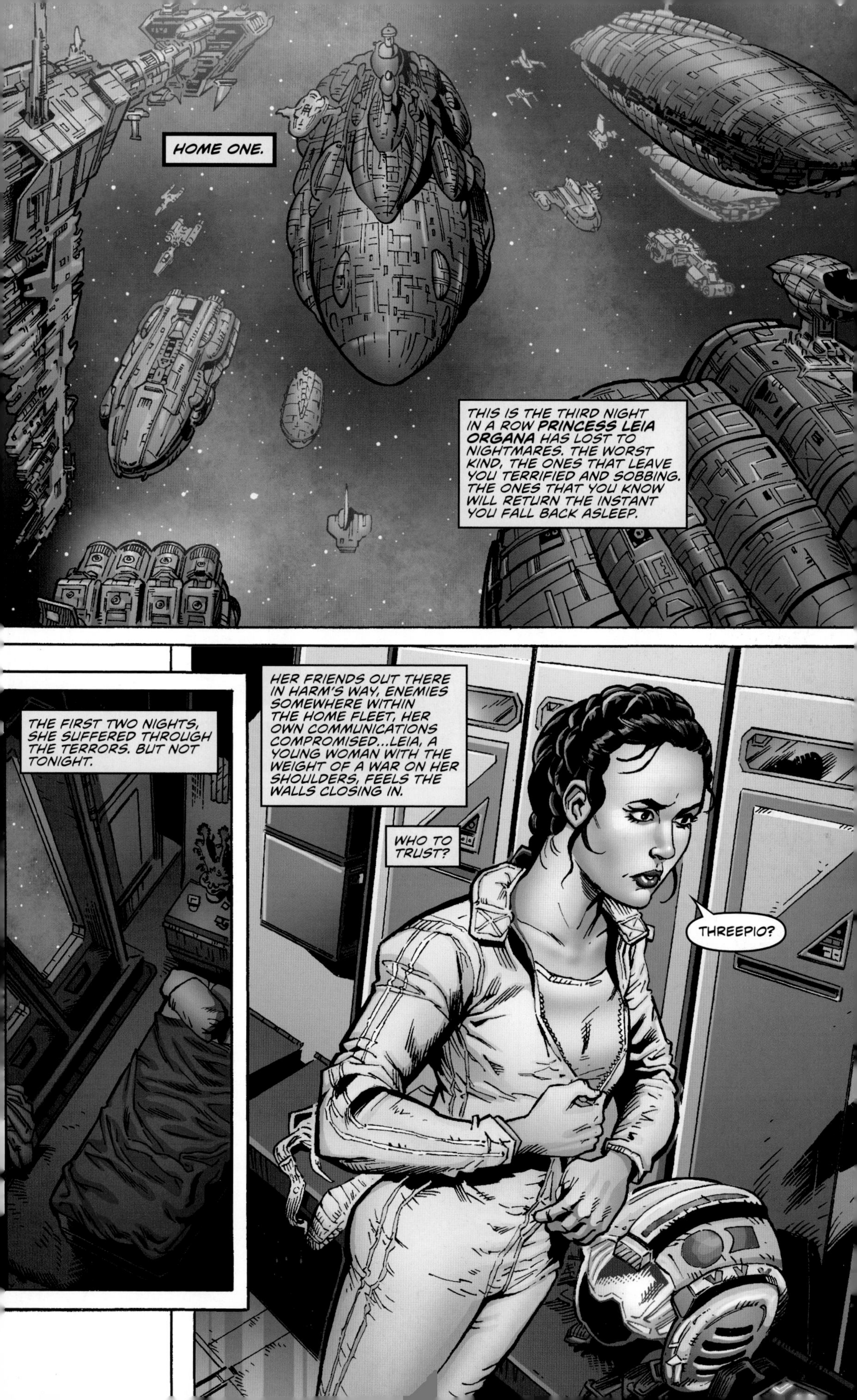
HOME ONE.
THIS IS THE THIRD NIGHT IN A ROW PRINCESS LEIA ORGANA HAS LOST TO NIGHTMARES. THE WORST KIND, THE ONES THAT LEAVE YOU TERRIFIED AND SOBBING. THE ONES THAT YOU KNOW WILL RETURN THE INSTANT YOU FALL BACK ASLEEP.
THE FIRST TWO NIGHTS, SHE SUFFERED THROUGH THE TERRORS. BUT NOT TONIGHT.
HER FRIENDS OUT THERE IN HARM'S WAY, ENEMIES SOMEWHERE WITHIN THE HOME FLEET, HER OWN COMMUNICATIONS COMPROMISED...LEIA, A YOUNG WOMAN WITH THE WEIGHT OF A WAR ON HER SHOULDERS, FEELS THE WALLS CLOSING IN.
WHO TO TRUST?
THREEPIO?

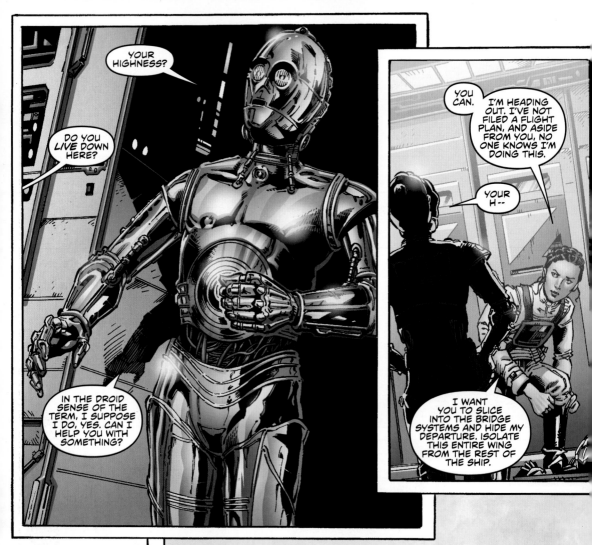

YOUR HIGHNESS?

DO YOU LIVE DOWN HERE?

IN THE DROID SENSE OF THE TERM, I SUPPOSE I DO, YES. CAN I HELP YOU WITH SOMETHING?

YOU CAN. I'M HEADING OUT. I'VE NOT FILED A FLIGHT PLAN, AND ASIDE FROM YOU, NO ONE KNOWS I'M DOING THIS.

YOUR H--

I WANT YOU TO SLICE INTO THE BRIDGE SYSTEMS AND HIDE MY DEPARTURE. ISOLATE THIS ENTIRE WING FROM THE REST OF THE SHIP.

I'M SURE I CANNOT DO THAT, PRINCESS. WE HAVE PROTOCOLS--

YOU CAN DO IT. THIS FALLS WELL WITHIN YOUR MANDATE TO FACILITATE THE RUNNING OF STEALTH SQUADRON.

SO: NO RECORD, NO FLIGHT LOG. WIPE THE SECURITY FEEDS. NO ONE KNOWS, NOT EVEN MON MOTHMA. VANISH ME.

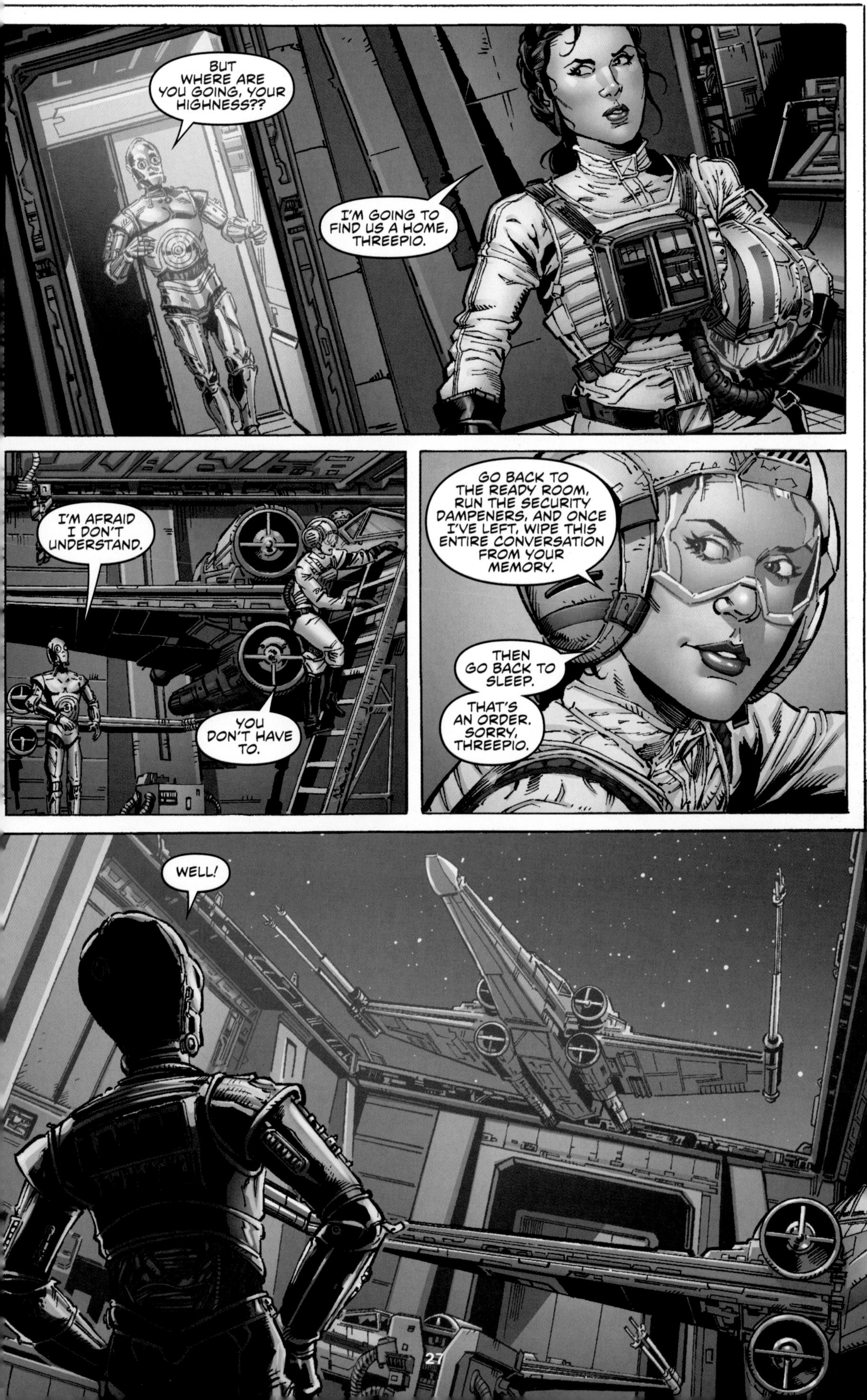
BUT WHERE ARE YOU GOING, YOUR HIGHNESS??
I'M GOING TO FIND US A HOME, THREEPIO.
I'M AFRAID I DON'T UNDERSTAND.
YOU DON'T HAVE TO.
GO BACK TO THE READY ROOM, RUN THE SECURITY DAMPENERS, AND ONCE I'VE LEFT, WIPE THIS ENTIRE CONVERSATION FROM YOUR MEMORY.
THEN GO BACK TO SLEEP.
THAT'S AN ORDER. SORRY, THREEPIO.
WELL!

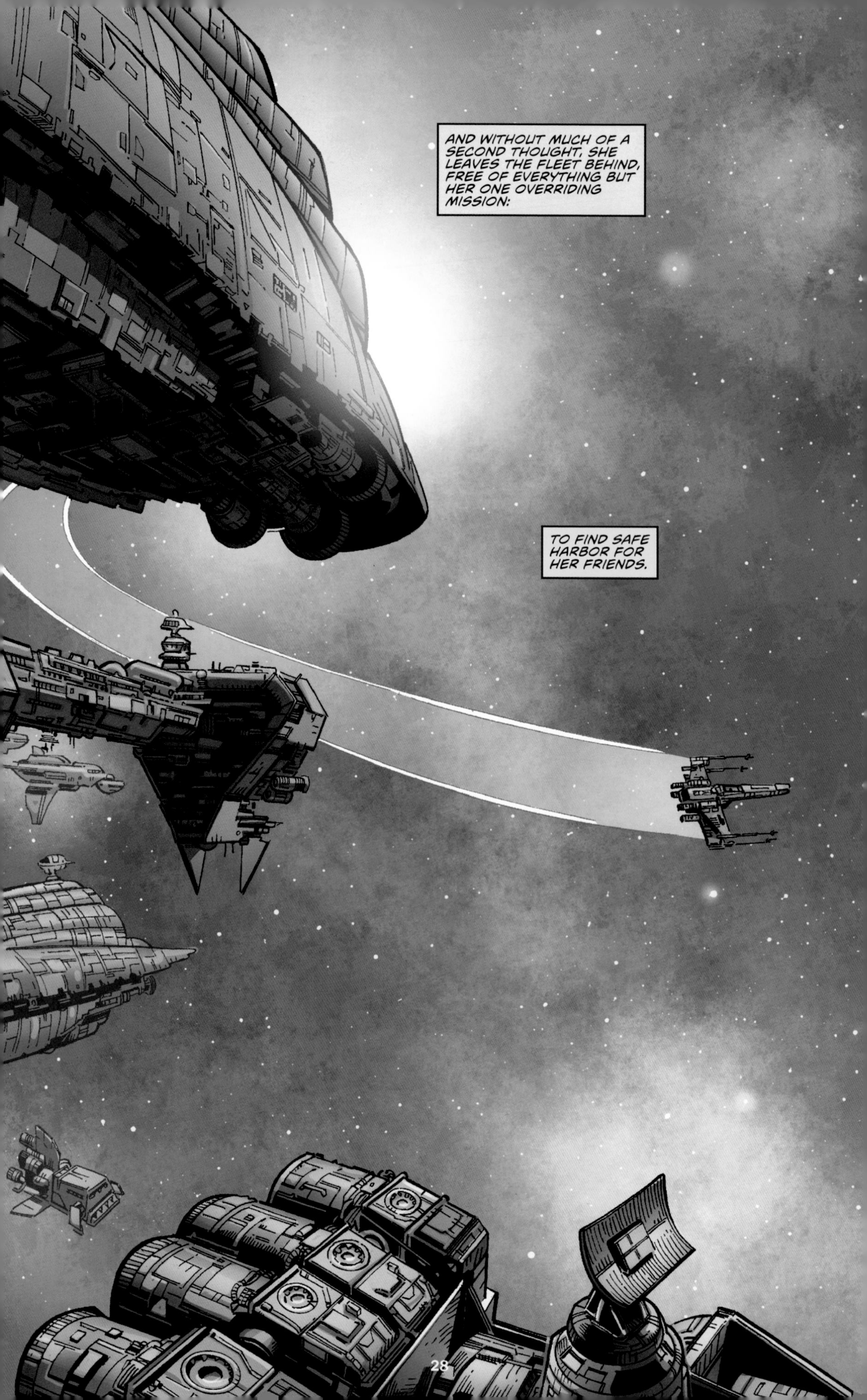
AND WITHOUT MUCH OF A SECOND THOUGHT, SHE LEAVES THE FLEET BEHIND, FREE OF EVERYTHING BUT HER ONE OVERRIDING MISSION:
TO FIND SAFE HARBOR FOR HER FRIENDS.

THE STAR
DESTROYER
DEVASTATOR.

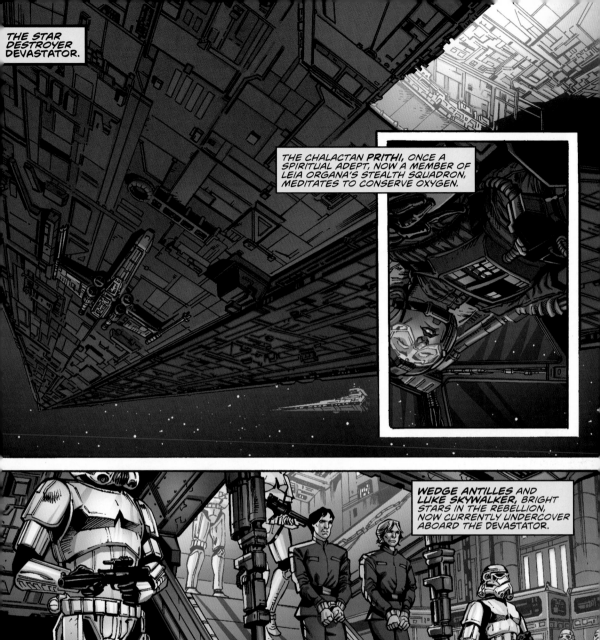

THE CHALACTAN **PRITHI**, ONCE A SPIRITUAL ADEPT, NOW A MEMBER OF LEIA ORGANA'S STEALTH SQUADRON, MEDITATES TO CONSERVE OXYGEN.

WEDGE ANTILLES AND **LUKE SKYWALKER**, BRIGHT STARS IN THE REBELLION, NOW CURRENTLY UNDERCOVER ABOARD THE DEVASTATOR.

ONE HAS NO RECORD AT ALL. THE OTHER IS A CORELLIAN, MINOR CRIMES, KID STUFF. POSSIBLE REBEL TIES...

...BUT UNCONFIRMED.

INDEED. DETAIN THEM, HIGHEST POSSIBLE SECURITY LEVEL. AND SWEEP THAT FREIGHTER.

HMM.

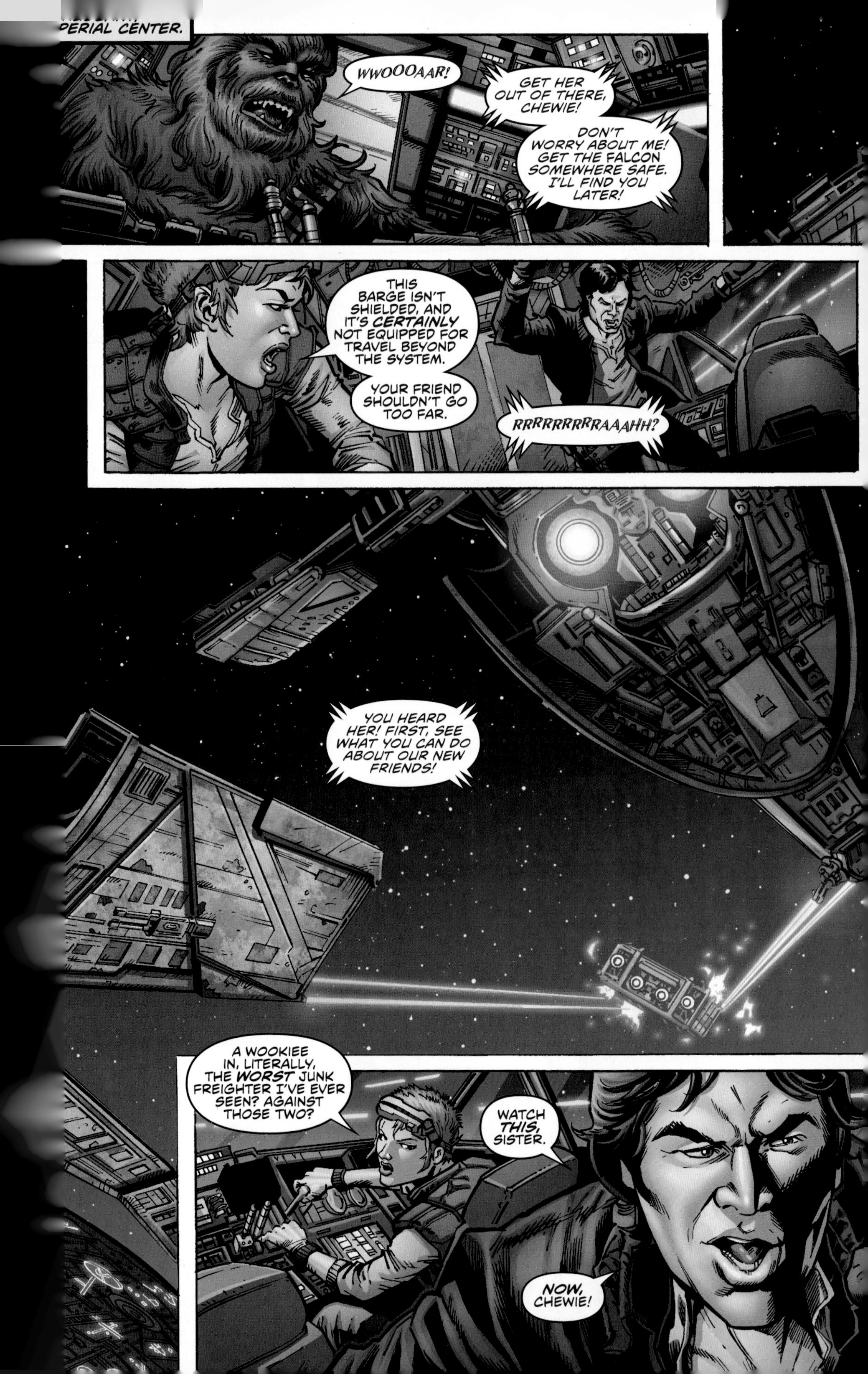
...PERIAL CENTER.
WWOOOAAR!
GET HER OUT OF THERE, CHEWIE!
DON'T WORRY ABOUT ME! GET THE FALCON SOMEWHERE SAFE. I'LL FIND YOU LATER!
THIS BARGE ISN'T SHIELDED, AND IT'S CERTAINLY NOT EQUIPPED FOR TRAVEL BEYOND THE SYSTEM.
YOUR FRIEND SHOULDN'T GO TOO FAR.
RRRRRRRRAAAHH?
YOU HEARD HER! FIRST, SEE WHAT YOU CAN DO ABOUT OUR NEW FRIENDS!
A WOOKIEE IN, LITERALLY, THE WORST JUNK FREIGHTER I'VE EVER SEEN? AGAINST THOSE TWO?
WATCH THIS, SISTER.
NOW, CHEWIE!

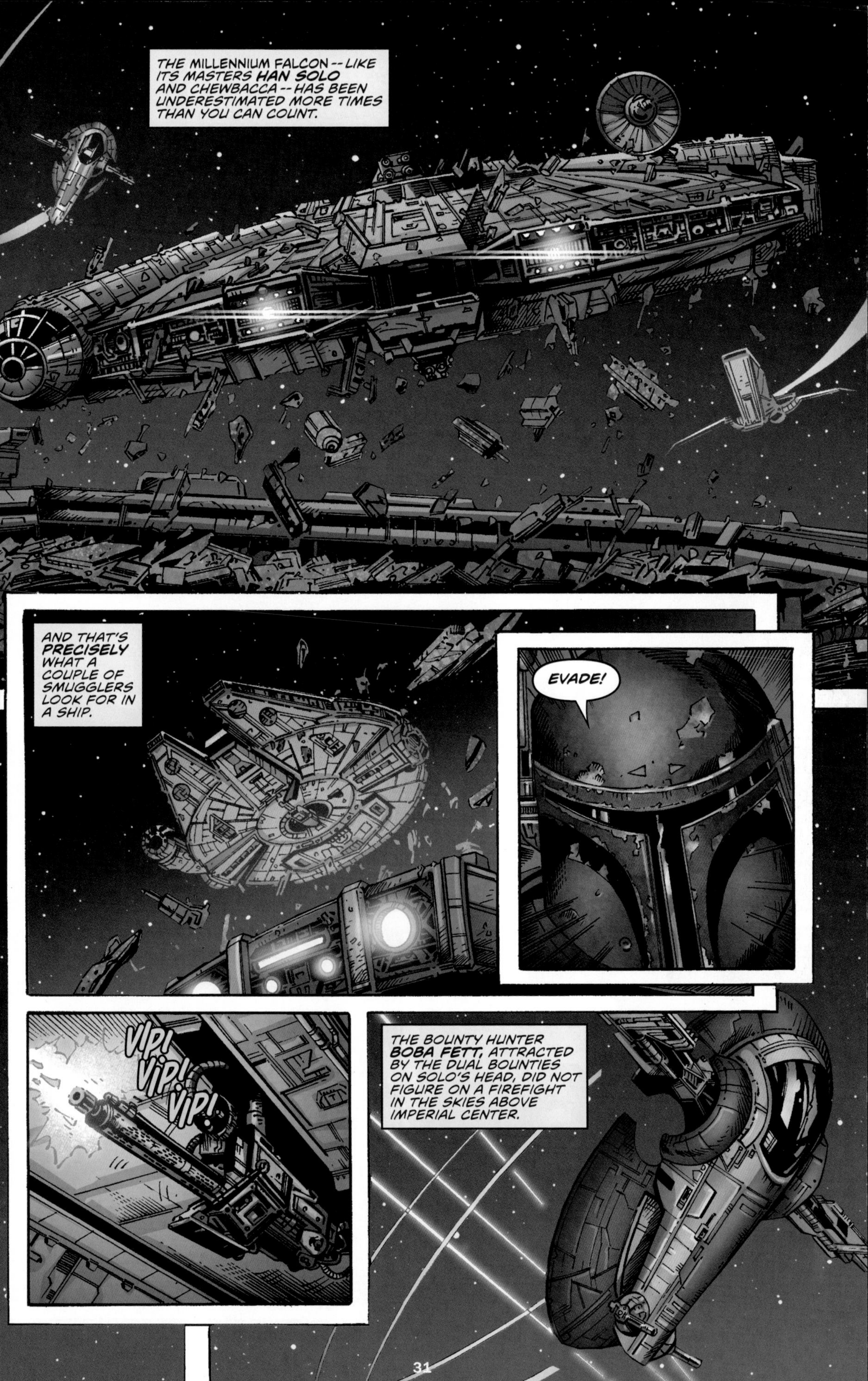
THE MILLENNIUM FALCON--LIKE ITS MASTERS HAN SOLO AND CHEWBACCA--HAS BEEN UNDERESTIMATED MORE TIMES THAN YOU CAN COUNT.
AND THAT'S PRECISELY WHAT A COUPLE OF SMUGGLERS LOOK FOR IN A SHIP.
EVADE!
VIP! VIP! VIP!
THE BOUNTY HUNTER BOBA FETT, ATTRACTED BY THE DUAL BOUNTIES ON SOLO'S HEAD, DID NOT FIGURE ON A FIREFIGHT IN THE SKIES ABOVE IMPERIAL CENTER.

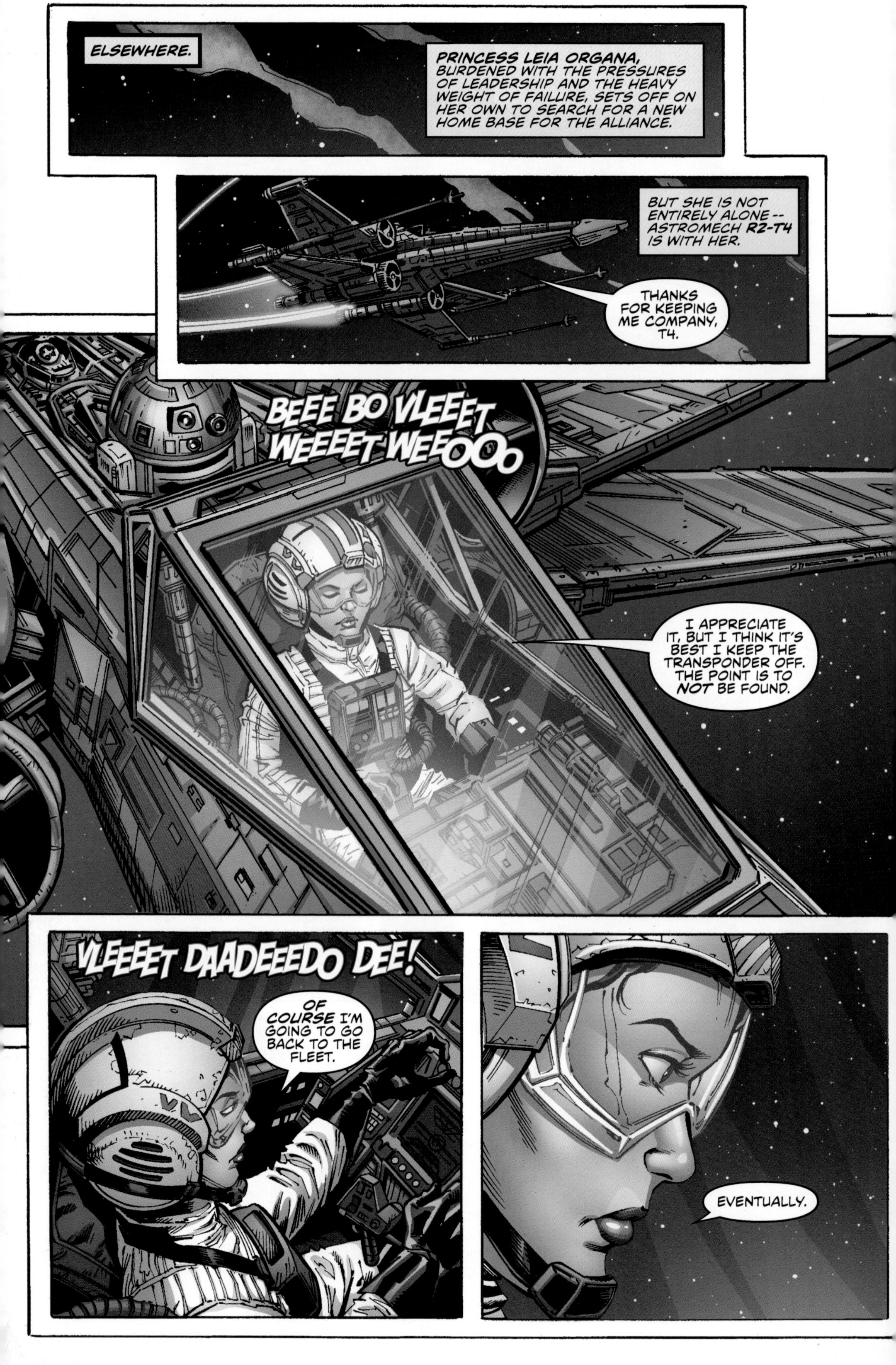
ELSEWHERE.
PRINCESS LEIA ORGANA, BURDENED WITH THE PRESSURES OF LEADERSHIP AND THE HEAVY WEIGHT OF FAILURE, SETS OFF ON HER OWN TO SEARCH FOR A NEW HOME BASE FOR THE ALLIANCE.
BUT SHE IS NOT ENTIRELY ALONE -- ASTROMECH R2-T4 IS WITH HER.
THANKS FOR KEEPING ME COMPANY, T4.
BEEE BO VLEEET WEEEET WEEOOo
I APPRECIATE IT, BUT I THINK IT'S BEST I KEEP THE TRANSPONDER OFF. THE POINT IS TO NOT BE FOUND.
VLEEEET DAADEEEDO DEE!
OF COURSE I'M GOING TO GO BACK TO THE FLEET.
EVENTUALLY.

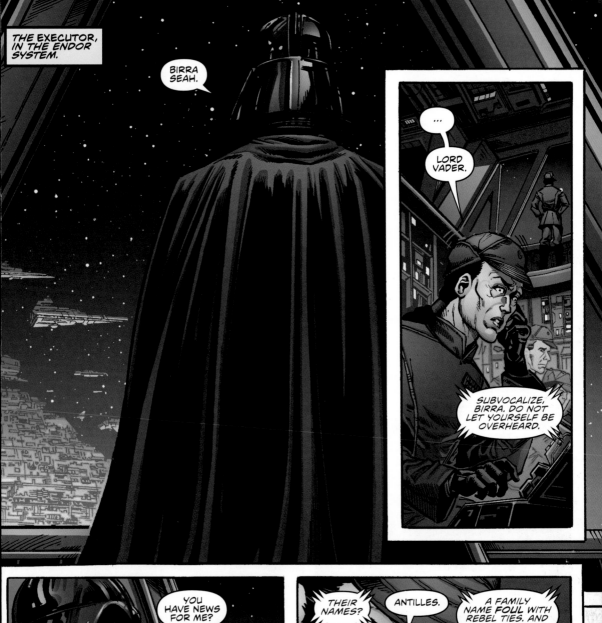

THE EXECUTOR, IN THE ENDOR SYSTEM.

BIRRA SEAH.

...LORD VADER.

SUBVOCALIZE, BIRRA. DO NOT LET YOURSELF BE OVERHEARD.

YOU HAVE NEWS FOR ME?

WE HAVE CAPTIVES, LORD VADER. COLONEL BIRCHER HAS DETAINED TWO COURIERS ACCUSED OF BEING REBEL COLLABORATORS.

THEIR NAMES?

ANTILLES.

A FAMILY NAME FOUL WITH REBEL TIES. AND THE OTHER?

I DON'T KNOW.

FIND OUT.

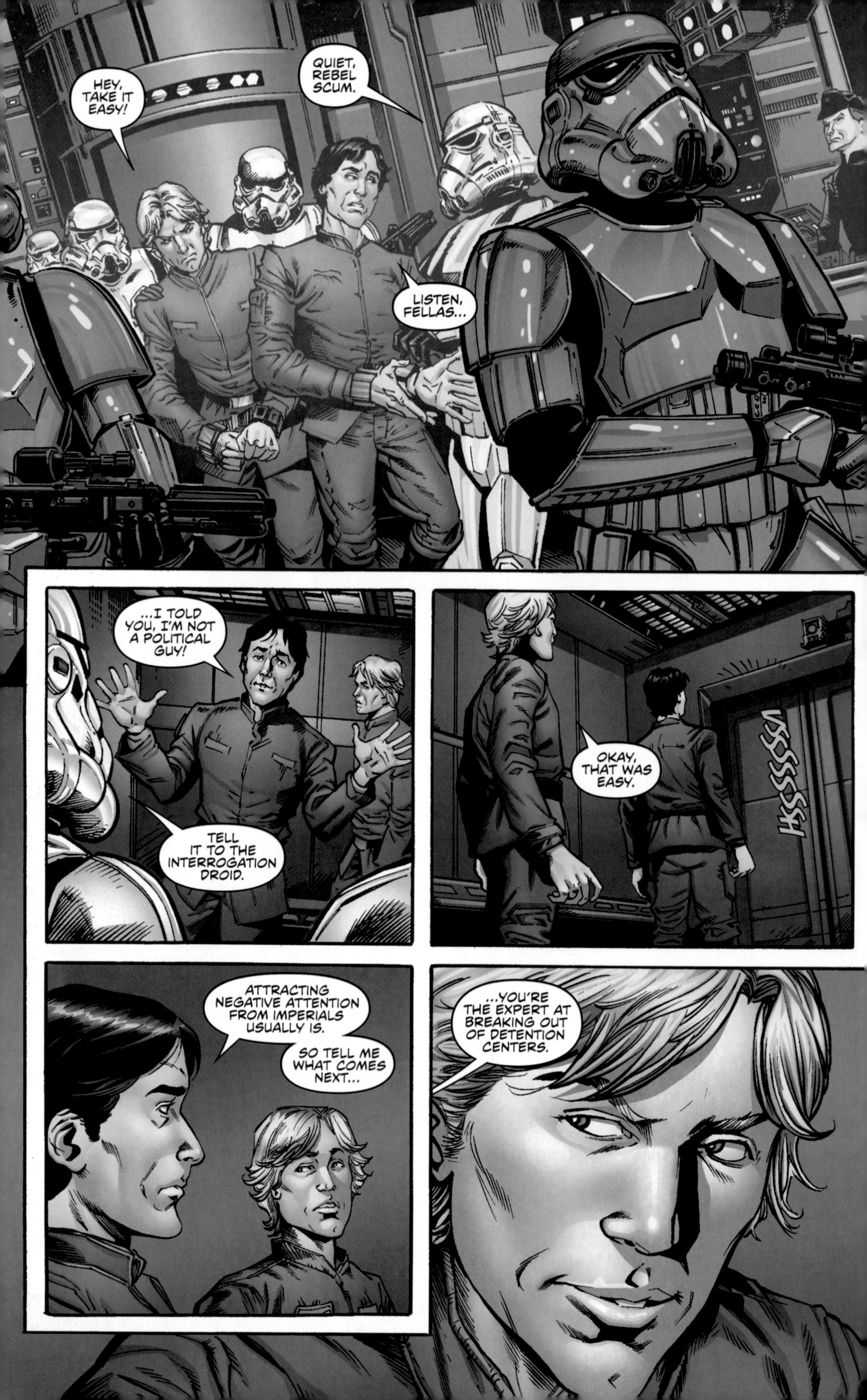
HEY, TAKE IT EASY!
QUIET, REBEL SCUM.
LISTEN, FELLAS...
...I TOLD YOU, I'M NOT A POLITICAL GUY!
TELL IT TO THE INTERROGATION DROID.
OKAY, THAT WAS EASY.
HSSSSSS
ATTRACTING NEGATIVE ATTENTION FROM IMPERIALS USUALLY IS.
SO TELL ME WHAT COMES NEXT...
...YOU'RE THE EXPERT AT BREAKING OUT OF DETENTION CENTERS.

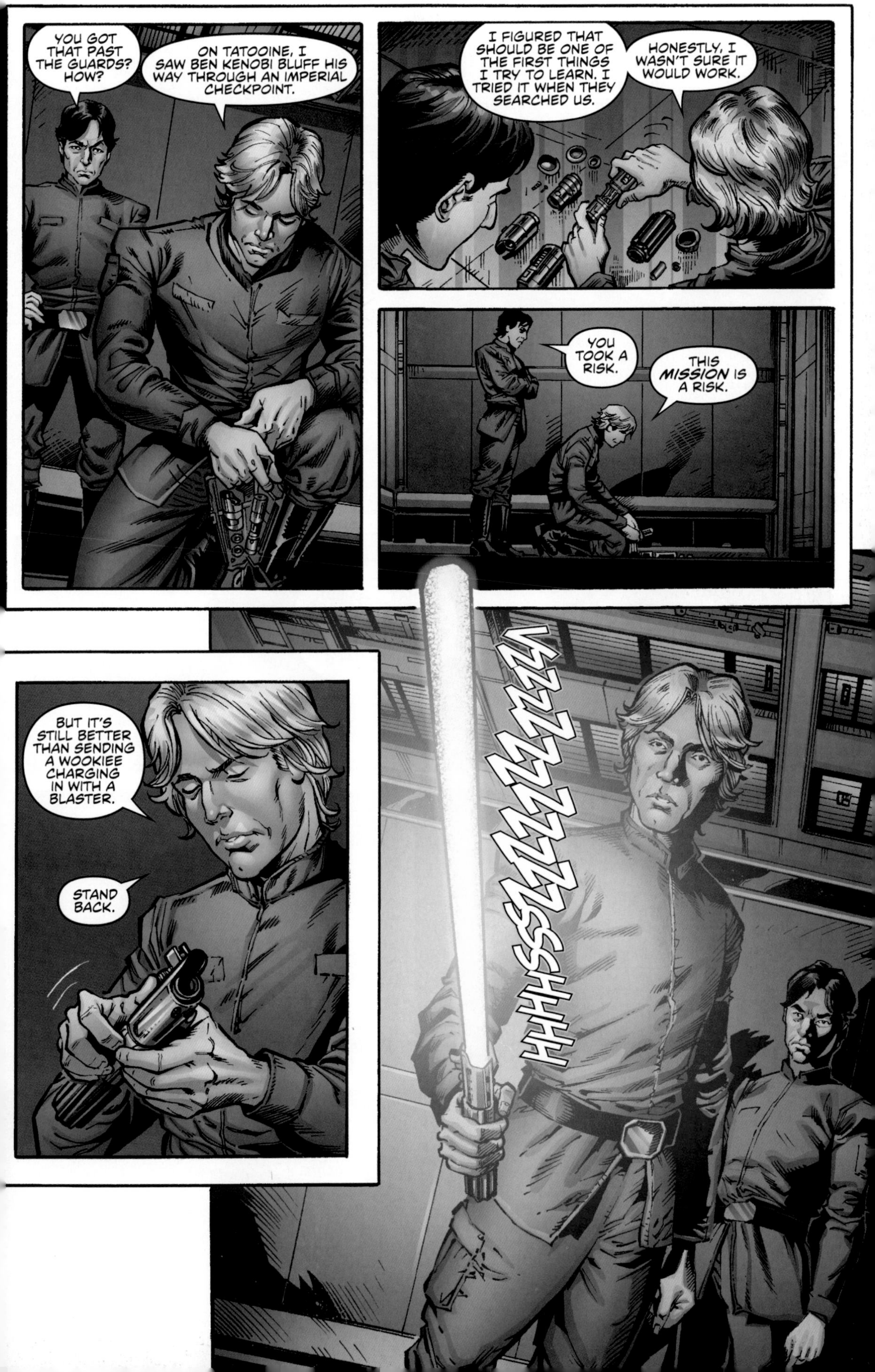
YOU GOT THAT PAST THE GUARDS? HOW?
ON TATOOINE, I SAW BEN KENOBI BLUFF HIS WAY THROUGH AN IMPERIAL CHECKPOINT.
I FIGURED THAT SHOULD BE ONE OF THE FIRST THINGS I TRY TO LEARN. I TRIED IT WHEN THEY SEARCHED US.
HONESTLY, I WASN'T SURE IT WOULD WORK.
YOU TOOK A RISK.
THIS *MISSION* IS A RISK.
BUT IT'S STILL BETTER THAN SENDING A WOOKIEE CHARGING IN WITH A BLASTER.
STAND BACK.
SSZZZZZZZMMMHHHH

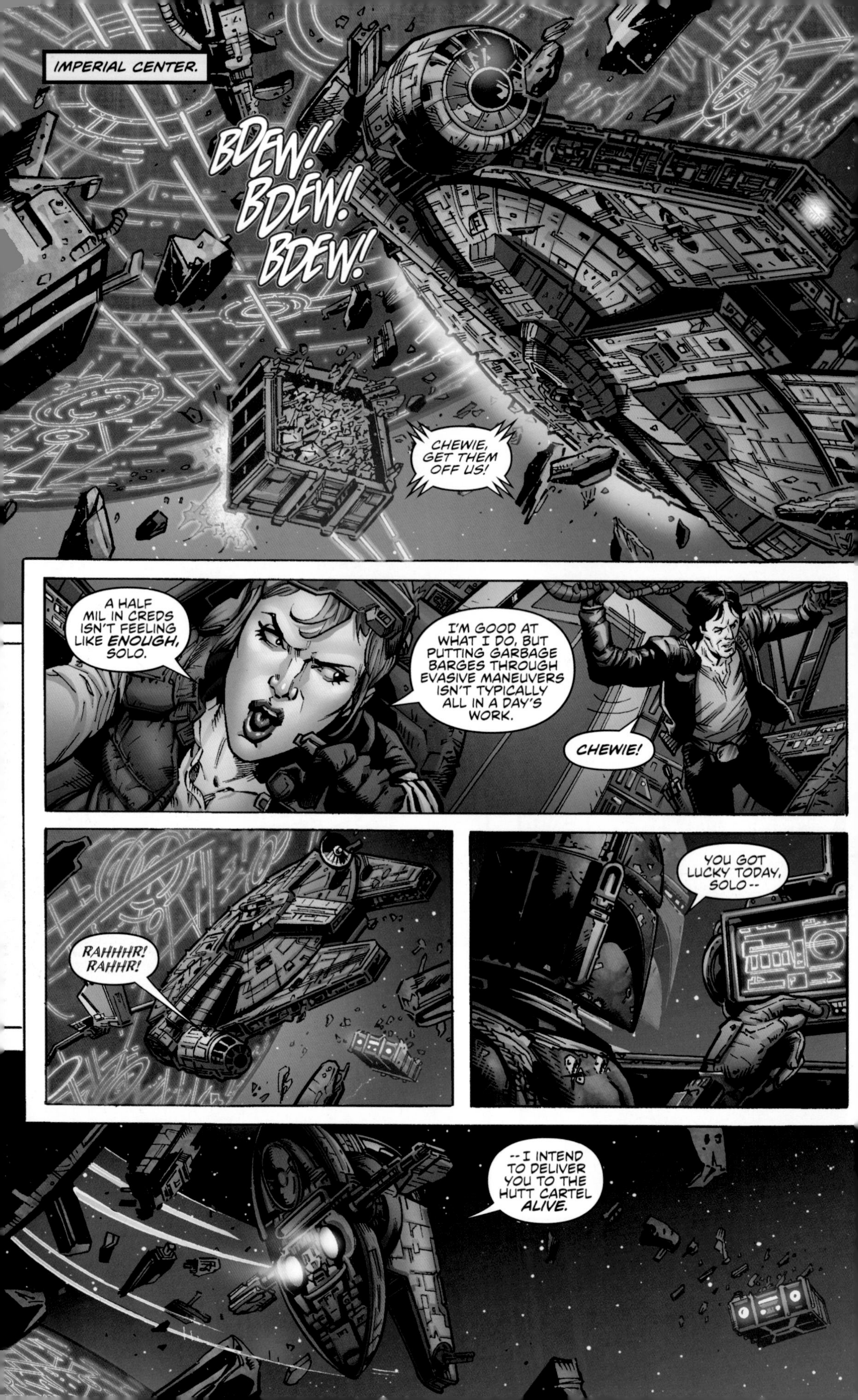
IMPERIAL CENTER.
BDEW! BDEW! BDEW!
CHEWIE, GET THEM OFF US!
A HALF MIL IN CREDS ISN'T FEELING LIKE ENOUGH, SOLO.
I'M GOOD AT WHAT I DO, BUT PUTTING GARBAGE BARGES THROUGH EVASIVE MANEUVERS ISN'T TYPICALLY ALL IN A DAY'S WORK.
CHEWIE!
RAHHHR! RAHHR!
YOU GOT LUCKY TODAY, SOLO--
--I INTEND TO DELIVER YOU TO THE HUTT CARTEL ALIVE.

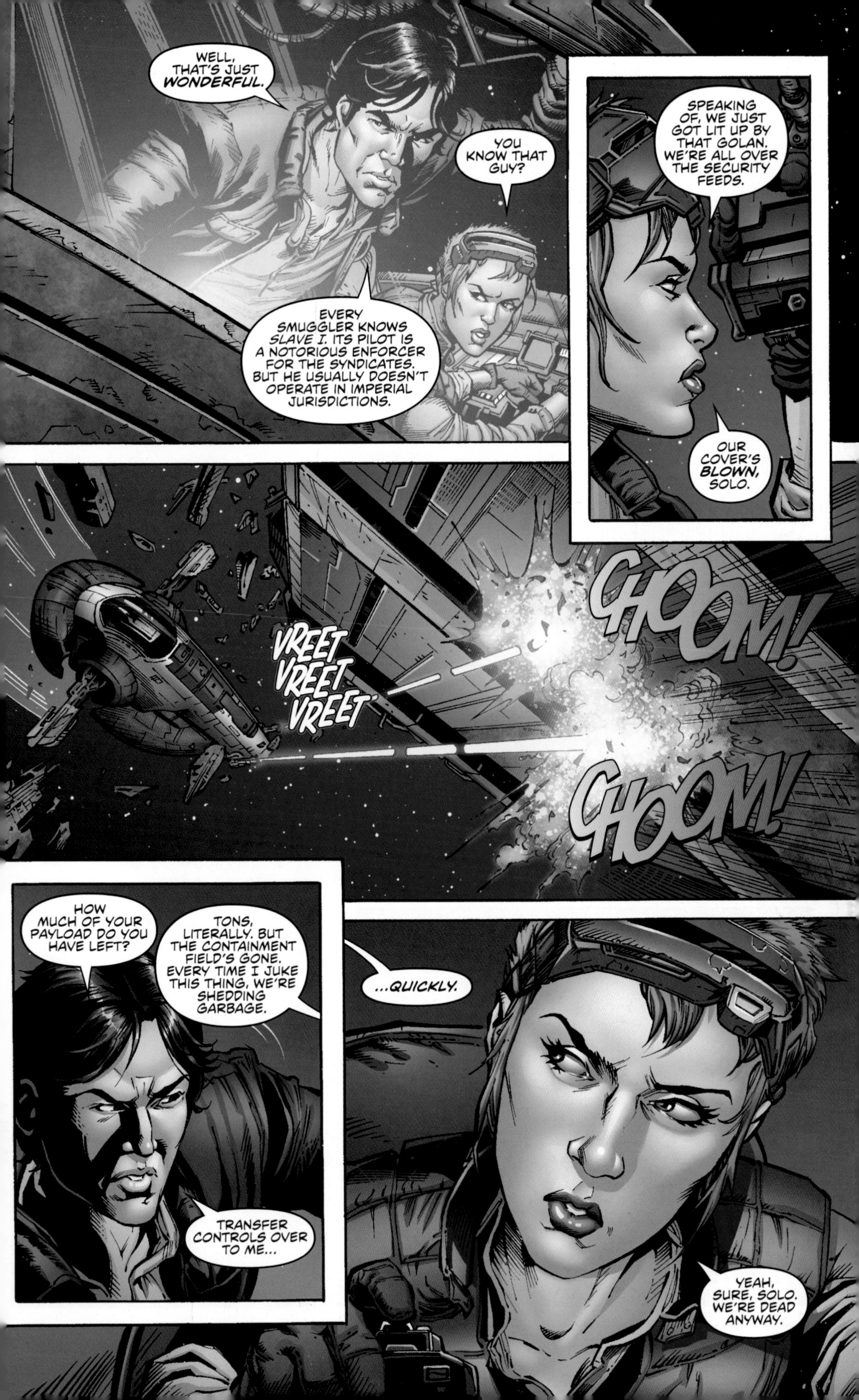
WELL, THAT'S JUST *WONDERFUL.*
YOU KNOW THAT GUY?
EVERY SMUGGLER KNOWS *SLAVE I.* ITS PILOT IS A NOTORIOUS ENFORCER FOR THE SYNDICATES. BUT HE USUALLY DOESN'T OPERATE IN IMPERIAL JURISDICTIONS.
SPEAKING OF, WE JUST GOT LIT UP BY THAT GOLAN. WE'RE ALL OVER THE SECURITY FEEDS.
OUR COVER'S *BLOWN,* SOLO.
VREET VREET VREET
CHOOM!
CHOOM!
HOW MUCH OF YOUR PAYLOAD DO YOU HAVE LEFT?
TONS, LITERALLY. BUT THE CONTAINMENT FIELD'S GONE. EVERY TIME I JUKE THIS THING, WE'RE SHEDDING GARBAGE.
TRANSFER CONTROLS OVER TO ME...
...QUICKLY.
YEAH, SURE, SOLO. WE'RE DEAD ANYWAY.

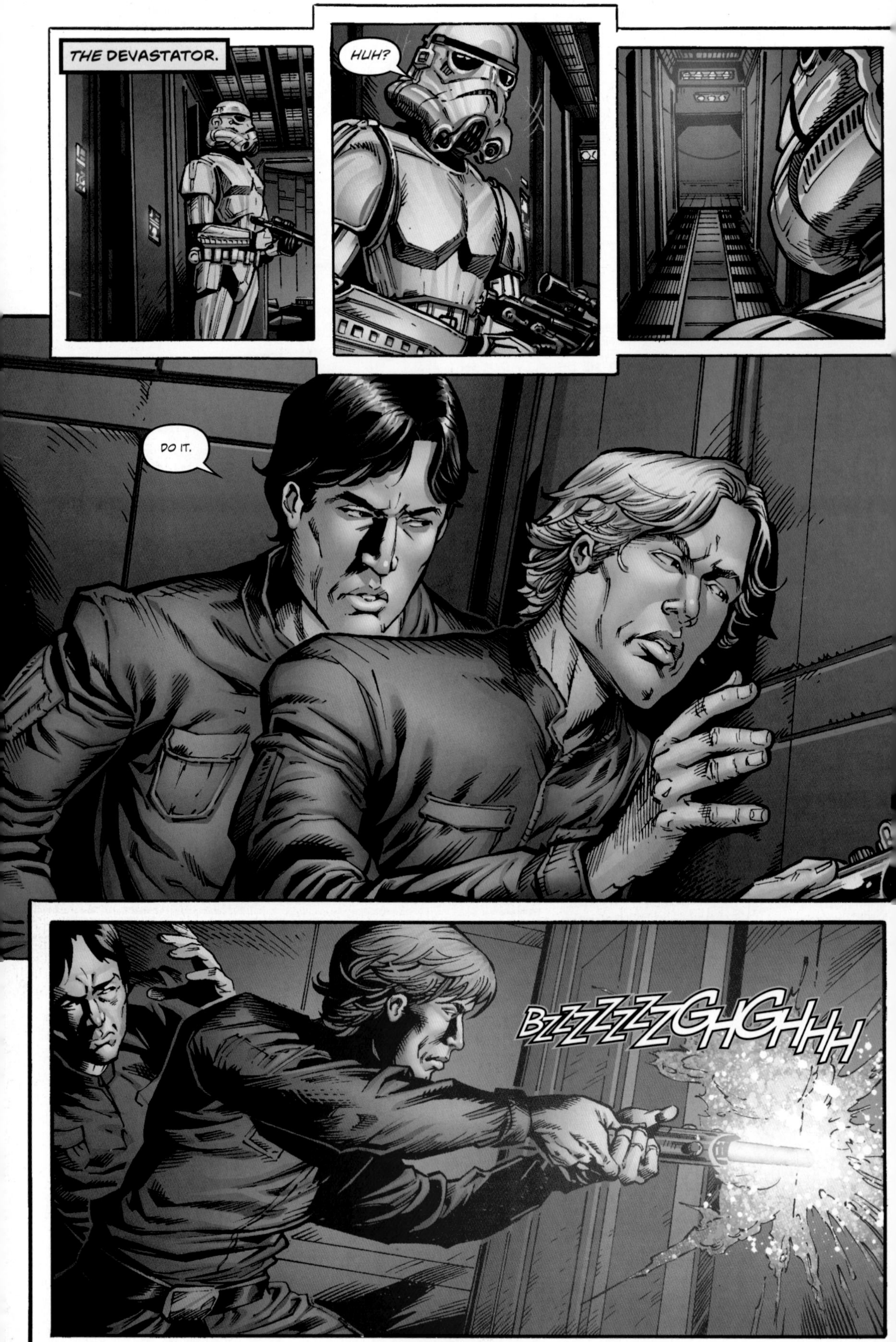
THE DEVASTATOR.
HUH?
DO IT.
BZZZZZZGHGHHH

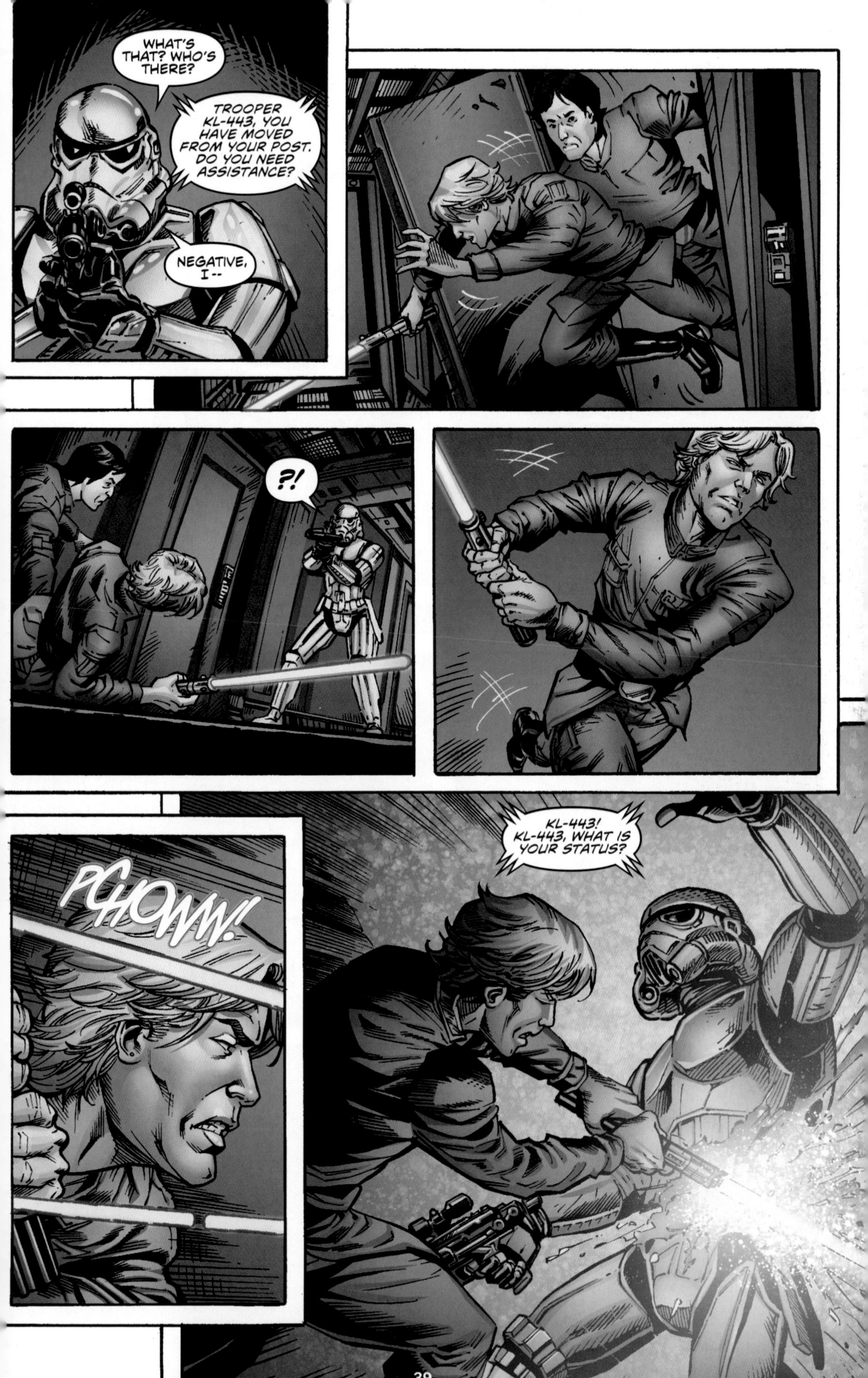
WHAT'S THAT? WHO'S THERE?
TROOPER KL-443, YOU HAVE MOVED FROM YOUR POST. DO YOU NEED ASSISTANCE?
NEGATIVE, I--
?!
PCHOWW!
KL-443! KL-443, WHAT IS YOUR STATUS?

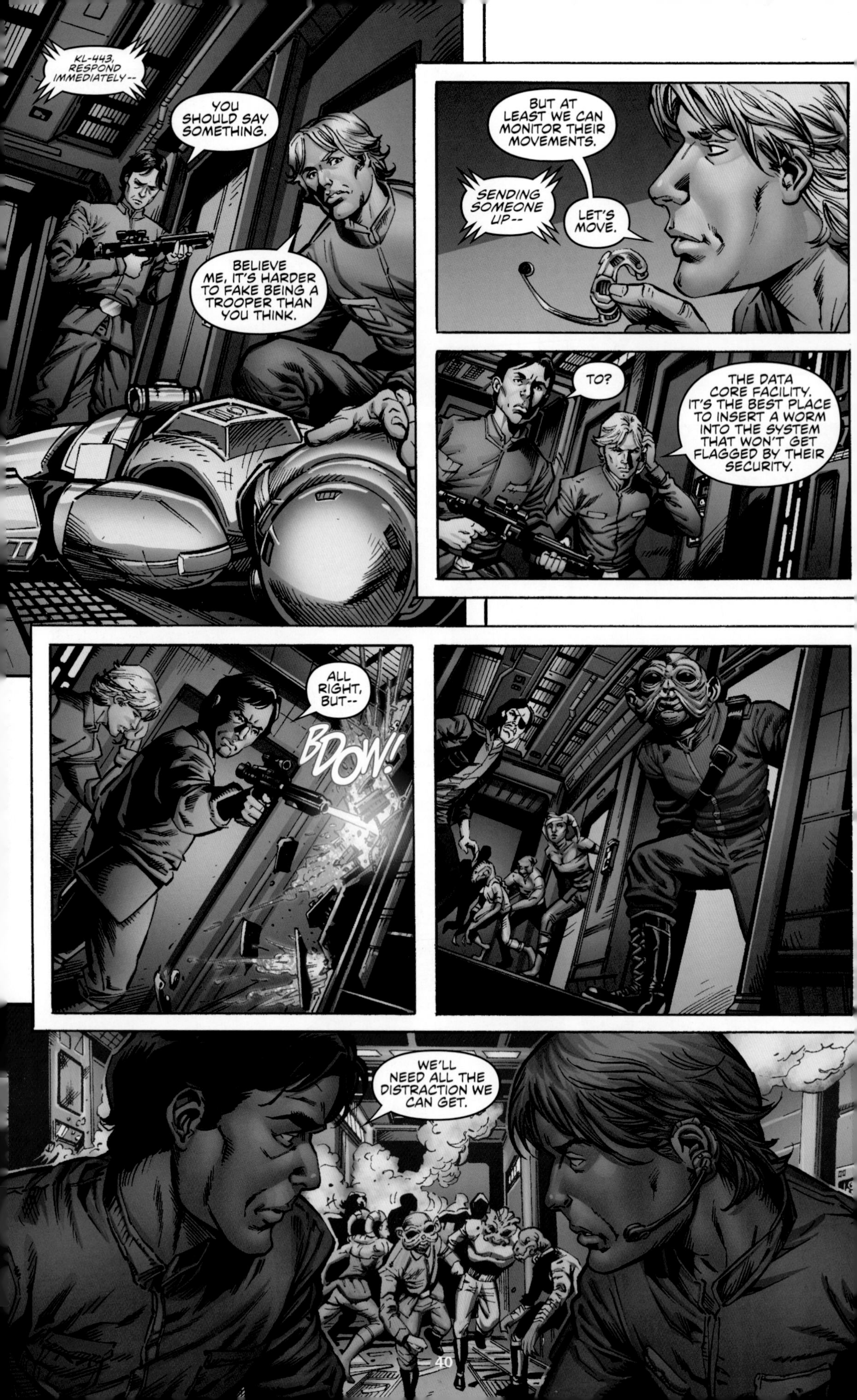
KL-443, RESPOND IMMEDIATELY--
YOU SHOULD SAY SOMETHING.
BELIEVE ME, IT'S HARDER TO FAKE BEING A TROOPER THAN YOU THINK.
SENDING SOMEONE UP--
BUT AT LEAST WE CAN MONITOR THEIR MOVEMENTS.
LET'S MOVE.
TO?
THE DATA CORE FACILITY. IT'S THE BEST PLACE TO INSERT A WORM INTO THE SYSTEM THAT WON'T GET FLAGGED BY THEIR SECURITY.
ALL RIGHT, BUT--
BDOW!
WE'LL NEED ALL THE DISTRACTION WE CAN GET.

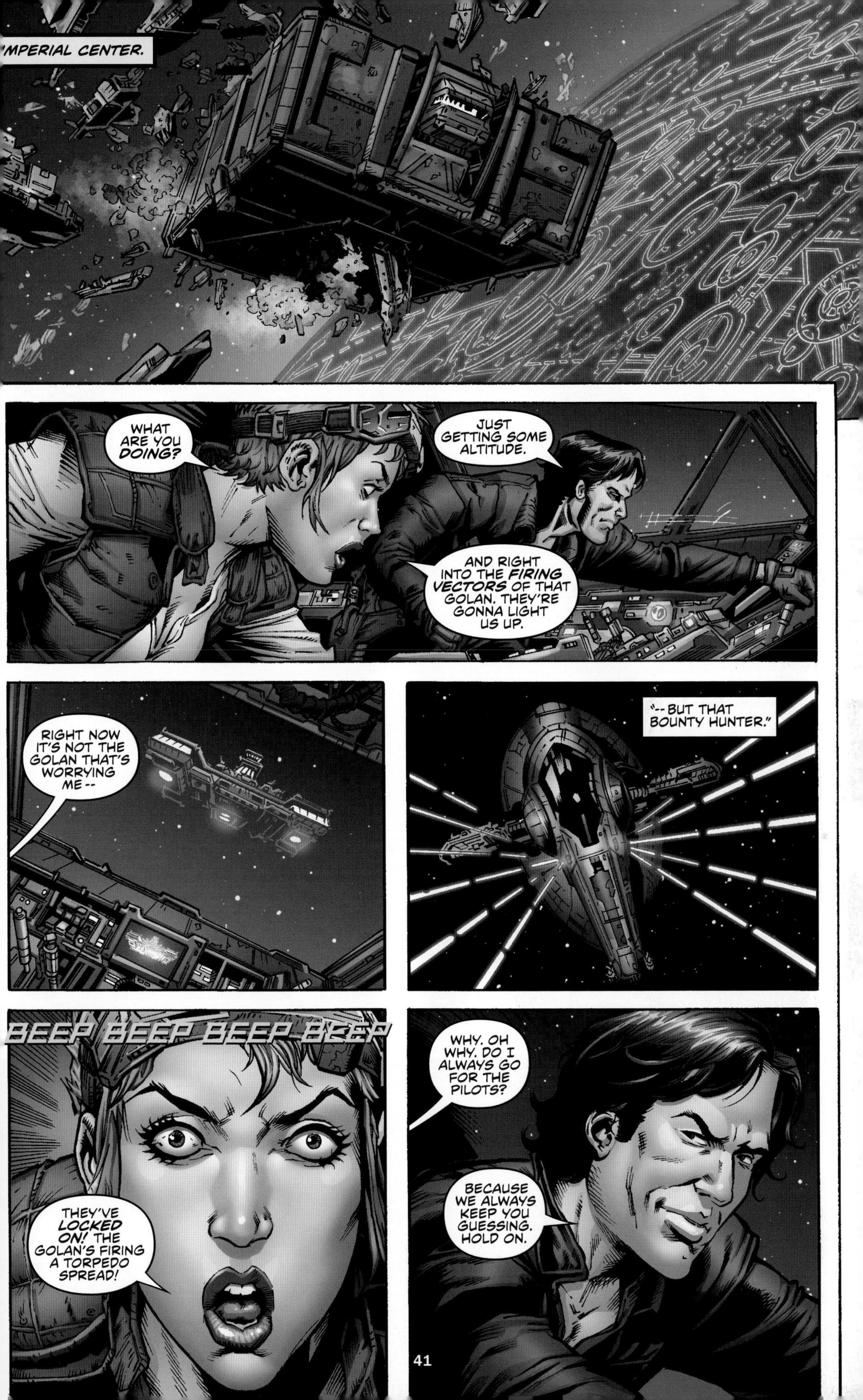
'MPERIAL CENTER.
WHAT ARE YOU DOING?
JUST GETTING SOME ALTITUDE.
AND RIGHT INTO THE FIRING VECTORS OF THAT GOLAN. THEY'RE GONNA LIGHT US UP.
RIGHT NOW IT'S NOT THE GOLAN THAT'S WORRYING ME --
"-- BUT THAT BOUNTY HUNTER."
BEEP BEEP BEEP BEEP
THEY'VE LOCKED ON! THE GOLAN'S FIRING A TORPEDO SPREAD!
WHY. OH WHY. DO I ALWAYS GO FOR THE PILOTS?
BECAUSE WE ALWAYS KEEP YOU GUESSING. HOLD ON.

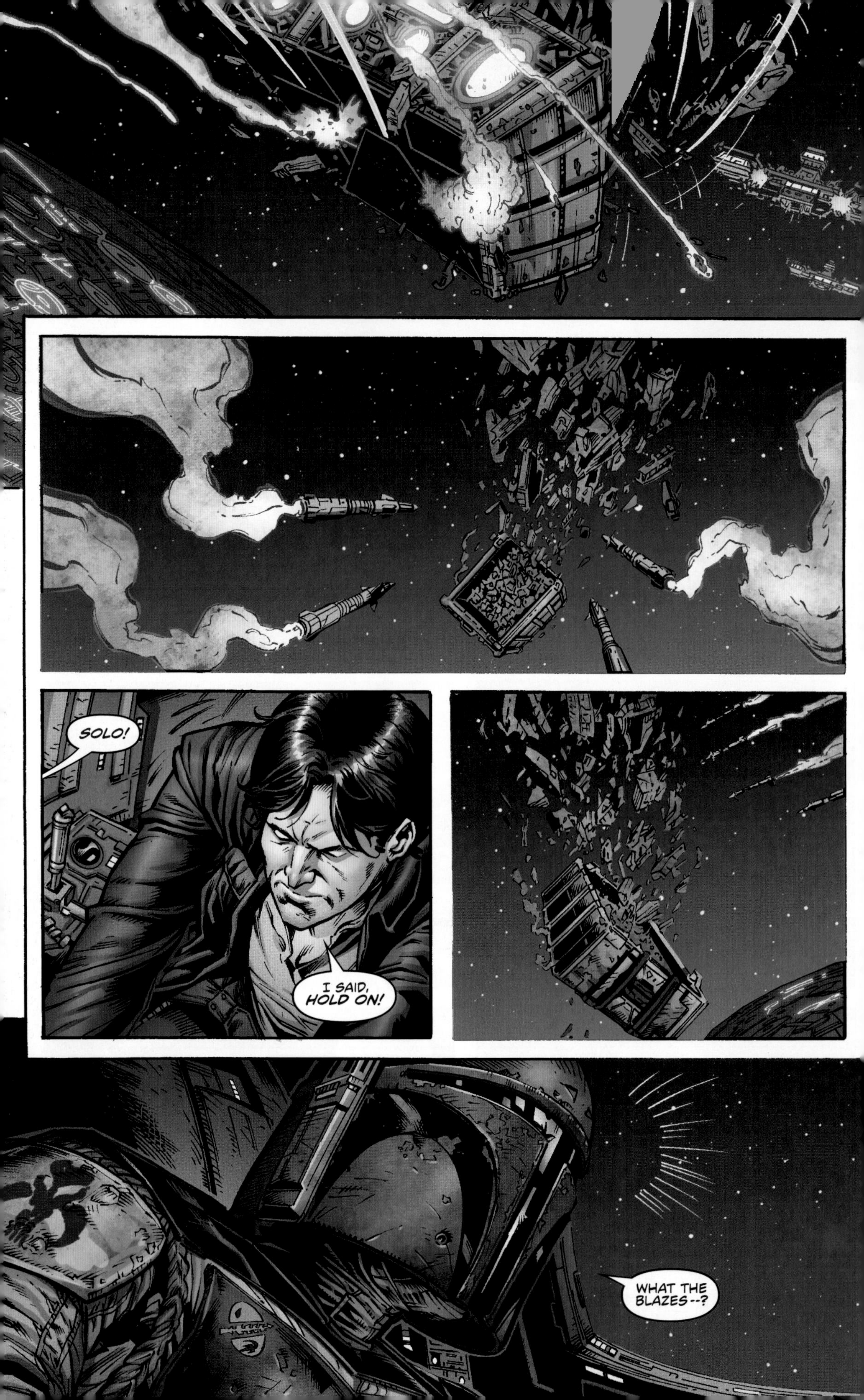
SOLO!
I SAID, HOLD ON!
WHAT THE BLAZES--?

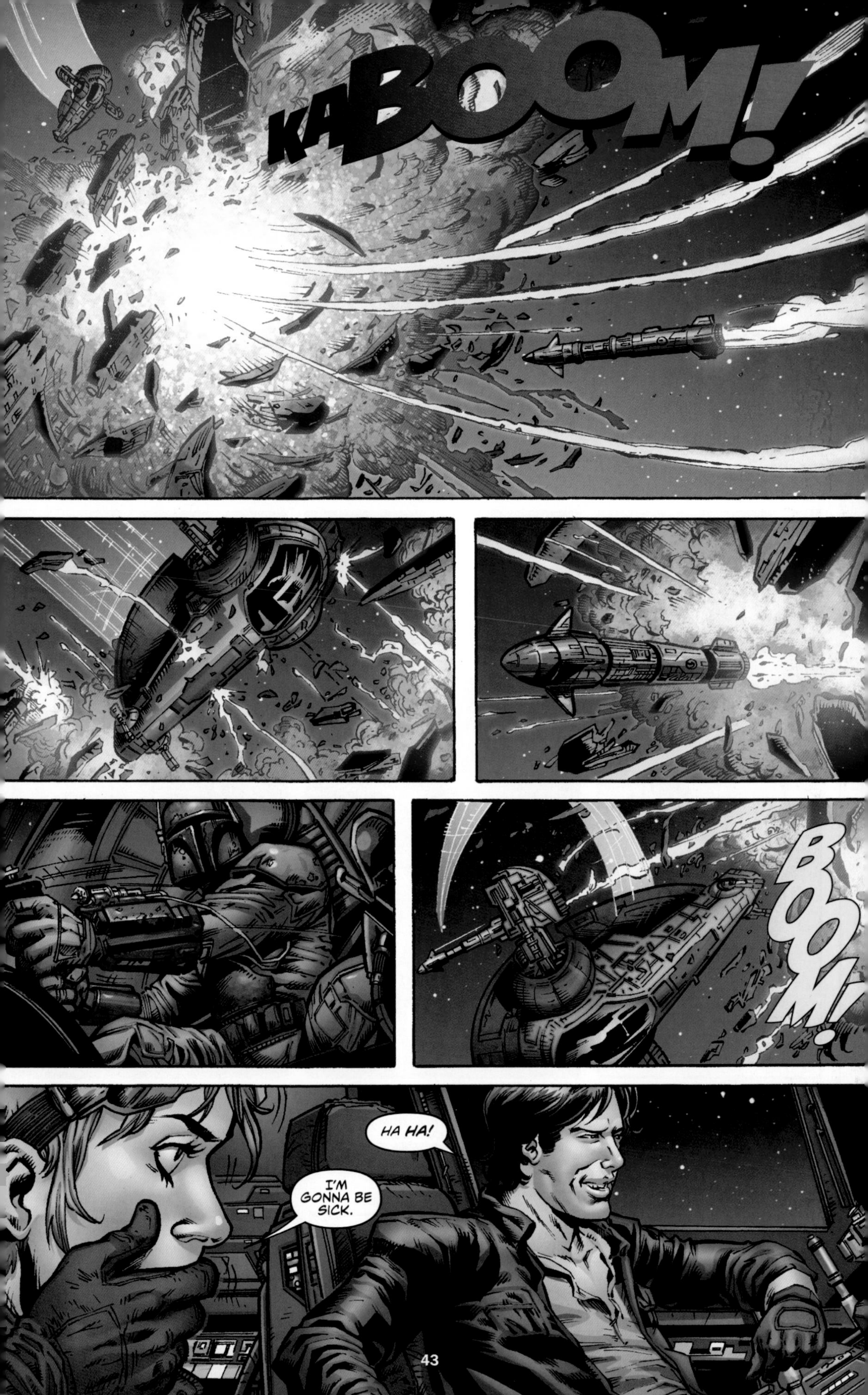
KABOOM!
BOOM!
HA HA!
I'M GONNA BE SICK.

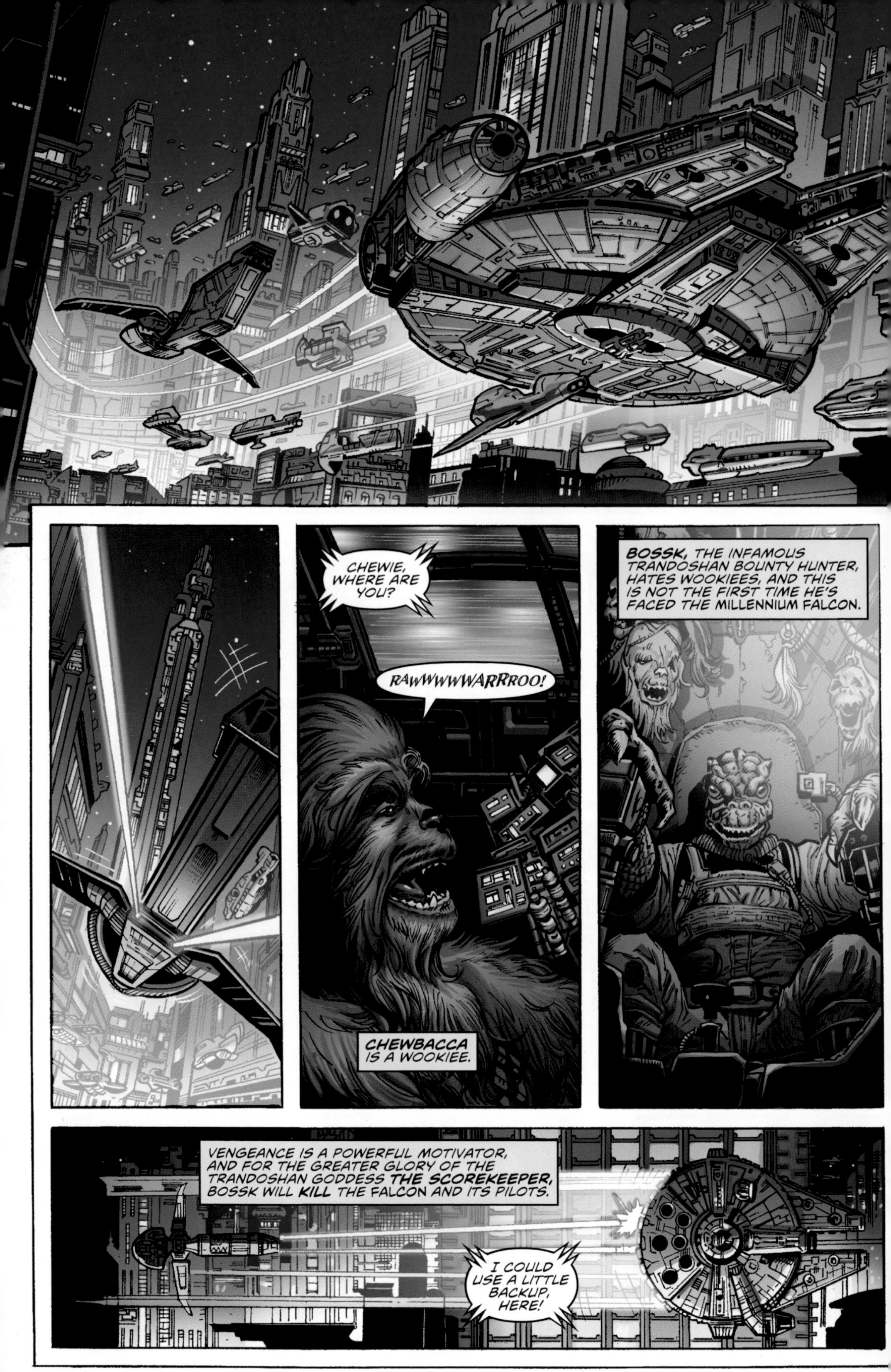
CHEWIE, WHERE ARE YOU?
RAWWWWWARRROO!
CHEWBACCA IS A WOOKIEE.
BOSSK, THE INFAMOUS TRANDOSHAN BOUNTY HUNTER, HATES WOOKIEES, AND THIS IS NOT THE FIRST TIME HE'S FACED THE MILLENNIUM FALCON.
VENGEANCE IS A POWERFUL MOTIVATOR, AND FOR THE GREATER GLORY OF THE TRANDOSHAN GODDESS THE SCOREKEEPER, BOSSK WILL KILL THE FALCON AND ITS PILOTS.
I COULD USE A LITTLE BACKUP, HERE!

THE ALDERAAN SYSTEM.

EEEEOOOOOWHEEEE?

MAINTAIN THIS POSITION, T4.

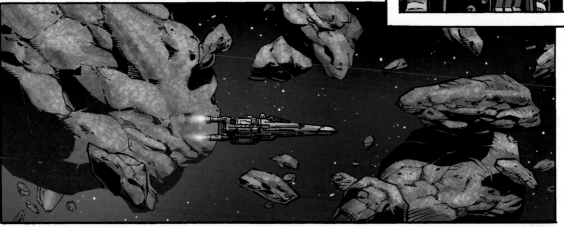

BEEEOOOOOOOOOOOOOOO

THANK YOU.

T4, I'M GOING TO SEND YOU A DATA PACKET...

...HARD CODE IT ONTO A CAPSULE AND EJECT IT FOR ME?

DEEET DAH DA DEEE DA!

IT'S A SURVIVOR'S THING.

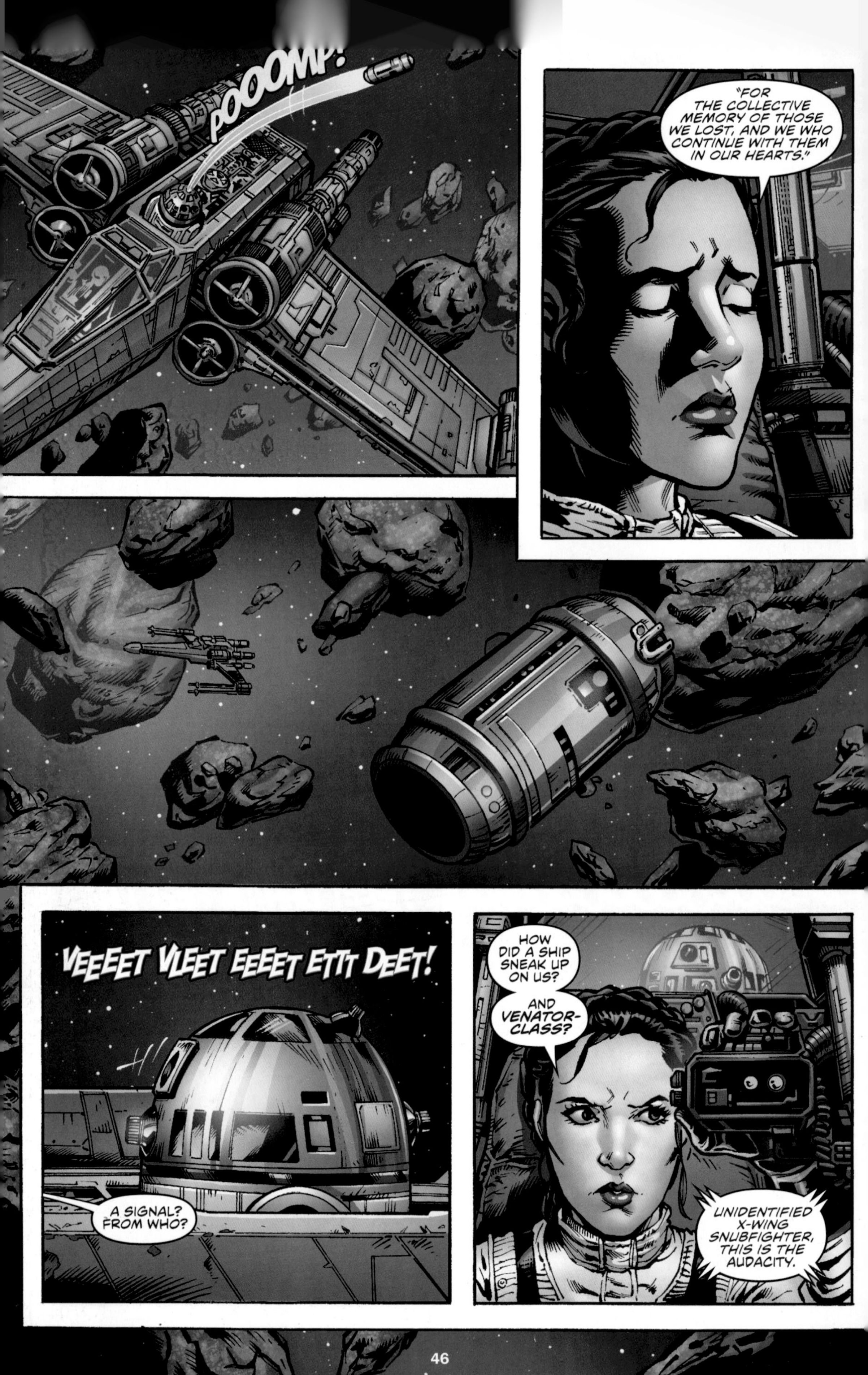
POOOMP!
"FOR THE COLLECTIVE MEMORY OF THOSE WE LOST, AND WE WHO CONTINUE WITH THEM IN OUR HEARTS."
VEEEET VLEET EEEET ETTT DEET!
A SIGNAL? FROM WHO?
HOW DID A SHIP SNEAK UP ON US?
AND VENATOR-CLASS?
UNIDENTIFIED X-WING SNUBFIGHTER, THIS IS THE AUDACITY.

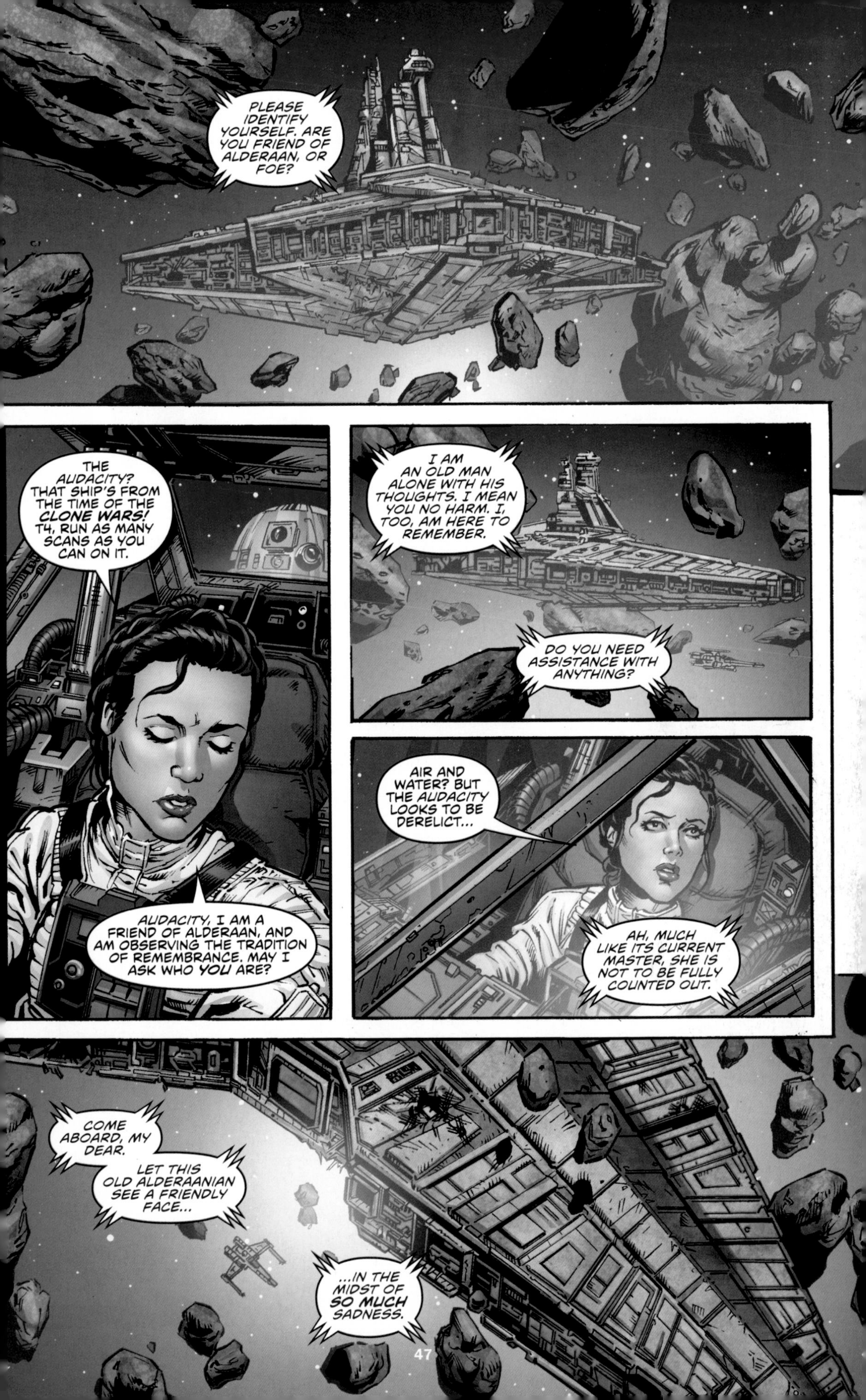
PLEASE IDENTIFY YOURSELF. ARE YOU FRIEND OF ALDERAAN, OR FOE?
THE *AUDACITY*? THAT SHIP'S FROM THE TIME OF THE **CLONE WARS!** T4, RUN AS MANY SCANS AS YOU CAN ON IT.
AUDACITY, I AM A FRIEND OF ALDERAAN, AND AM OBSERVING THE TRADITION OF REMEMBRANCE. MAY I ASK WHO **YOU** ARE?
I AM AN OLD MAN ALONE WITH HIS THOUGHTS. I MEAN YOU NO HARM. I, TOO, AM HERE TO REMEMBER.
DO YOU NEED ASSISTANCE WITH ANYTHING?
AIR AND WATER? BUT THE *AUDACITY* LOOKS TO BE DERELICT...
AH, MUCH LIKE ITS CURRENT MASTER, SHE IS NOT TO BE FULLY COUNTED OUT.
COME ABOARD, MY DEAR.
LET THIS OLD ALDERAANIAN SEE A FRIENDLY FACE...
...IN THE MIDST OF **SO MUCH** SADNESS.

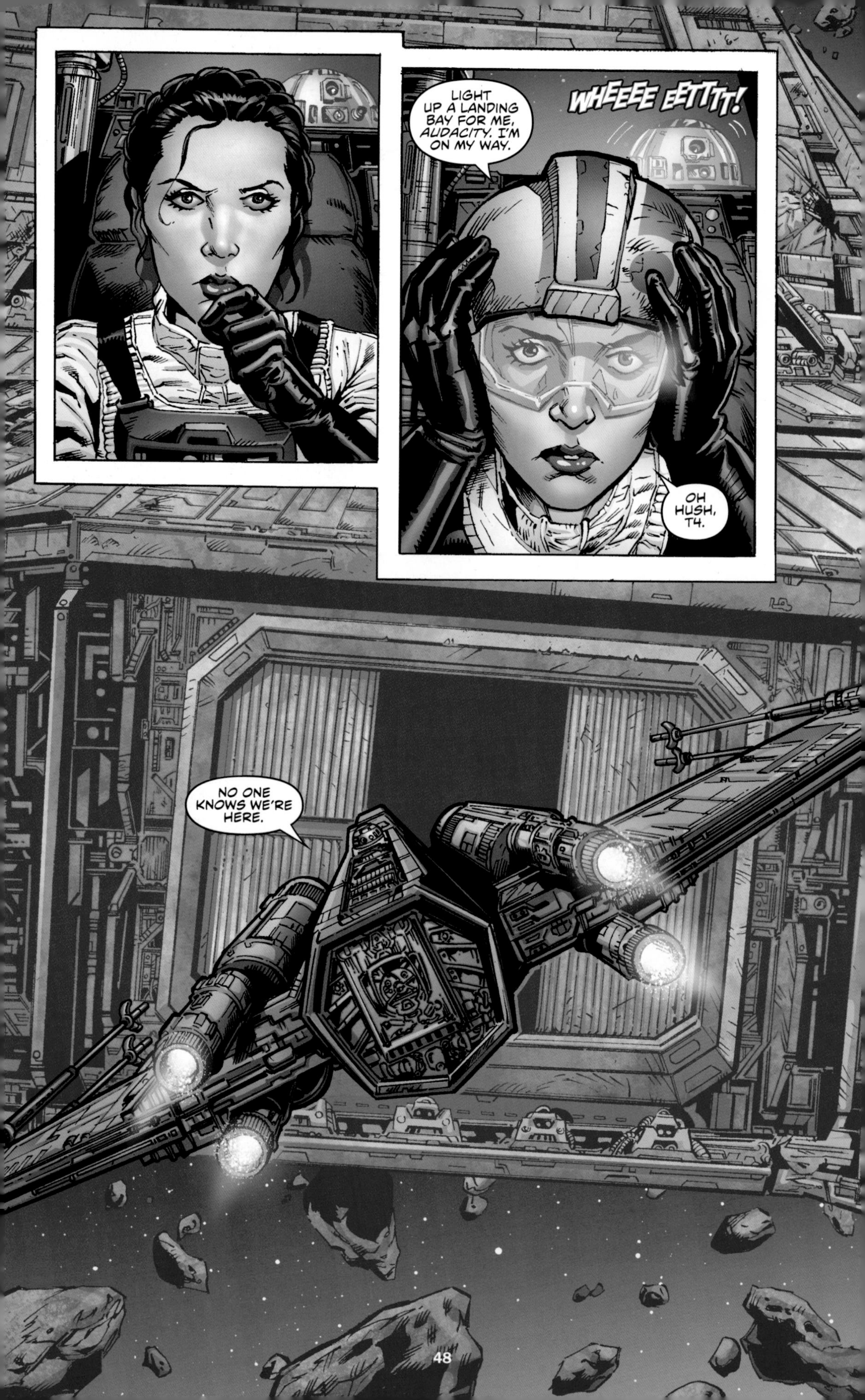
LIGHT UP A LANDING BAY FOR ME, AUDACITY. I'M ON MY WAY.
WHEEEE EETTTT!
OH HUSH, T4.
NO ONE KNOWS WE'RE HERE.

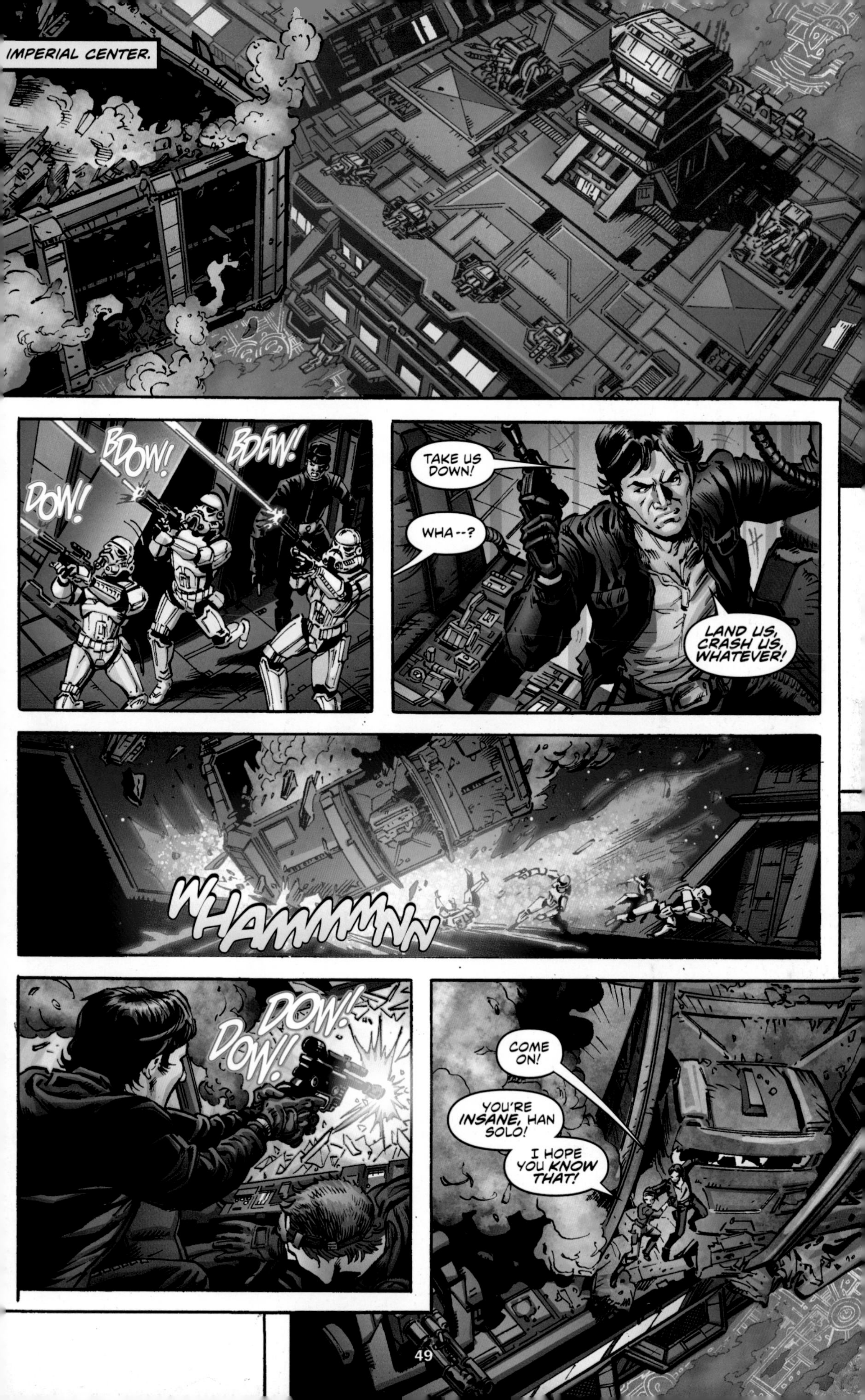
IMPERIAL CENTER.
DOW!
BDOW!
BDEW!
TAKE US DOWN!
WHA--?
LAND US, CRASH US, WHATEVER!
WHAMMMNN
DOW!
DOW!
COME ON!
YOU'RE INSANE, HAN SOLO!
I HOPE YOU KNOW THAT!

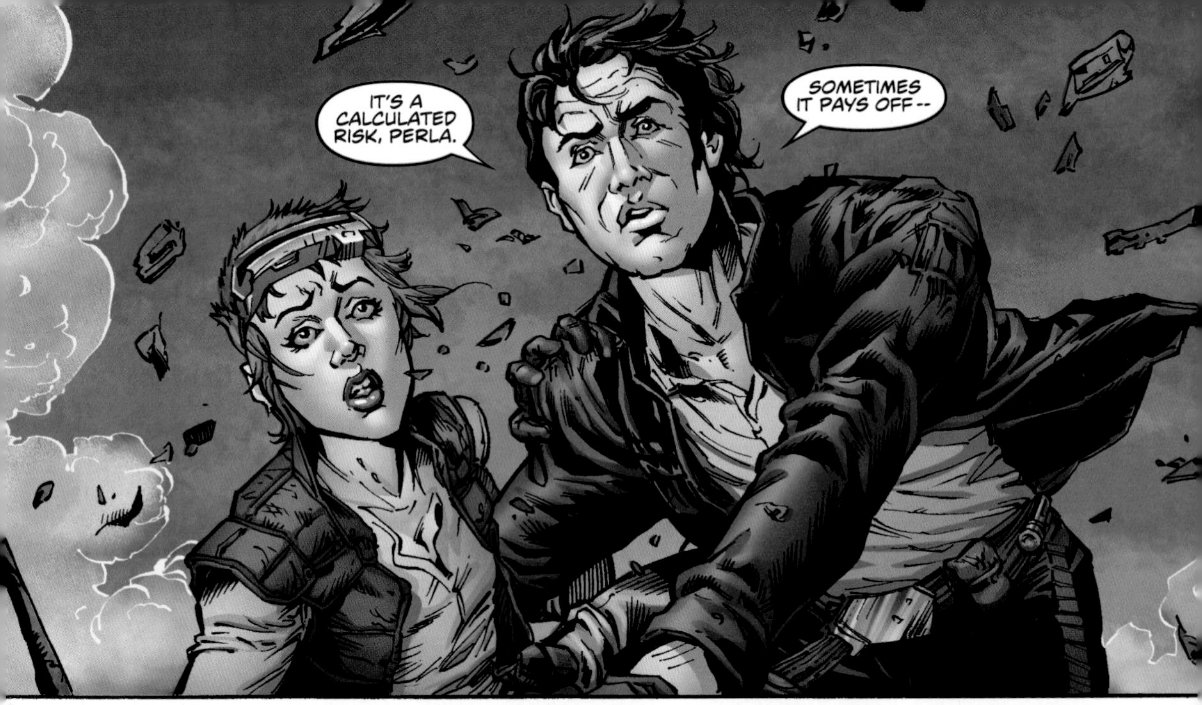
IT'S A CALCULATED RISK, PERLA.
SOMETIMES IT PAYS OFF--

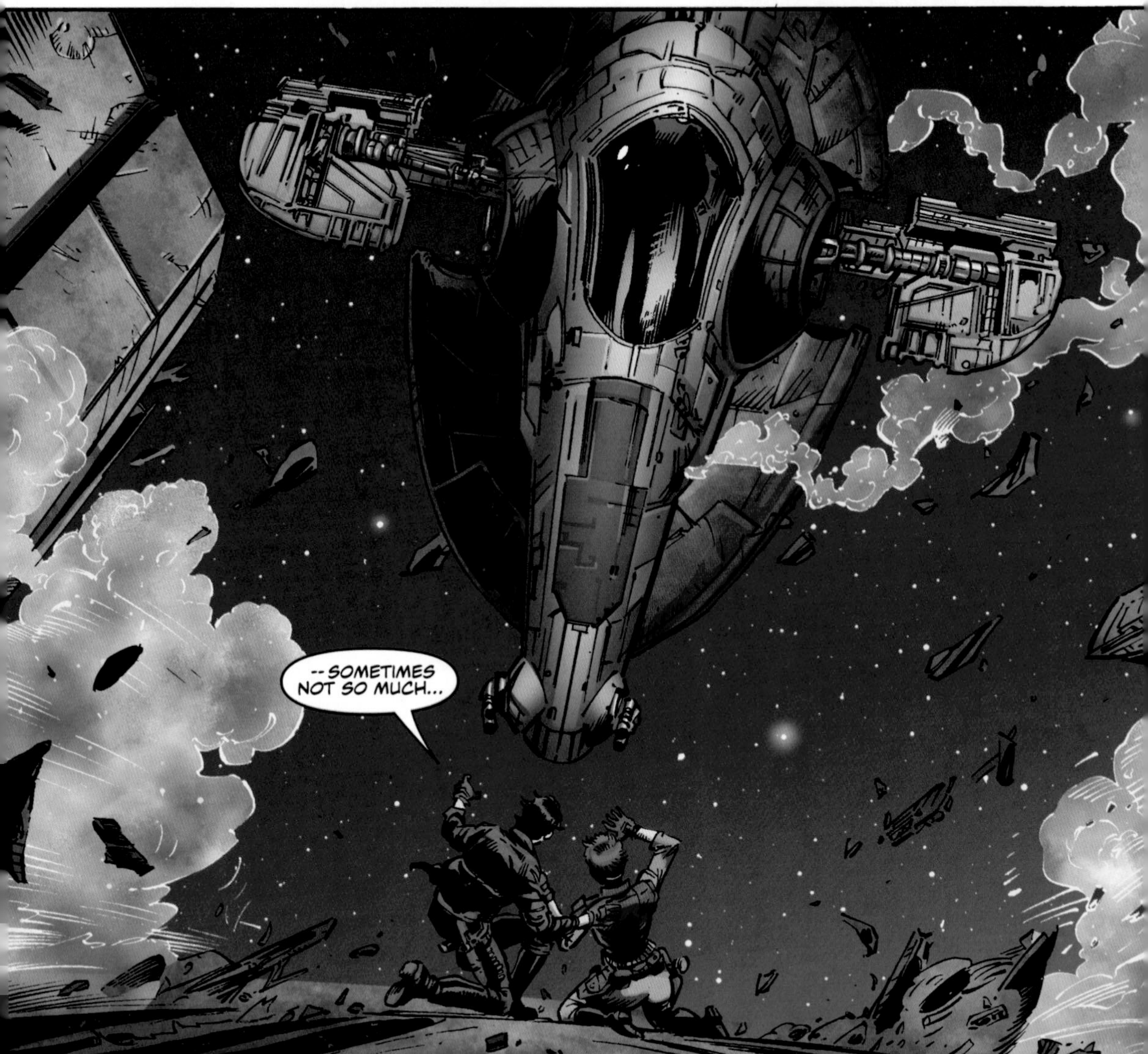
--SOMETIMES NOT SO MUCH...

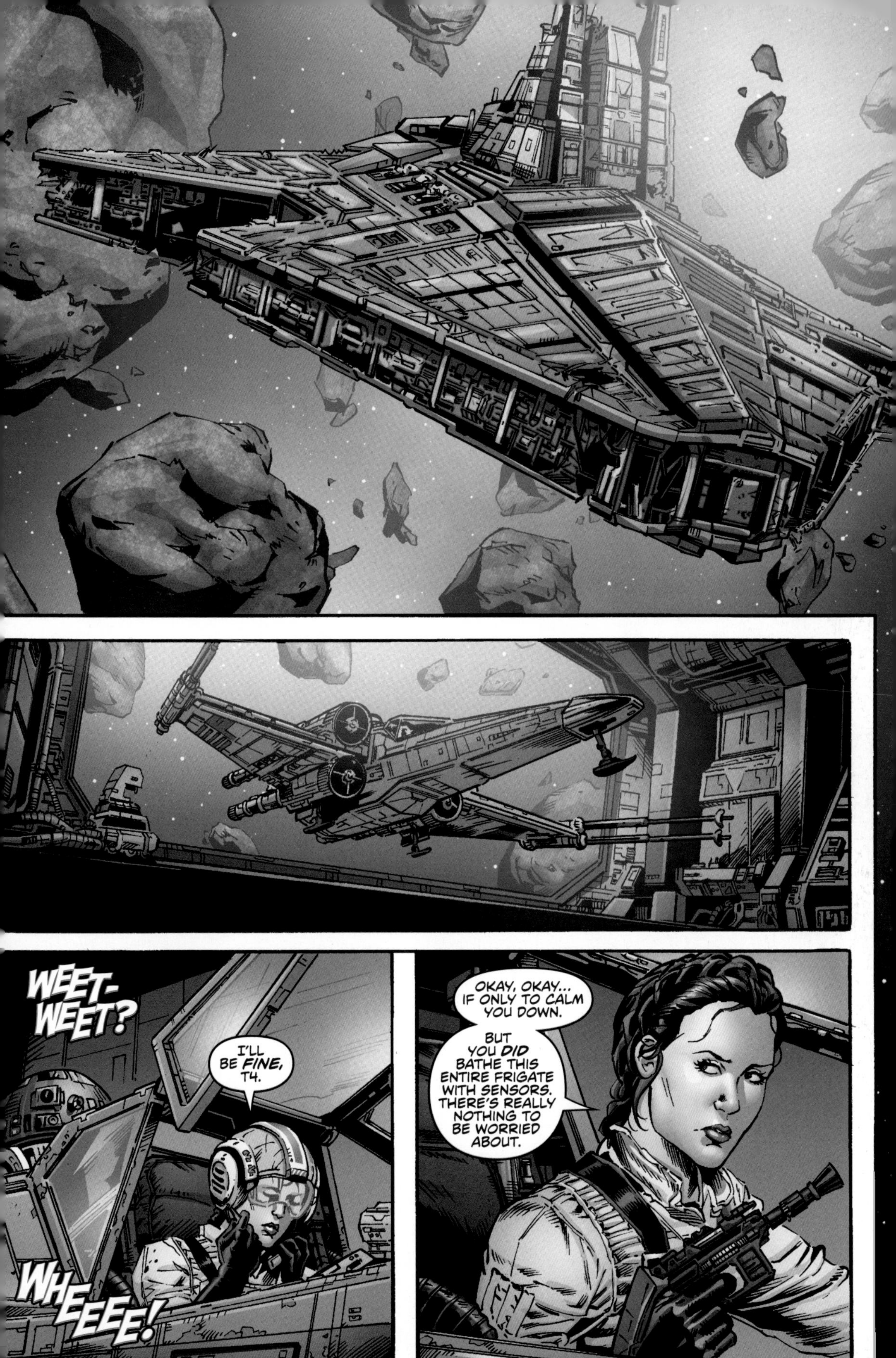
WEET-WEET?
I'LL BE FINE, T4.
WHEEEEE!
OKAY, OKAY... IF ONLY TO CALM YOU DOWN.
BUT YOU DID BATHE THIS ENTIRE FRIGATE WITH SENSORS. THERE'S REALLY NOTHING TO BE WORRIED ABOUT.

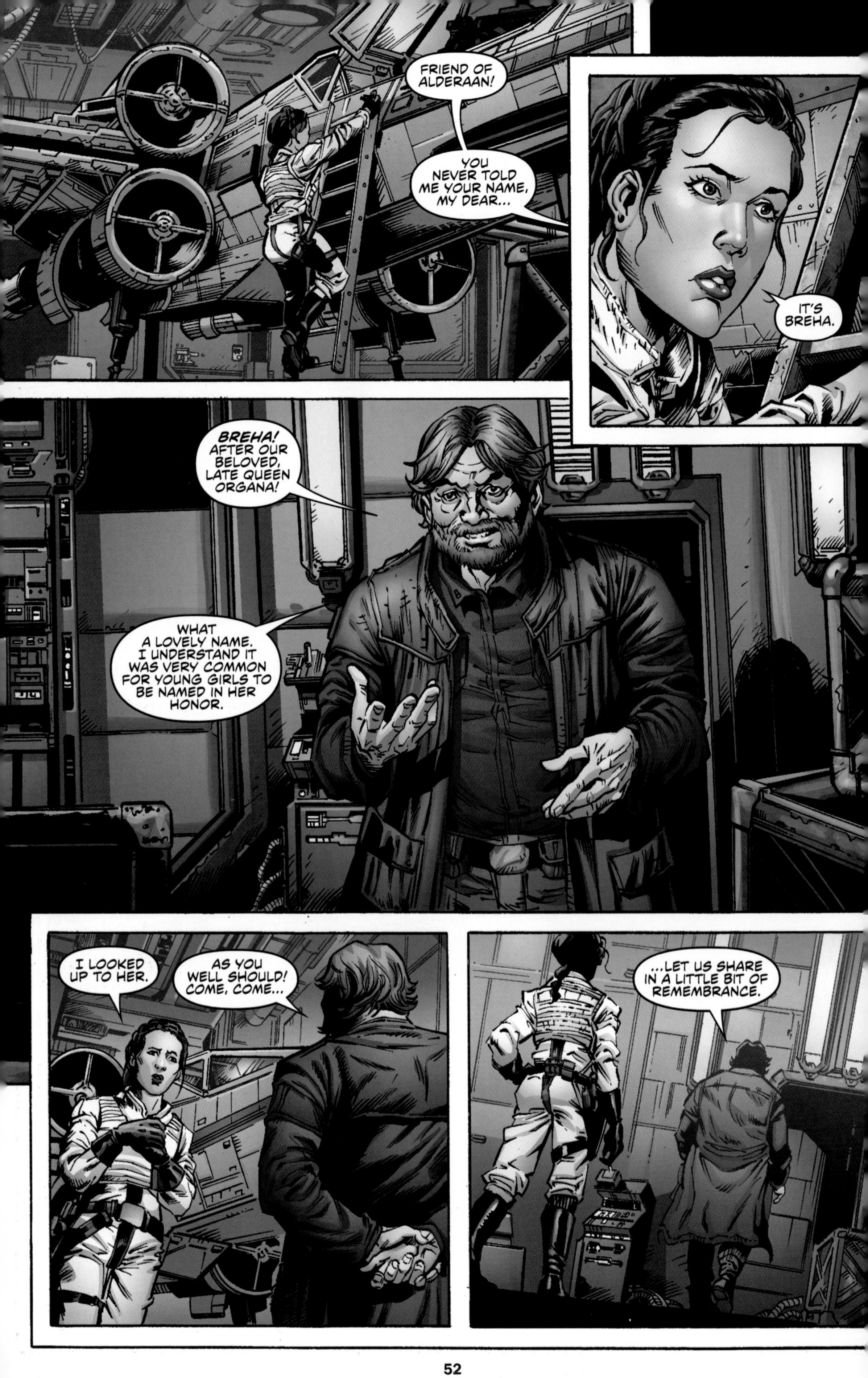
FRIEND OF ALDERAAN!
YOU NEVER TOLD ME YOUR NAME, MY DEAR...
IT'S BREHA.
BREHA! AFTER OUR BELOVED, LATE QUEEN ORGANA!
WHAT A LOVELY NAME. I UNDERSTAND IT WAS VERY COMMON FOR YOUNG GIRLS TO BE NAMED IN HER HONOR.
I LOOKED UP TO HER.
AS YOU WELL SHOULD! COME, COME...
...LET US SHARE IN A LITTLE BIT OF REMEMBRANCE.

WELCOME TO ALDERAAN, MY DEAR. OR WHAT I'VE BEEN ABLE TO SALVAGE.

SALVAGE... FROM THE WRECKAGE?

OH, NO...

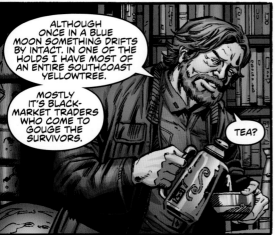

ALTHOUGH ONCE IN A BLUE MOON SOMETHING DRIFTS BY INTACT. IN ONE OF THE HOLDS I HAVE MOST OF AN ENTIRE SOUTHCOAST YELLOWTREE.

MOSTLY IT'S BLACK-MARKET TRADERS WHO COME TO GOUGE THE SURVIVORS.

TEA?

FLATLEAF. THIS IS EXPENSIVE.

BAH.

I AM AN OLD MAN. I HAVE SOME MEANS. WHAT BETTER WAY TO SPEND IT THAN TO SURROUND MYSELF WITH ALL OF THIS?

WE LIVE IN DARK TIMES, BREHA.

DO YOU MEAN THE EMPIRE?

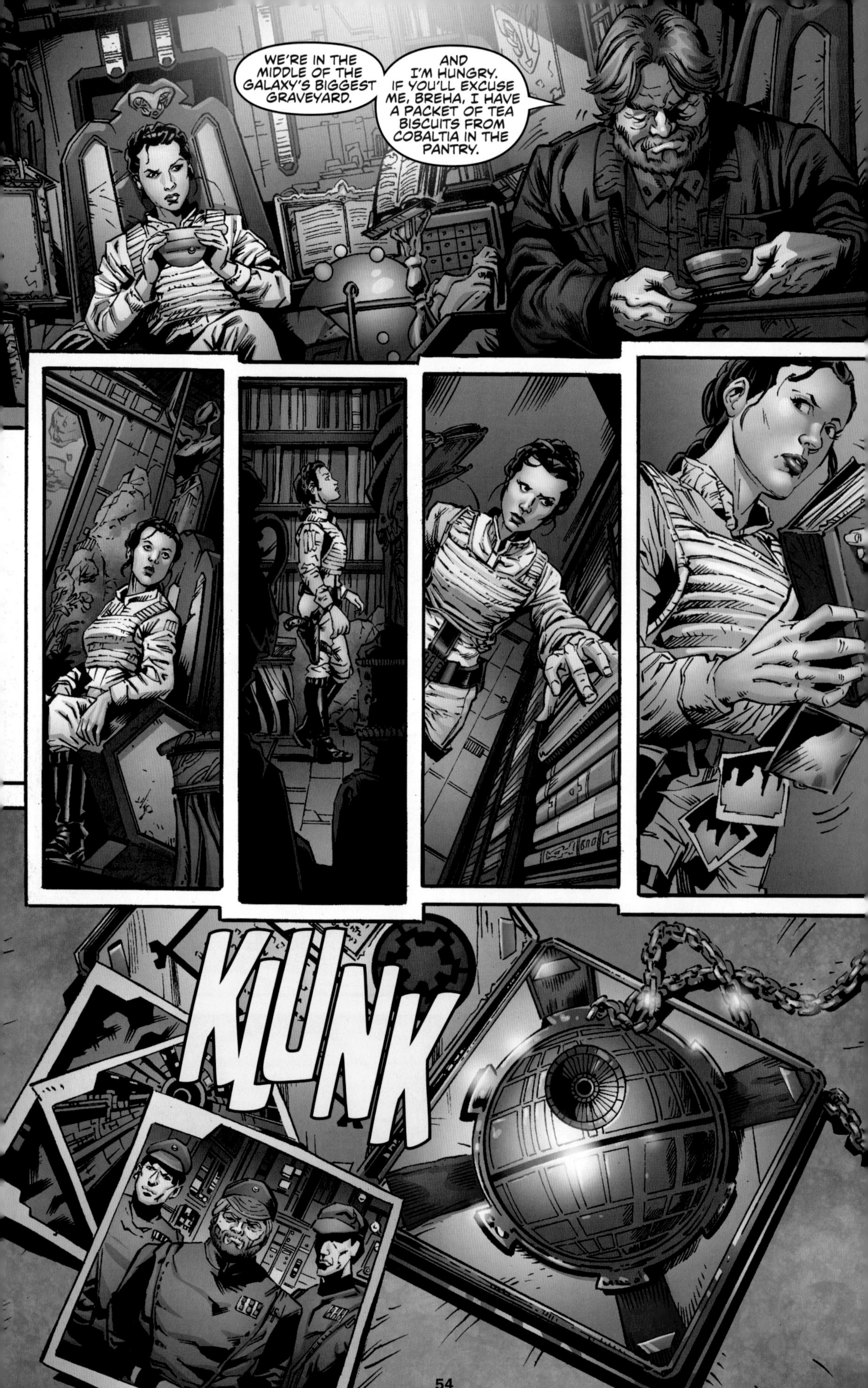
WE'RE IN THE MIDDLE OF THE GALAXY'S BIGGEST GRAVEYARD.
AND I'M HUNGRY. IF YOU'LL EXCUSE ME, BREHA, I HAVE A PACKET OF TEA BISCUITS FROM COBALTIA IN THE PANTRY.
KLUNK

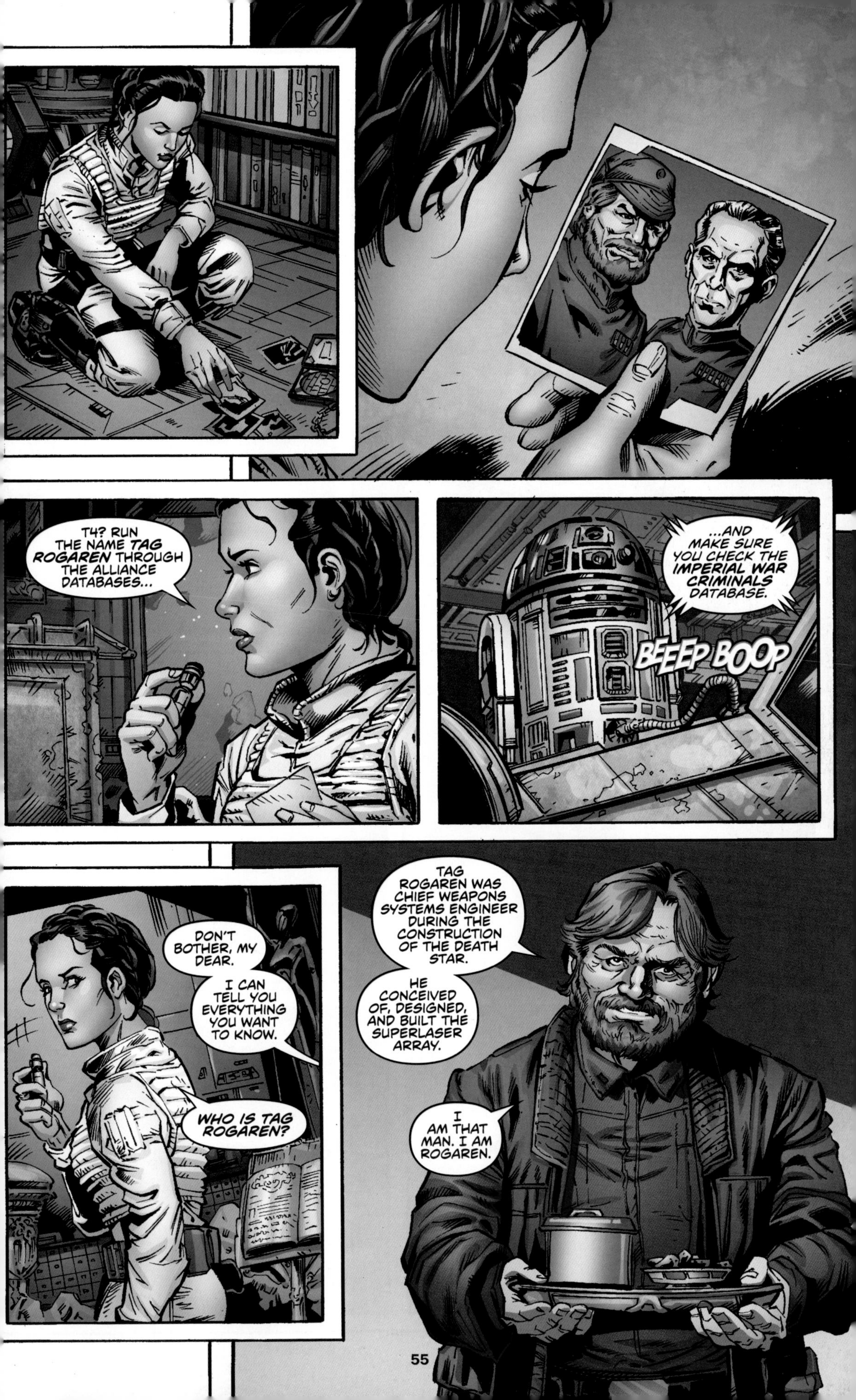
T4? RUN THE NAME TAG ROGAREN THROUGH THE ALLIANCE DATABASES...
...AND MAKE SURE YOU CHECK THE IMPERIAL WAR CRIMINALS DATABASE.
BEEEP BOOP
DON'T BOTHER, MY DEAR.
I CAN TELL YOU EVERYTHING YOU WANT TO KNOW.
WHO IS TAG ROGAREN?
TAG ROGAREN WAS CHIEF WEAPONS SYSTEMS ENGINEER DURING THE CONSTRUCTION OF THE DEATH STAR.
HE CONCEIVED OF, DESIGNED, AND BUILT THE SUPERLASER ARRAY.
I AM THAT MAN. I AM ROGAREN.

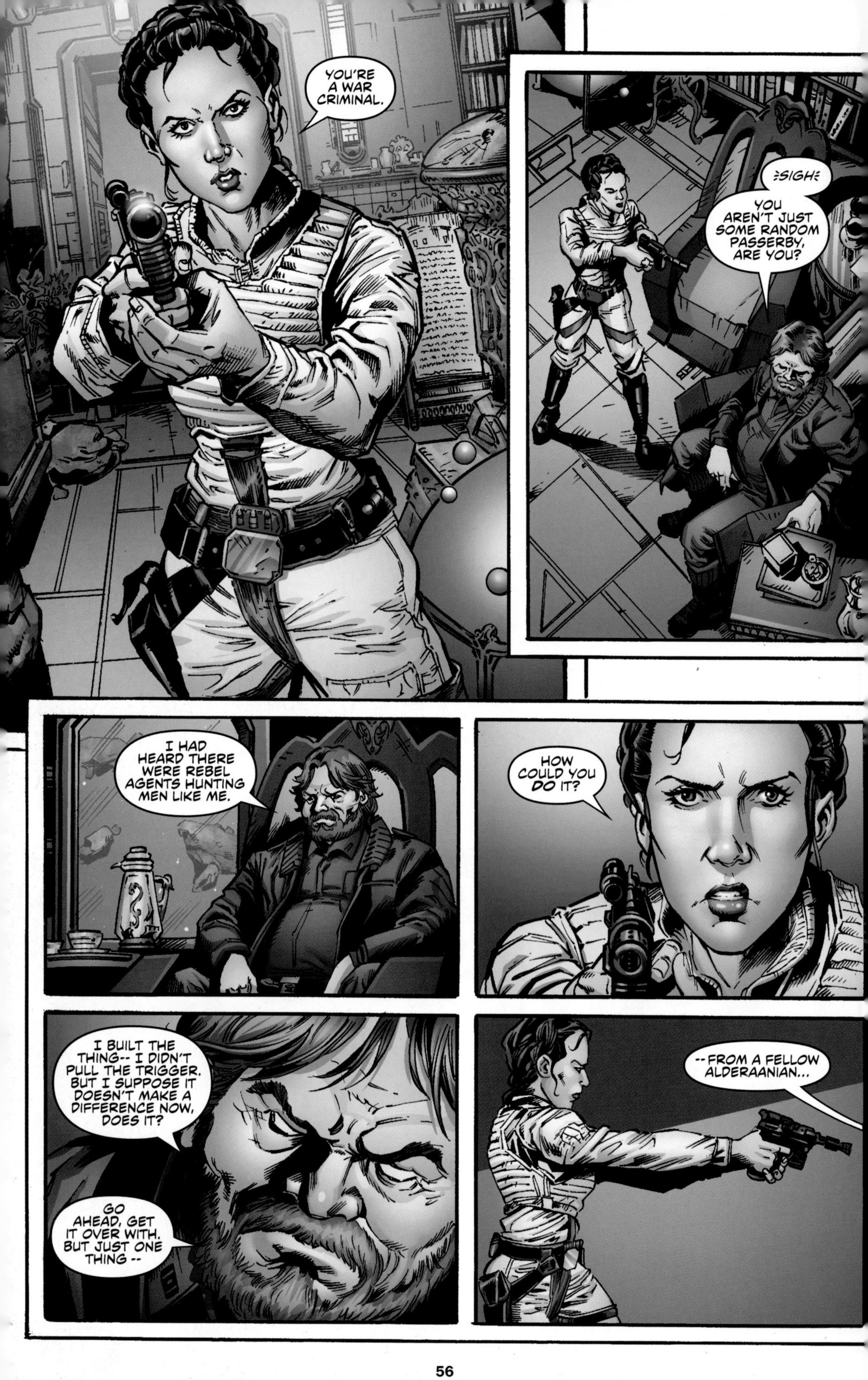
YOU'RE A WAR CRIMINAL.
SIGH
YOU AREN'T JUST SOME RANDOM PASSERBY, ARE YOU?
I HAD HEARD THERE WERE REBEL AGENTS HUNTING MEN LIKE ME.
HOW COULD YOU DO IT?
I BUILT THE THING-- I DIDN'T PULL THE TRIGGER. BUT I SUPPOSE IT DOESN'T MAKE A DIFFERENCE NOW, DOES IT?
GO AHEAD, GET IT OVER WITH. BUT JUST ONE THING --
--FROM A FELLOW ALDERAANIAN...

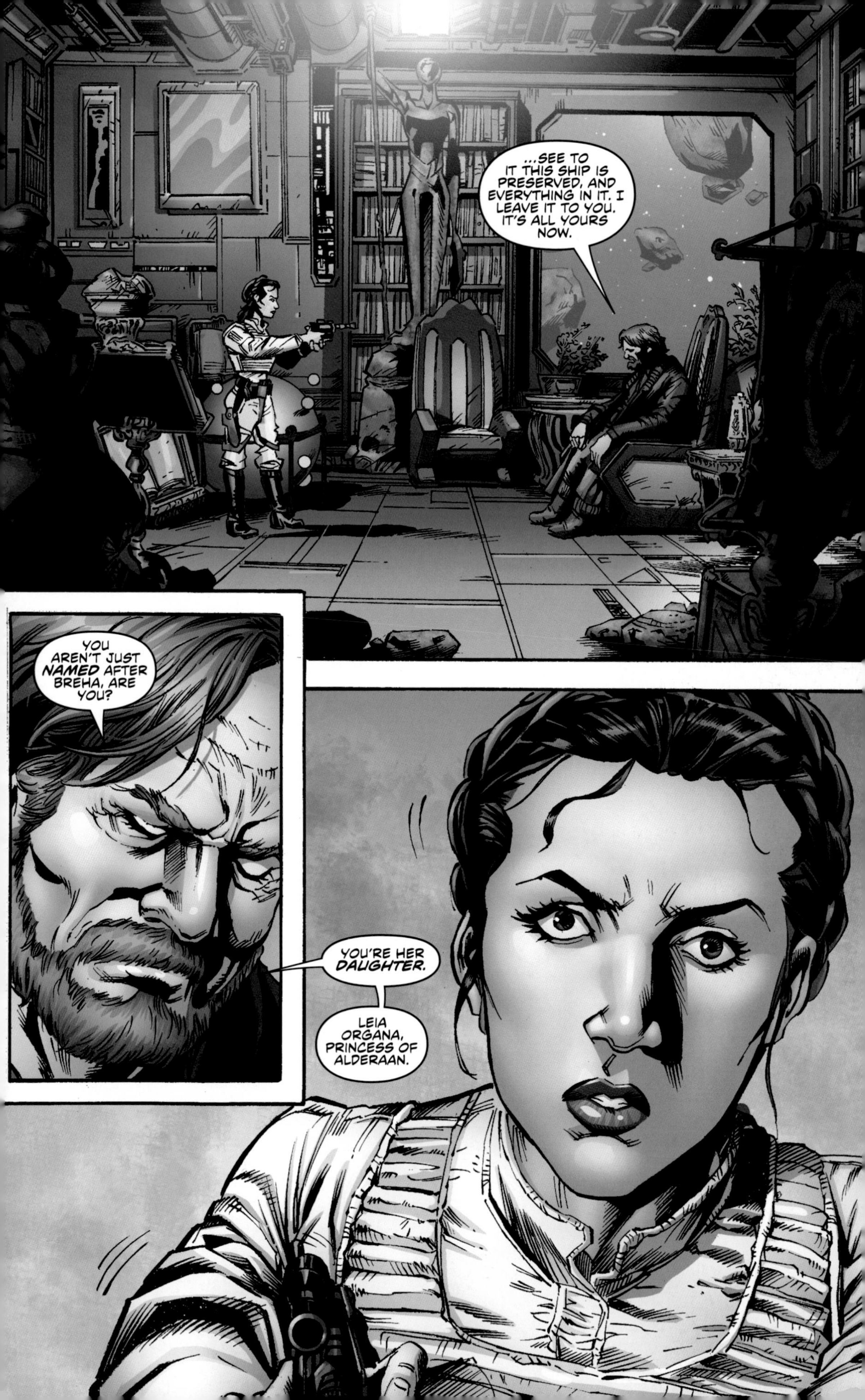
...SEE TO IT THIS SHIP IS PRESERVED, AND EVERYTHING IN IT. I LEAVE IT TO YOU. IT'S ALL YOURS NOW.
YOU AREN'T JUST *NAMED* AFTER BREHA, ARE YOU?
YOU'RE HER *DAUGHTER.*
LEIA ORGANA, PRINCESS OF ALDERAAN.

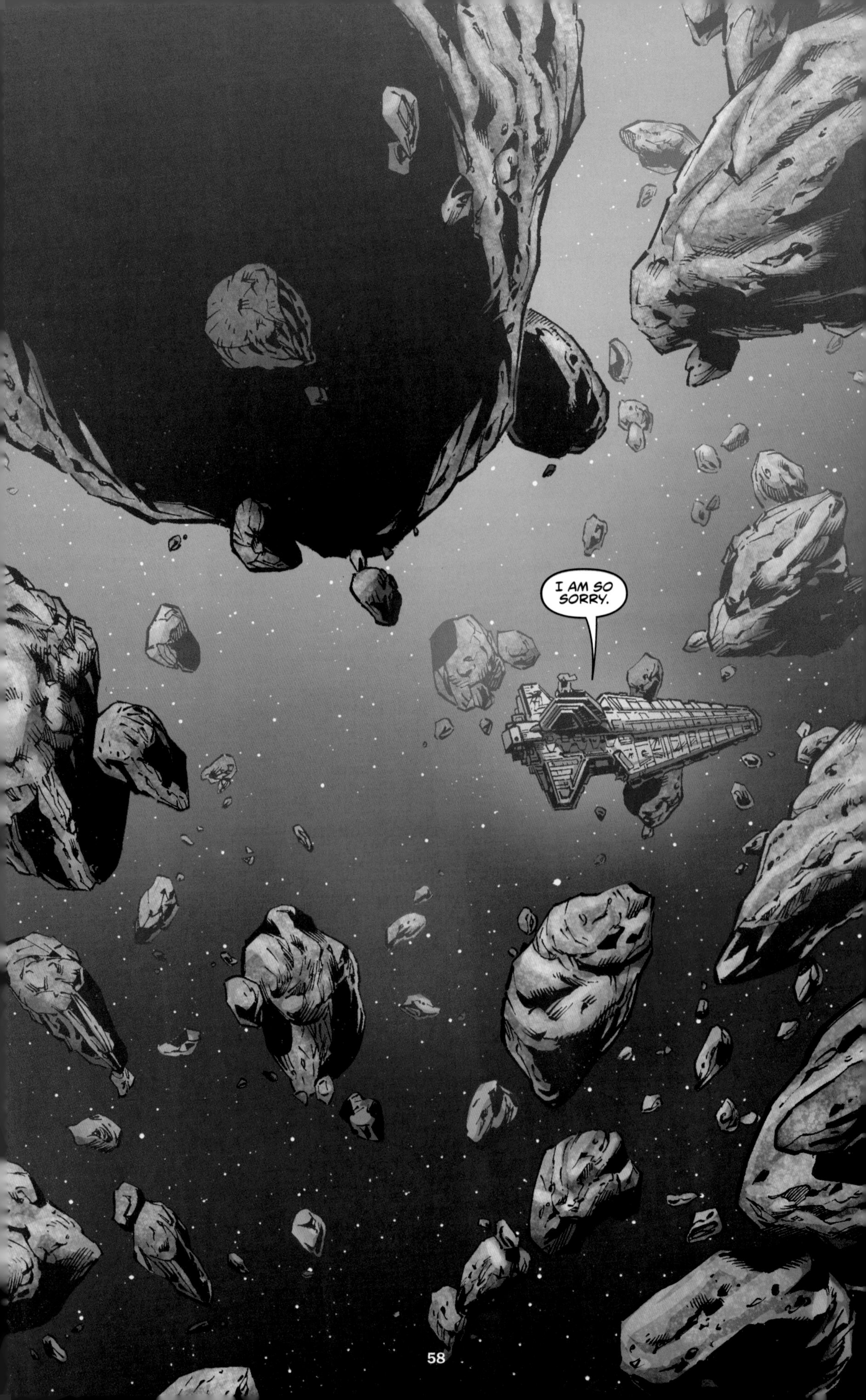
I AM SO SORRY.

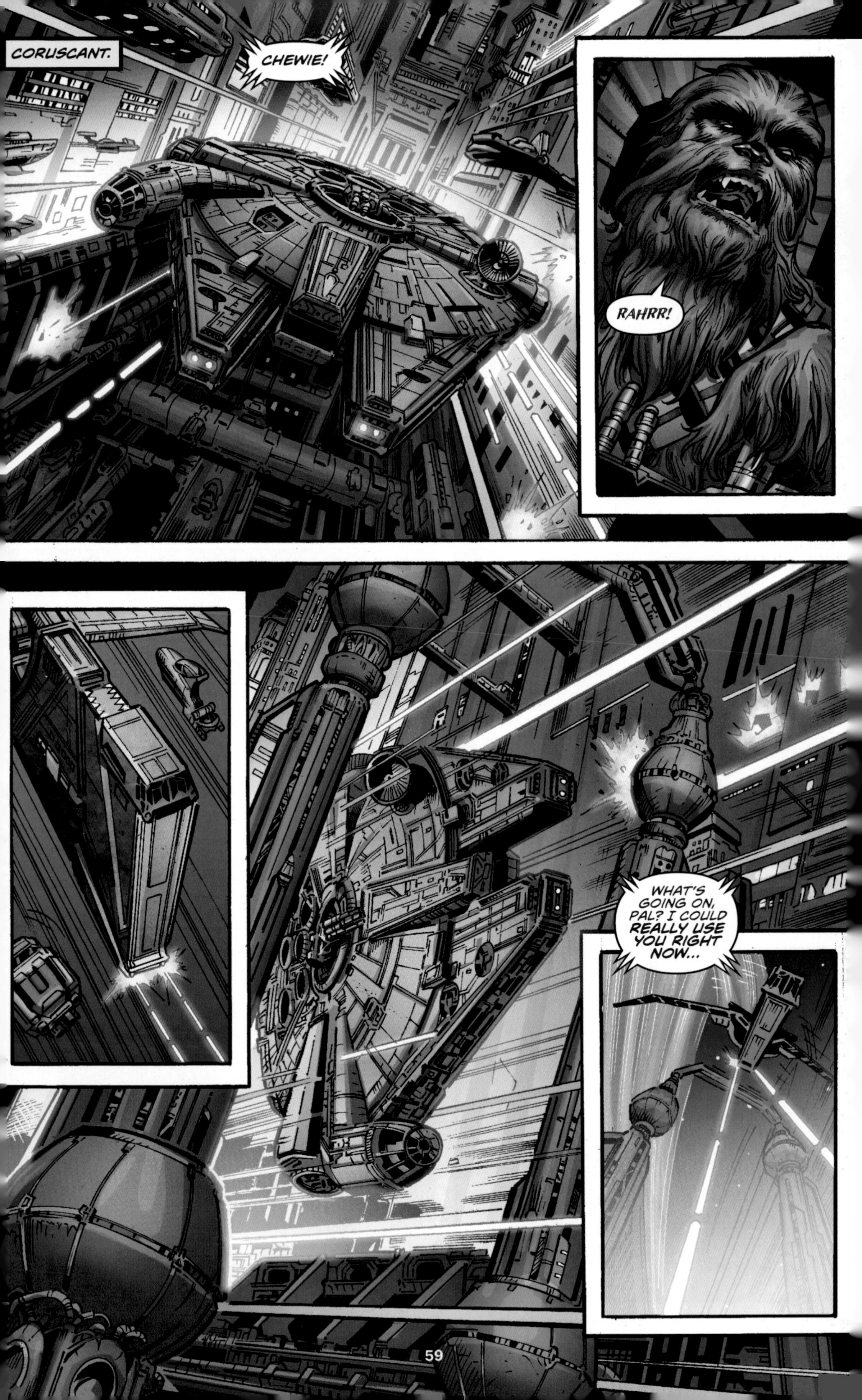
CORUSCANT.
CHEWIE!
RAHRR!
WHAT'S GOING ON, PAL? I COULD REALLY USE YOU RIGHT NOW...

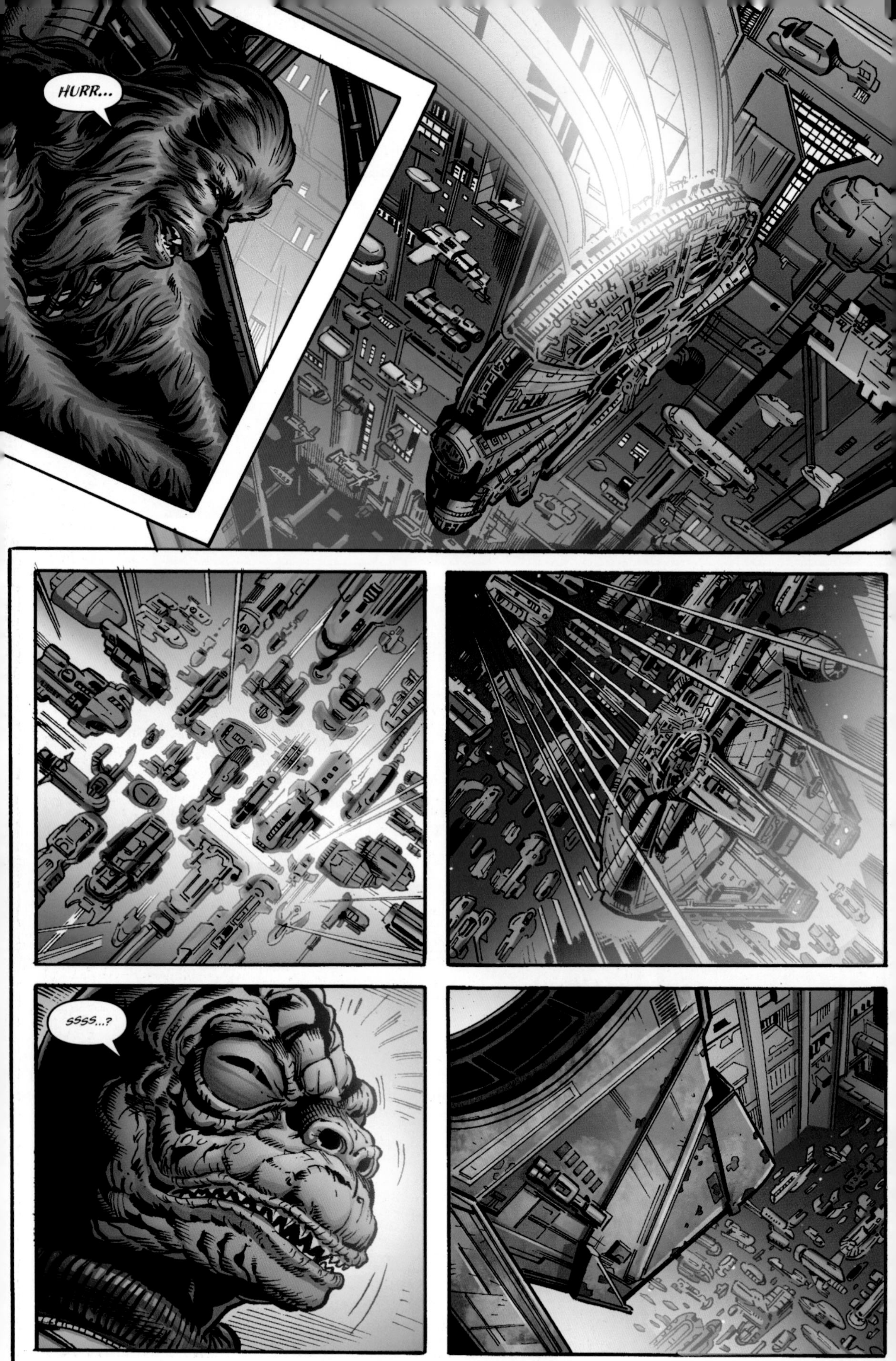
HURR...
SSSS...?

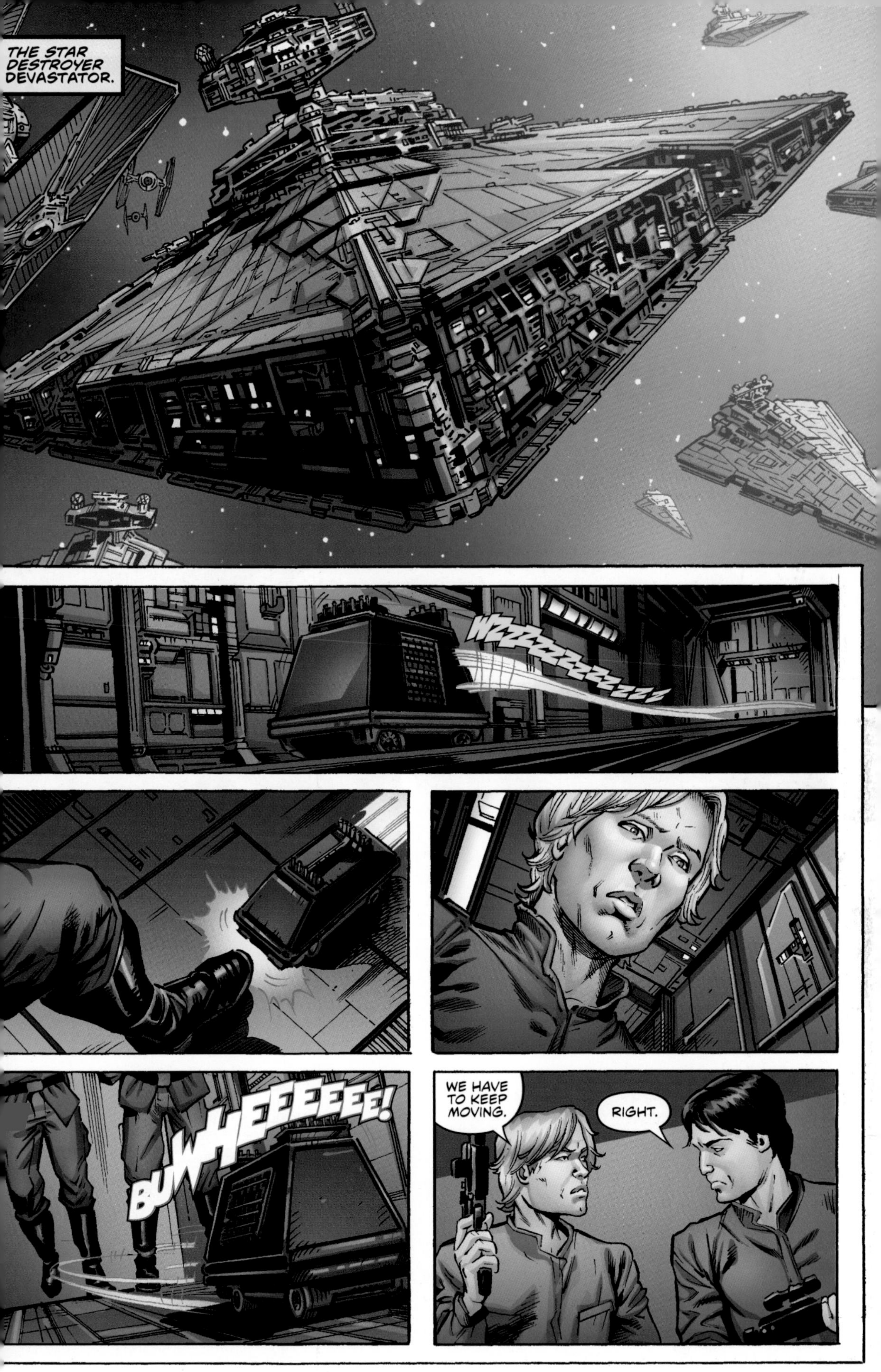
THE STAR DESTROYER DEVASTATOR.
WZZZZZZZZZZZZ
BUWHEEEEEEE!
WE HAVE TO KEEP MOVING.
RIGHT.

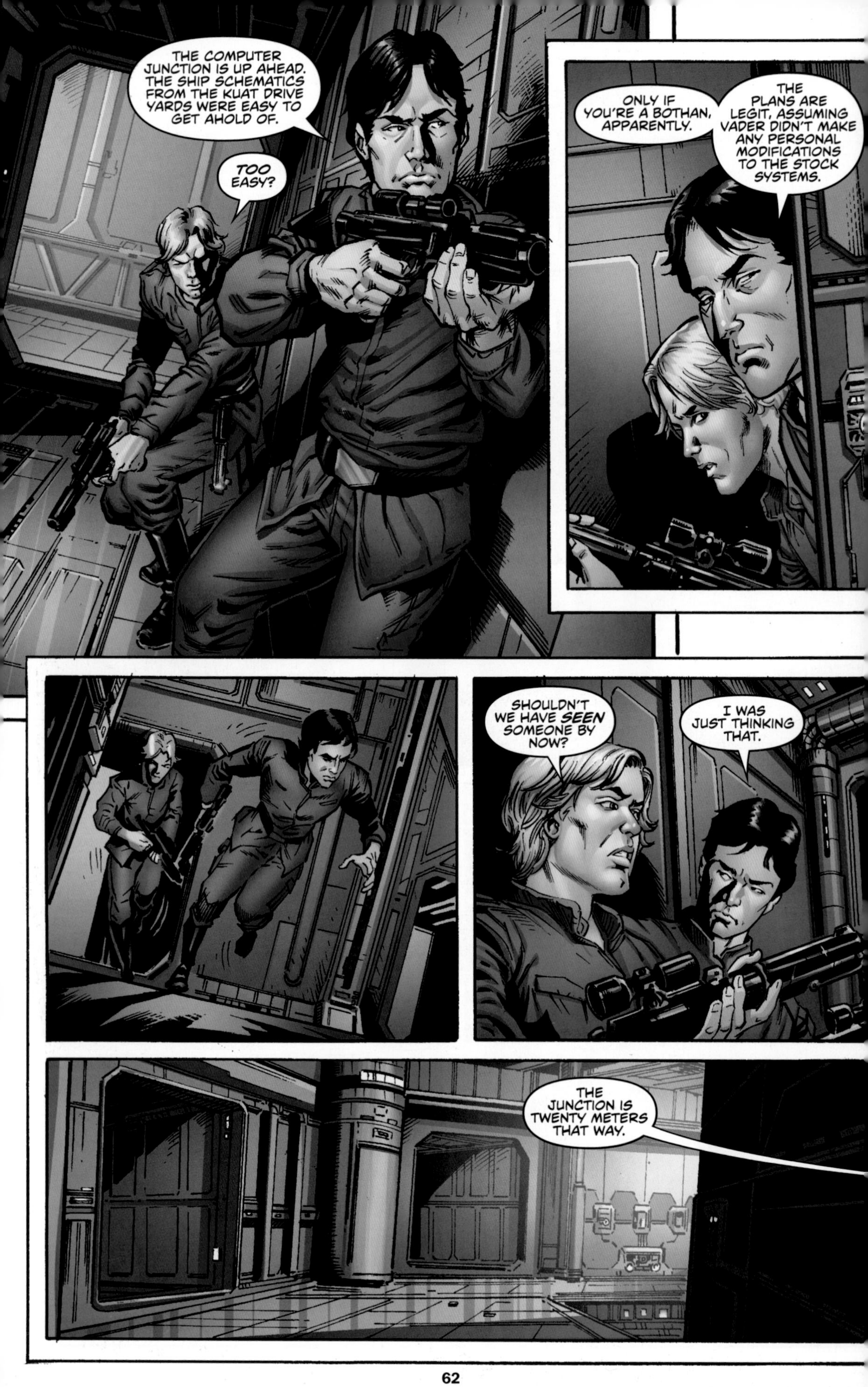
THE COMPUTER JUNCTION IS UP AHEAD. THE SHIP SCHEMATICS FROM THE KUAT DRIVE YARDS WERE EASY TO GET AHOLD OF.
TOO EASY?
ONLY IF YOU'RE A BOTHAN, APPARENTLY.
THE PLANS ARE LEGIT, ASSUMING VADER DIDN'T MAKE ANY PERSONAL MODIFICATIONS TO THE STOCK SYSTEMS.
SHOULDN'T WE HAVE SEEN SOMEONE BY NOW?
I WAS JUST THINKING THAT.
THE JUNCTION IS TWENTY METERS THAT WAY.

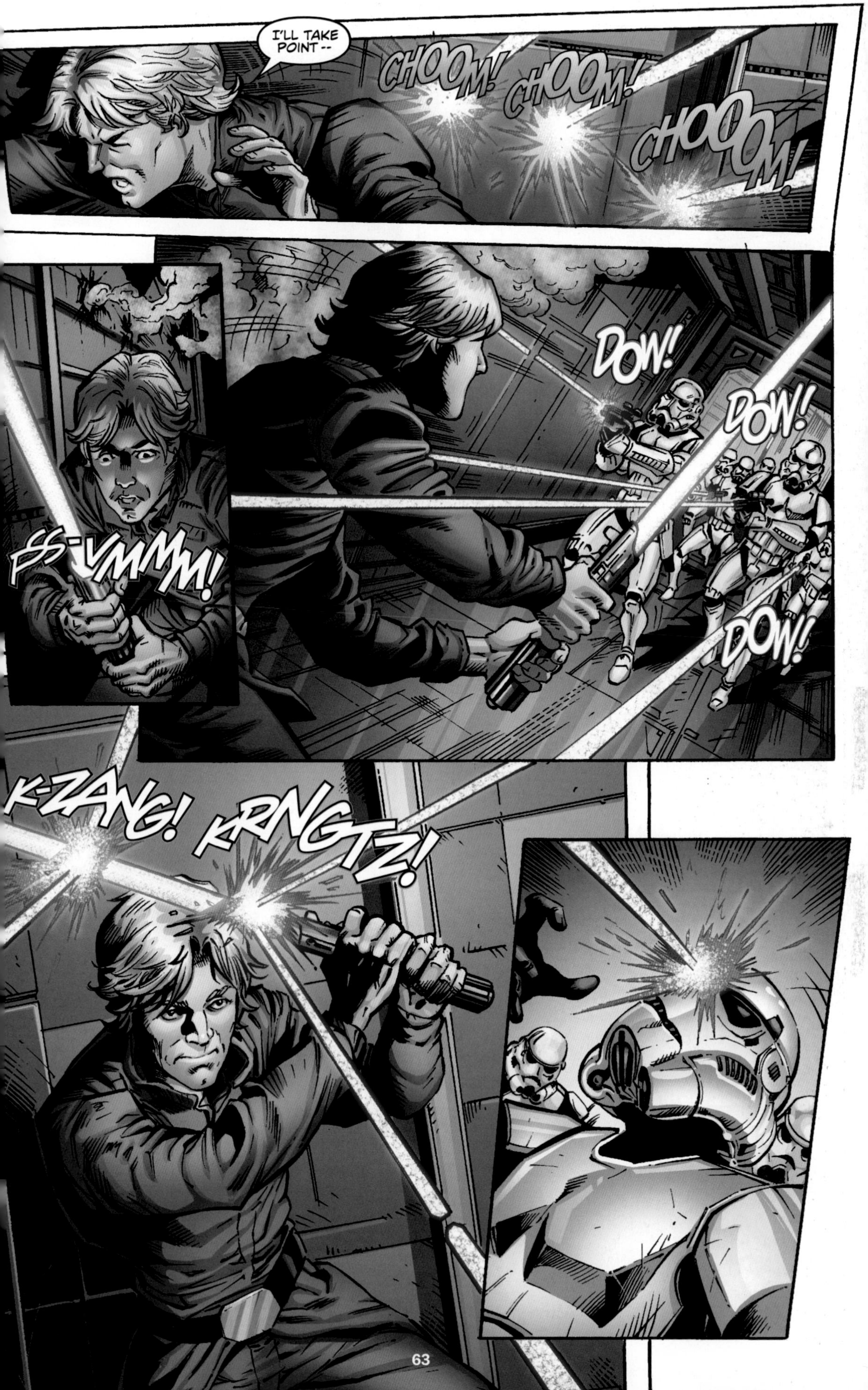
I'LL TAKE POINT --
CHOOOM! CHOOOM!
CHOOOOM!
DOW!
DOW!
DOW!
SS-VMMMM!
K-ZANG! KRNGTZ!

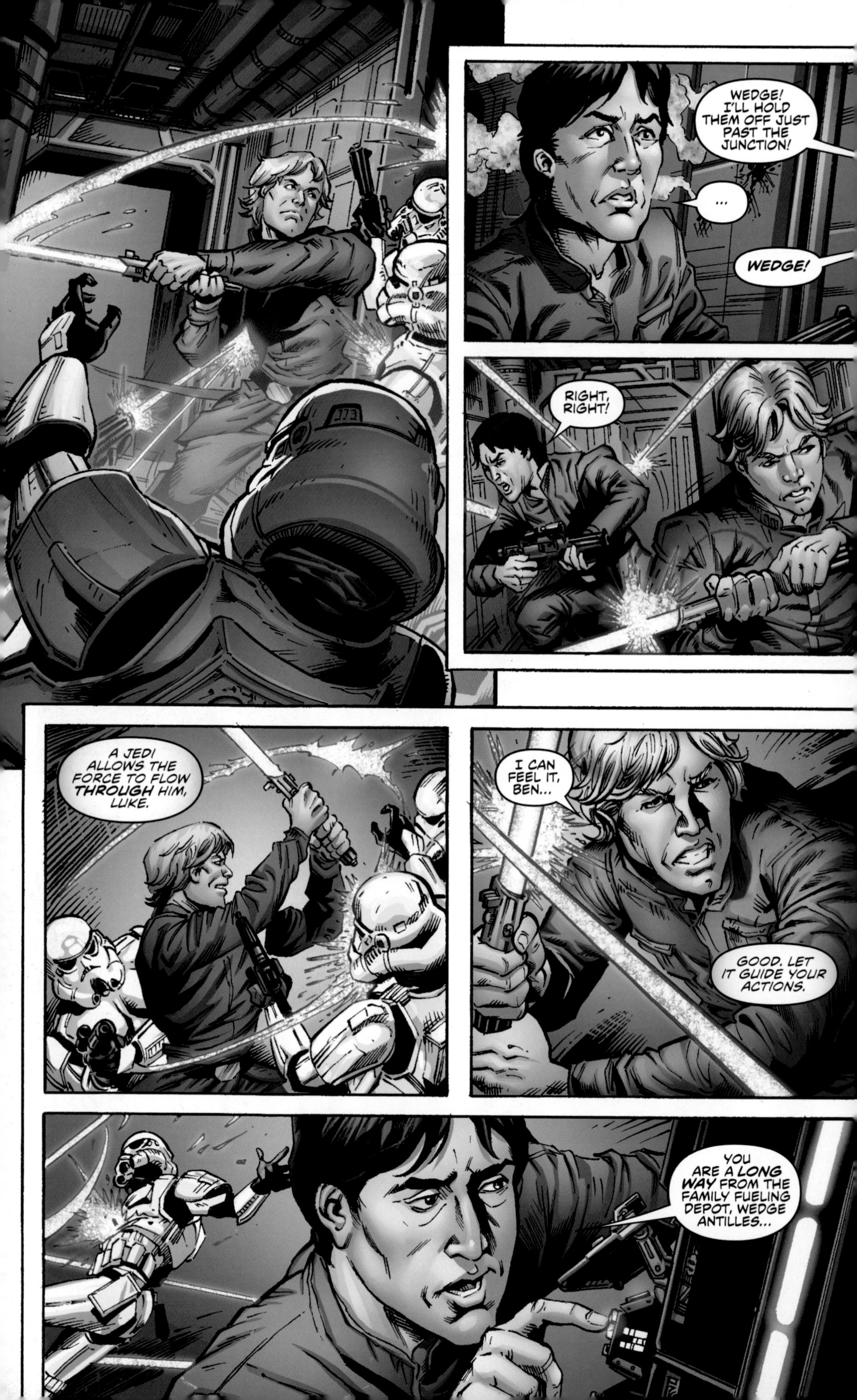
WEDGE! I'LL HOLD THEM OFF JUST PAST THE JUNCTION!
...
WEDGE!
RIGHT, RIGHT!
A JEDI ALLOWS THE FORCE TO FLOW THROUGH HIM, LUKE.
I CAN FEEL IT, BEN...
GOOD. LET IT GUIDE YOUR ACTIONS.
YOU ARE A LONG WAY FROM THE FAMILY FUELING DEPOT, WEDGE ANTILLES...

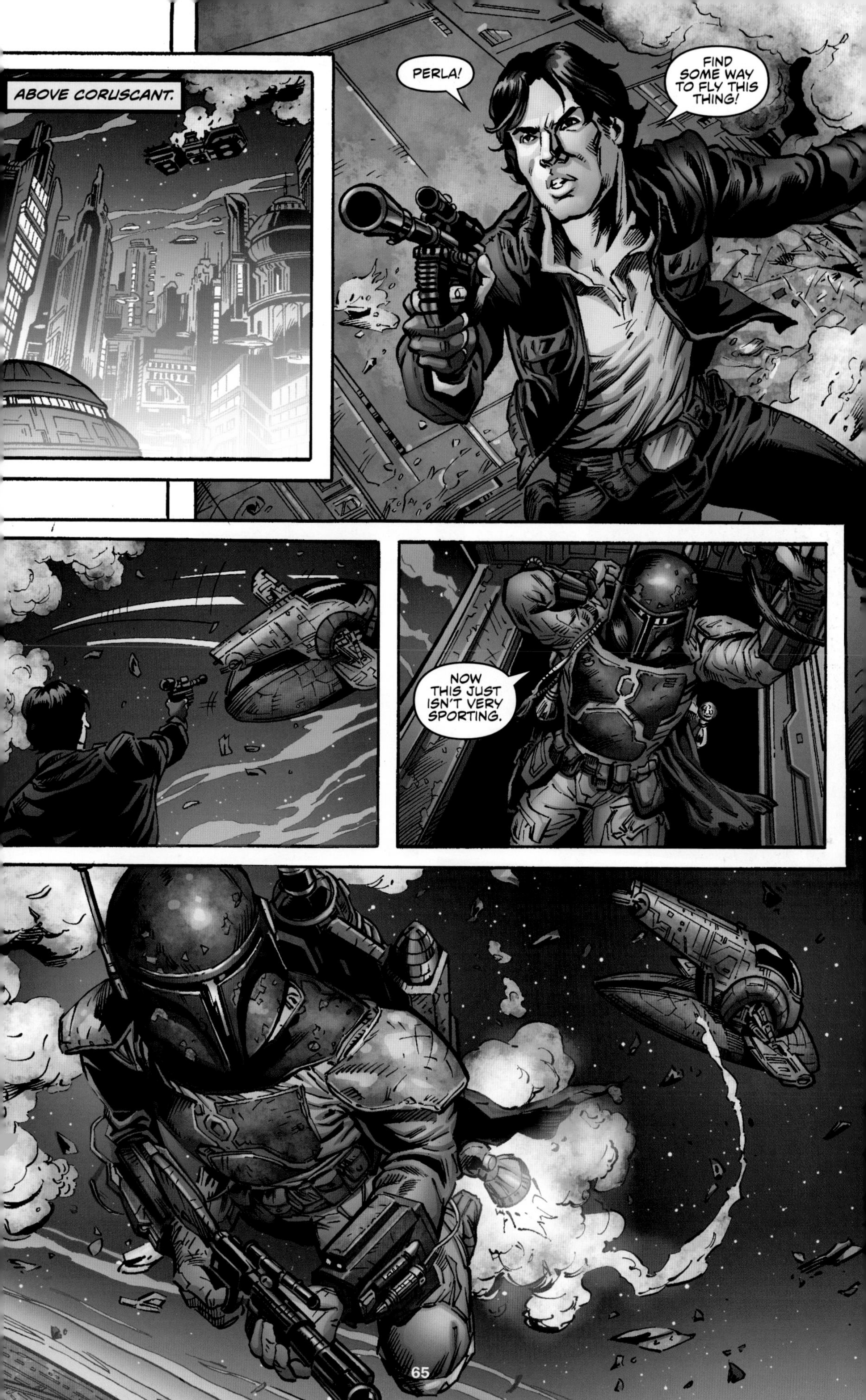
ABOVE CORUSCANT.
PERLA!
FIND SOME WAY TO FLY THIS THING!
NOW THIS JUST ISN'T VERY SPORTING.

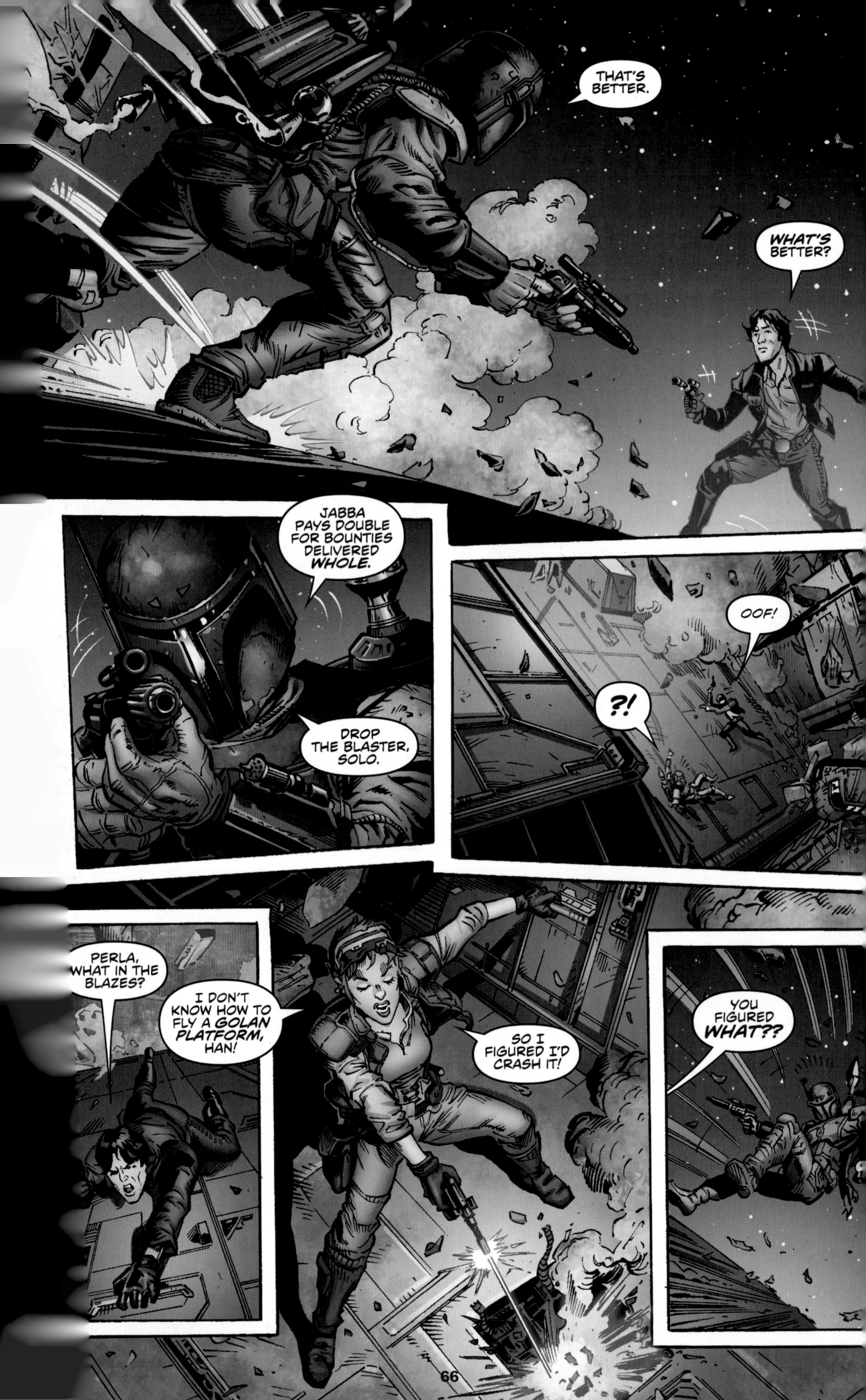
THAT'S BETTER.
WHAT'S BETTER?
JABBA PAYS DOUBLE FOR BOUNTIES DELIVERED WHOLE.
DROP THE BLASTER, SOLO.
OOF!
?!
PERLA, WHAT IN THE BLAZES?
I DON'T KNOW HOW TO FLY A GOLAN PLATFORM, HAN!
SO I FIGURED I'D CRASH IT!
YOU FIGURED WHAT??

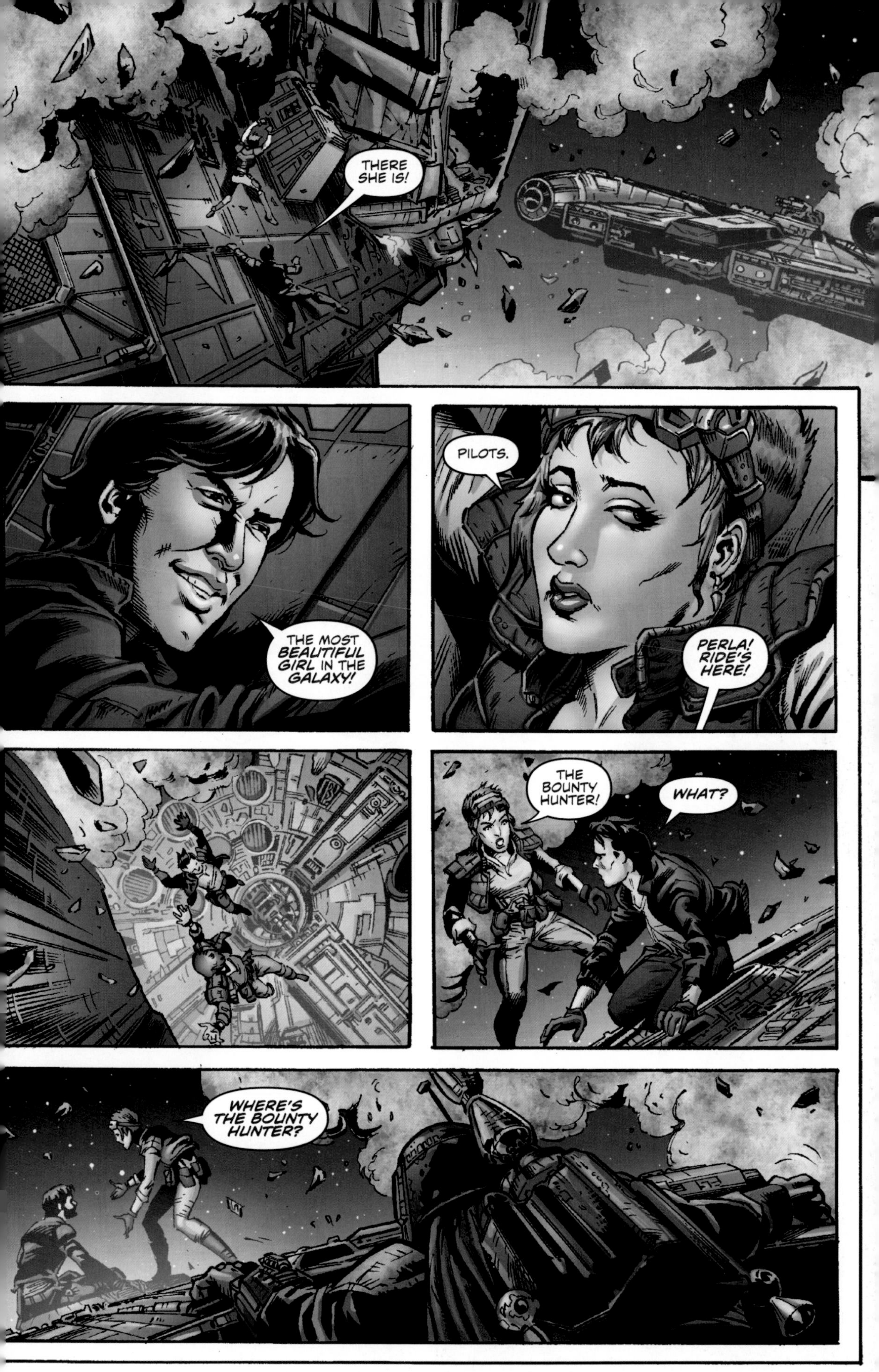
THERE SHE IS!
THE MOST BEAUTIFUL GIRL IN THE GALAXY!
PILOTS.
PERLA! RIDE'S HERE!
THE BOUNTY HUNTER!
WHAT?
WHERE'S THE BOUNTY HUNTER?

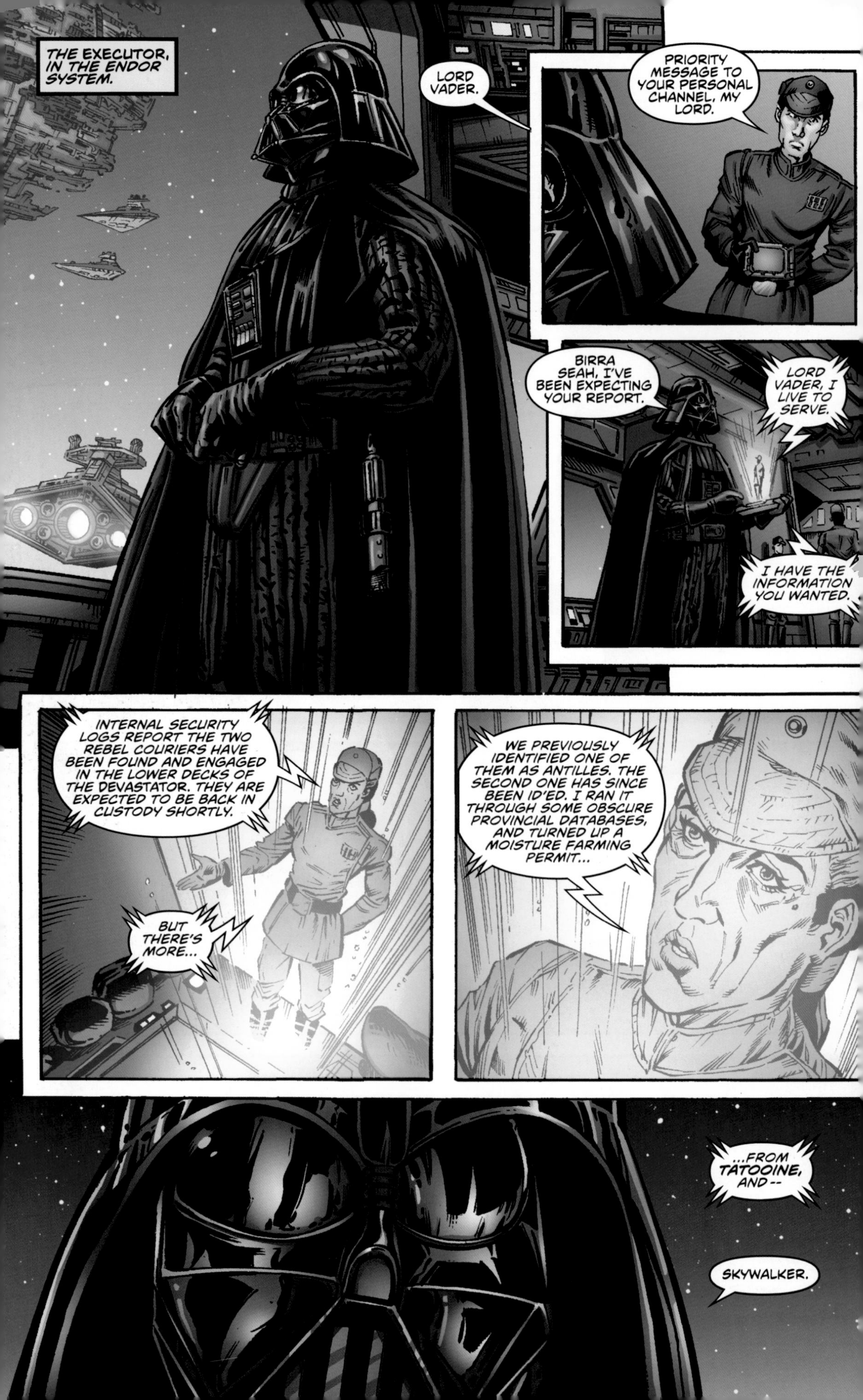
THE EXECUTOR, IN THE ENDOR SYSTEM.
LORD VADER.
PRIORITY MESSAGE TO YOUR PERSONAL CHANNEL, MY LORD.
BIRRA SEAH, I'VE BEEN EXPECTING YOUR REPORT.
LORD VADER, I LIVE TO SERVE.
I HAVE THE INFORMATION YOU WANTED.
INTERNAL SECURITY LOGS REPORT THE TWO REBEL COURIERS HAVE BEEN FOUND AND ENGAGED IN THE LOWER DECKS OF THE DEVASTATOR. THEY ARE EXPECTED TO BE BACK IN CUSTODY SHORTLY.
BUT THERE'S MORE...
WE PREVIOUSLY IDENTIFIED ONE OF THEM AS ANTILLES. THE SECOND ONE HAS SINCE BEEN ID'ED. I RAN IT THROUGH SOME OBSCURE PROVINCIAL DATABASES, AND TURNED UP A MOISTURE FARMING PERMIT...
...FROM TATOOINE, AND --
SKYWALKER.

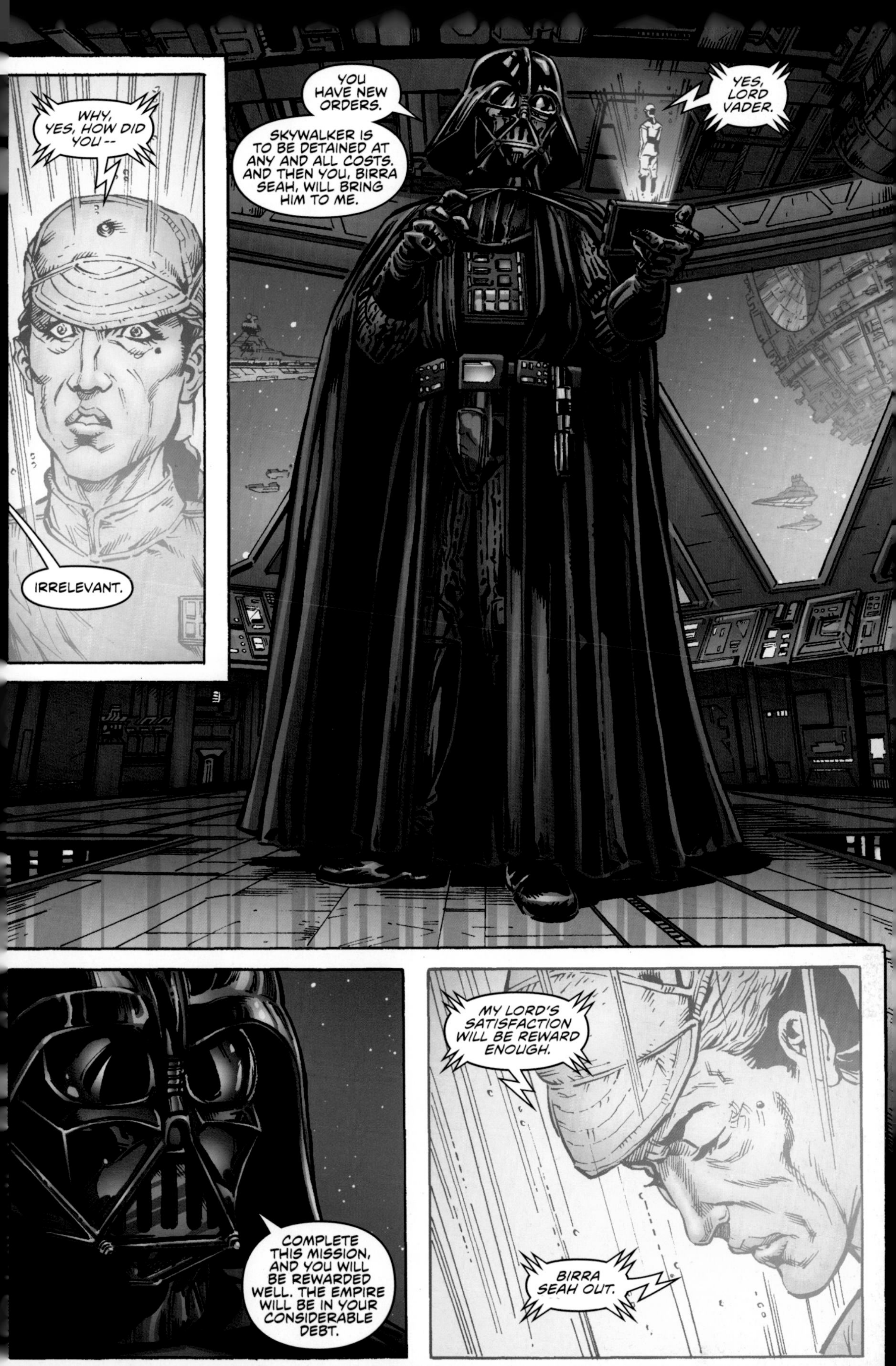
WHY, YES, HOW DID YOU --
IRRELEVANT.
YOU HAVE NEW ORDERS.
SKYWALKER IS TO BE DETAINED AT ANY AND ALL COSTS. AND THEN YOU, BIRRA SEAH, WILL BRING HIM TO ME.
YES, LORD VADER.
COMPLETE THIS MISSION, AND YOU WILL BE REWARDED WELL. THE EMPIRE WILL BE IN YOUR CONSIDERABLE DEBT.
MY LORD'S SATISFACTION WILL BE REWARD ENOUGH.
BIRRA SEAH OUT.

FOOLS.

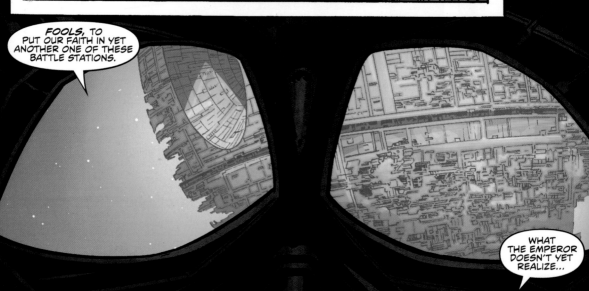

FOOLS, TO PUT OUR FAITH IN YET ANOTHER ONE OF THESE BATTLE STATIONS.

WHAT THE EMPEROR DOESN'T YET REALIZE...

...IS THE *ULTIMATE POWER* IN THE UNIVERSE LIES *ELSEWHERE.*

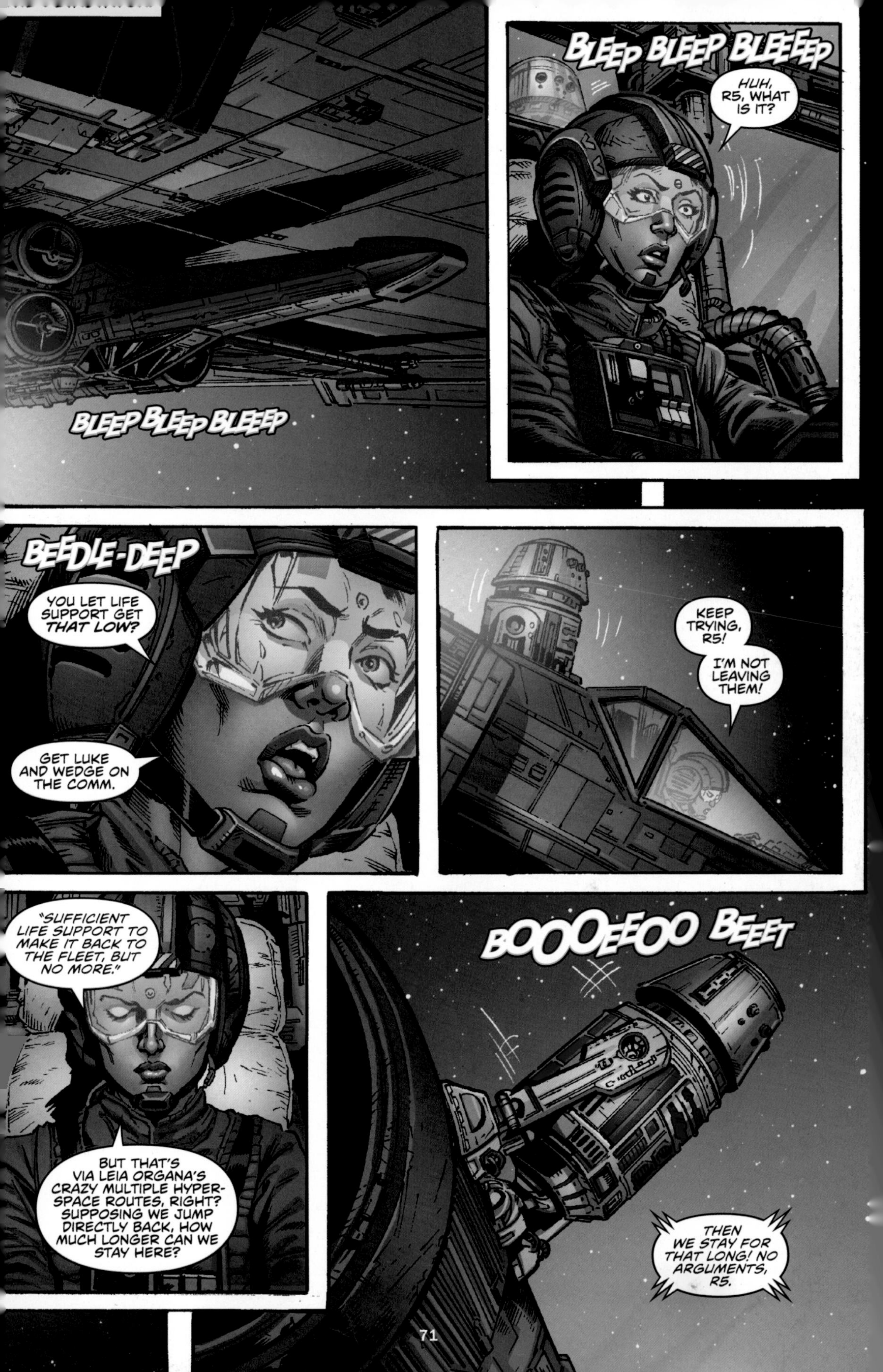
BLEEP BLEEP BLEEEP
BLEEP BLEEP BLEEEEP
HUH, R5, WHAT IS IT?
BEEDLE-DEEP
YOU LET LIFE SUPPORT GET *THAT LOW?*
GET LUKE AND WEDGE ON THE COMM.
KEEP TRYING, R5!
I'M NOT LEAVING THEM!
"SUFFICIENT LIFE SUPPORT TO MAKE IT BACK TO THE FLEET, BUT NO MORE."
BUT THAT'S VIA LEIA ORGANA'S CRAZY MULTIPLE HYPER-SPACE ROUTES, RIGHT? SUPPOSING WE JUMP DIRECTLY BACK, HOW MUCH LONGER CAN WE STAY HERE?
BOOOEEOO BEEET
THEN WE STAY FOR THAT LONG! NO ARGUMENTS, R5.

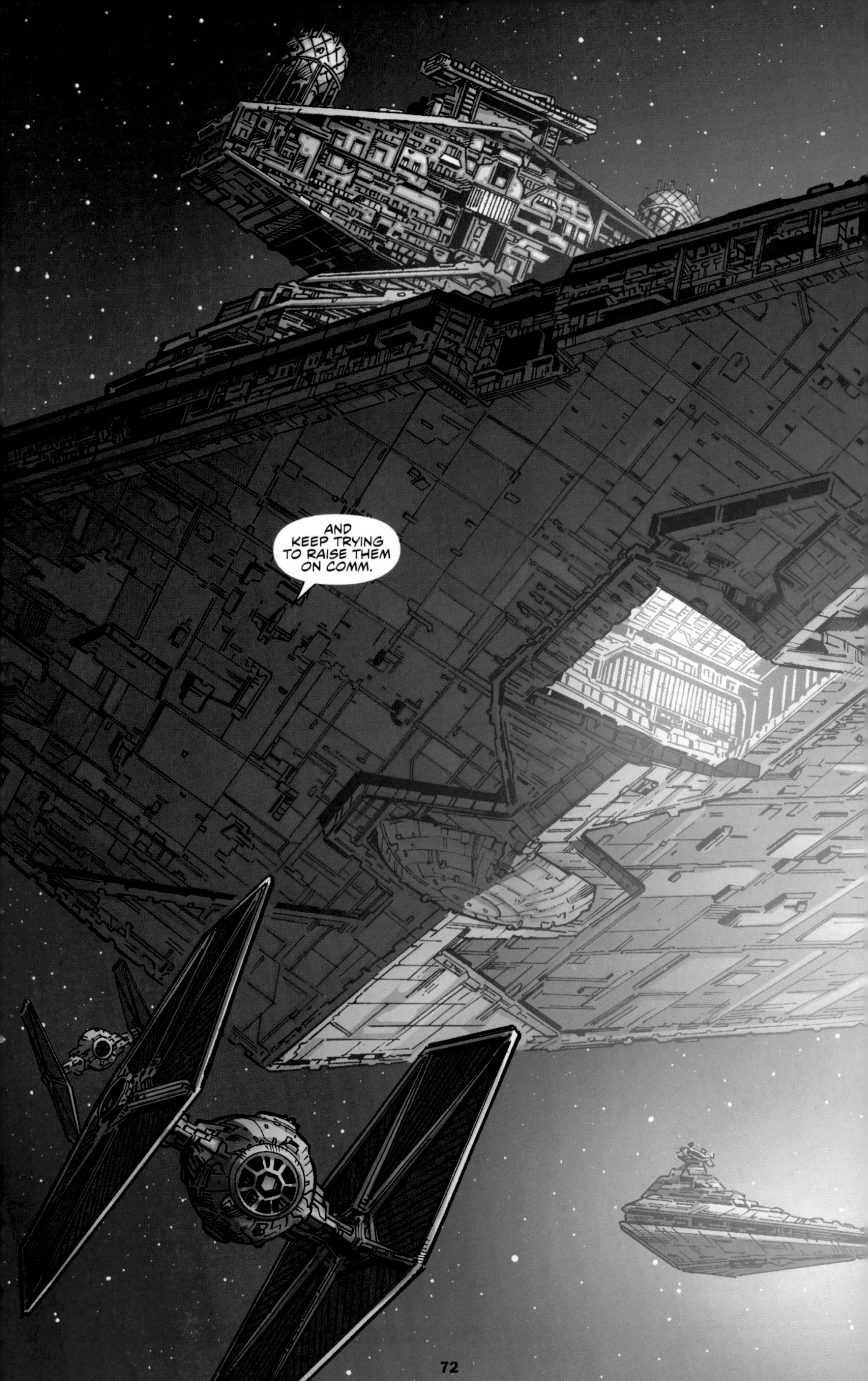
AND KEEP TRYING TO RAISE THEM ON COMM.

THE DEVASTATOR.

WE'RE WAY PAST RENDEZVOUS. PRITHI SHOULD HAVE LEFT BY NOW.

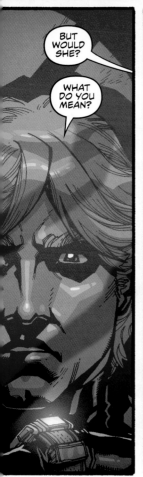

BUT WOULD SHE?

WHAT DO YOU MEAN?

IT'S NOT A *SECRET*, YOU AND HER.

SHE'LL HAVE FOLLOWED HER ORDERS, WEDGE. NO NEED TO WORRY.

NO, NO, DON'T MISUNDERSTAND...

...I *ENVY* YOU TWO.

73

MON MOTHMA MAY HAVE HER OWN OPINIONS ON FRATERNIZING WITHIN THE RANKS, BUT WITH ALL DUE RESPECT, MON MOTHMA DOESN'T FLY COMBAT.

...WHERE YOU LOSE *EVERYONE* YOU KNOW...

THE STATS ARE PRETTY SOBERING -- YOU FLY COMBAT, YOUR LIFE EXPECTANCY DROPS, AND FAST. IN THIS WAR? MOST OF US CAN EXPECT TO LIVE MAYBE SIX WEEKS.

AND THEN THERE ARE BATTLES LIKE YAVIN...

...AND YOU REGRET, *REALLY REGRET*, NOT MAKING A CONNECTION WHEN YOU HAD THE CHANCE.

WEDGE, WAS THERE SOMEONE?

YEAH, THERE WAS.

AND NOT A SHIFT GOES BY WITHOUT *MY* THINKING ABOUT HER.

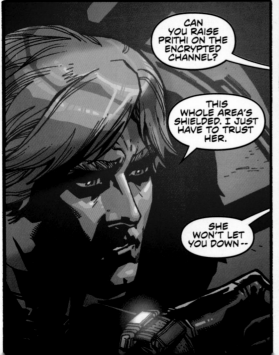

CAN YOU RAISE PRITHI ON THE ENCRYPTED CHANNEL?

THIS WHOLE AREA'S SHIELDED. I JUST HAVE TO TRUST HER.

SHE WON'T LET YOU DOWN --

-- SHE'S ROGUE SQUADRON.

...WHAT?

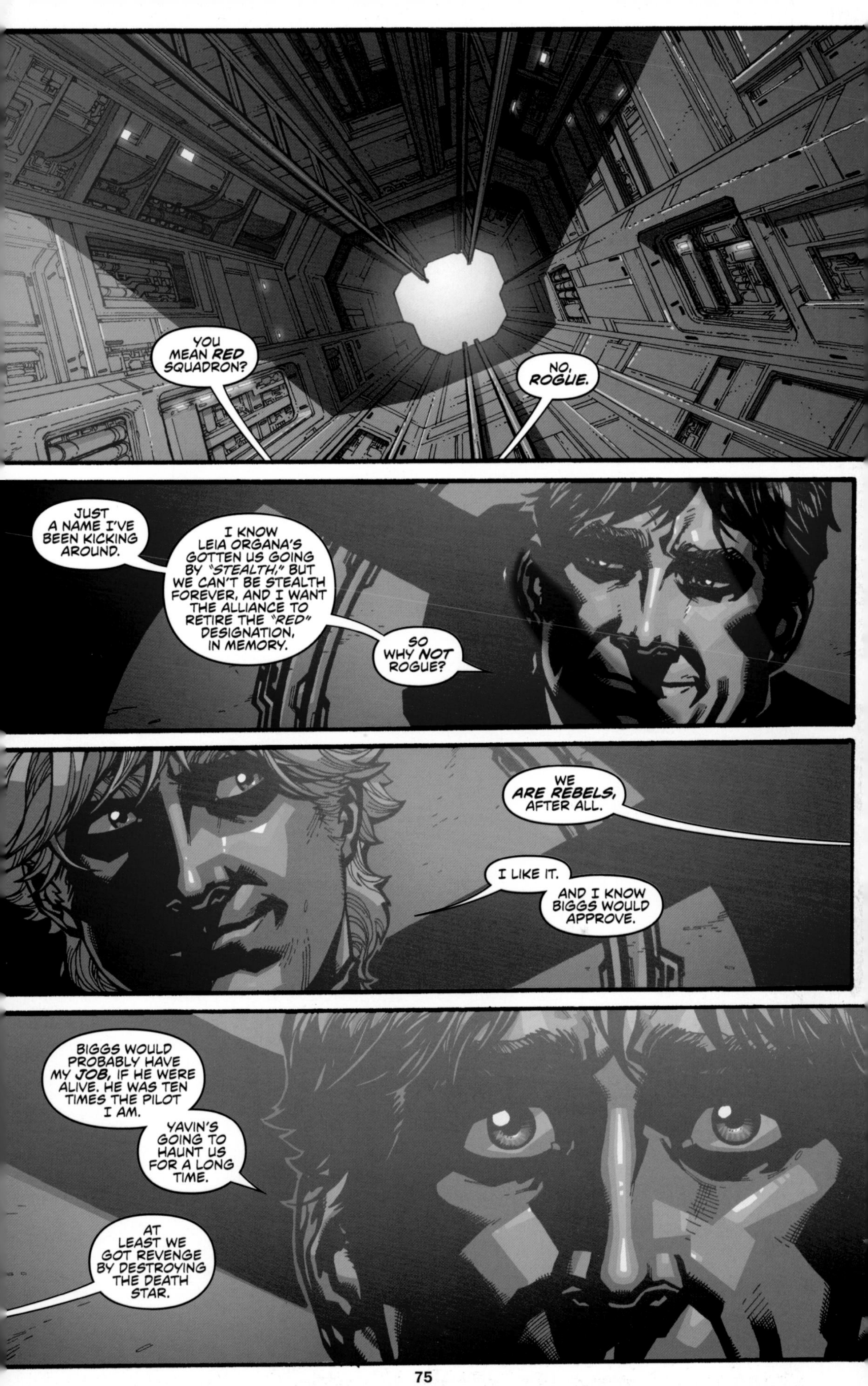
YOU MEAN RED SQUADRON?
NO, ROGUE.
JUST A NAME I'VE BEEN KICKING AROUND.
I KNOW LEIA ORGANA'S GOTTEN US GOING BY "STEALTH," BUT WE CAN'T BE STEALTH FOREVER, AND I WANT THE ALLIANCE TO RETIRE THE "RED" DESIGNATION, IN MEMORY.
SO WHY NOT ROGUE?
WE ARE REBELS, AFTER ALL.
I LIKE IT.
AND I KNOW BIGGS WOULD APPROVE.
BIGGS WOULD PROBABLY HAVE MY JOB, IF HE WERE ALIVE. HE WAS TEN TIMES THE PILOT I AM.
YAVIN'S GOING TO HAUNT US FOR A LONG TIME.
AT LEAST WE GOT REVENGE BY DESTROYING THE DEATH STAR.

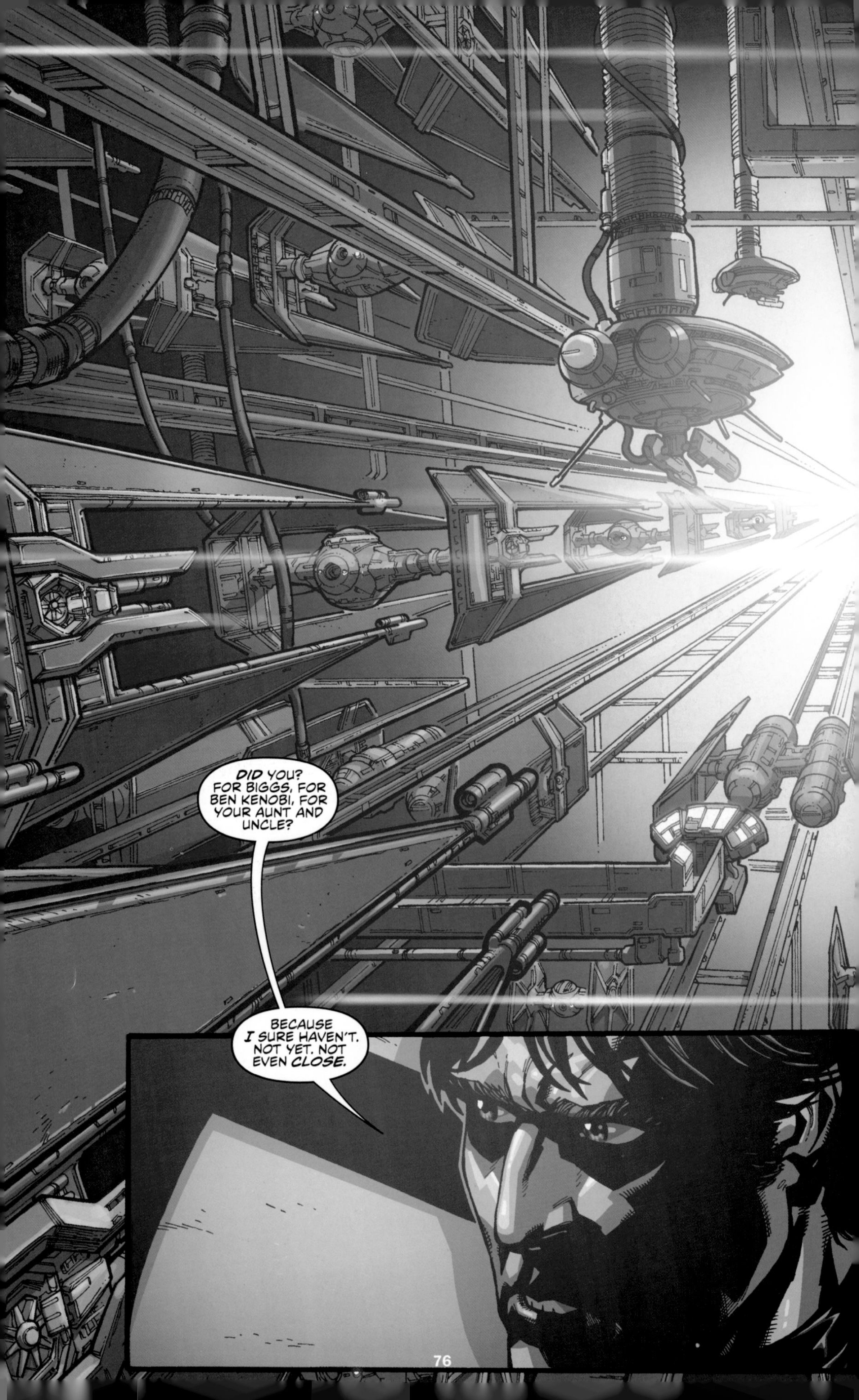
DID YOU? FOR BIGGS, FOR BEN KENOBI, FOR YOUR AUNT AND UNCLE?
BECAUSE I SURE HAVEN'T. NOT YET. NOT EVEN CLOSE.

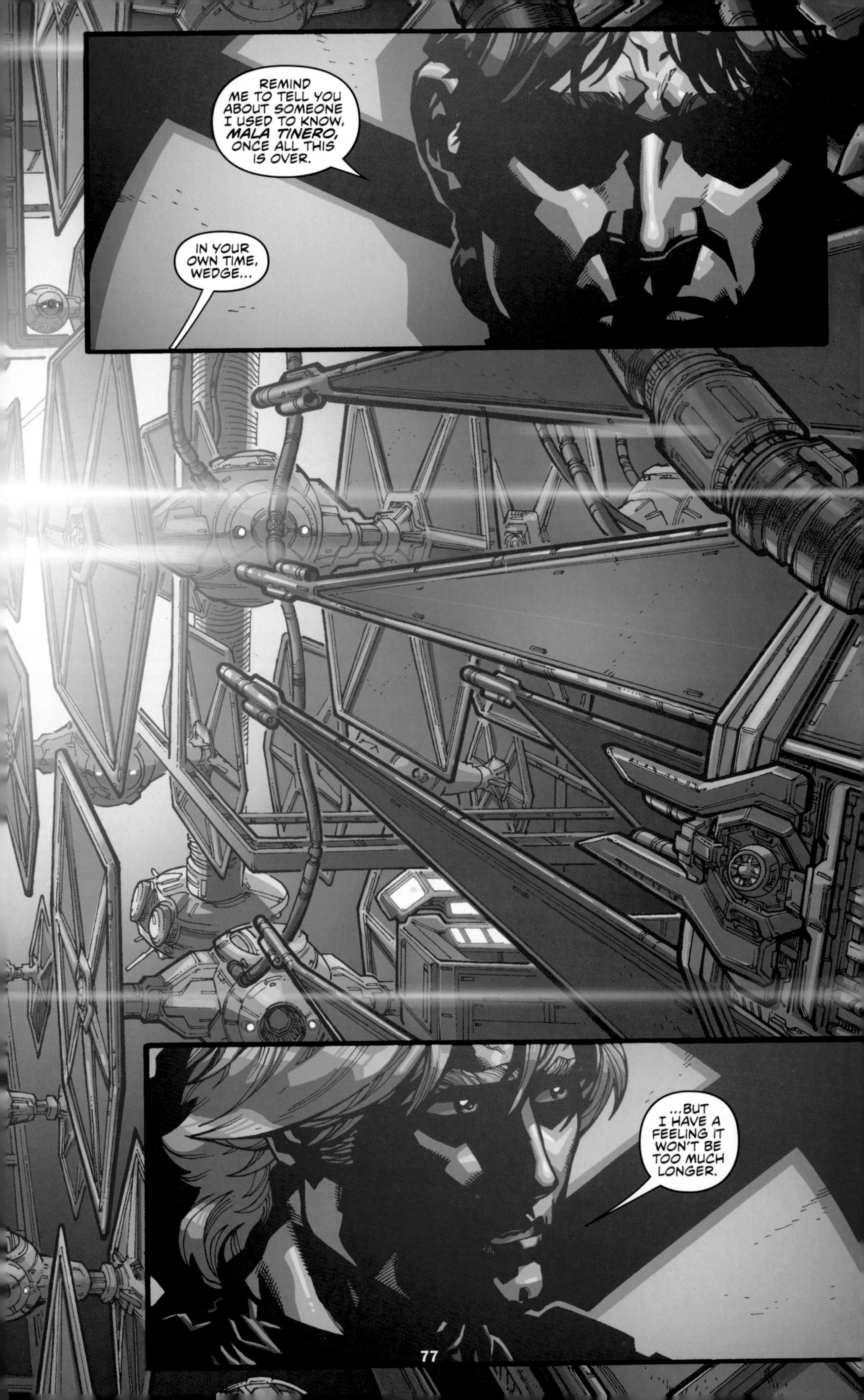
REMIND ME TO TELL YOU ABOUT SOMEONE I USED TO KNOW, MALA TINERO, ONCE ALL THIS IS OVER.
IN YOUR OWN TIME, WEDGE...
...BUT I HAVE A FEELING IT WON'T BE TOO MUCH LONGER.

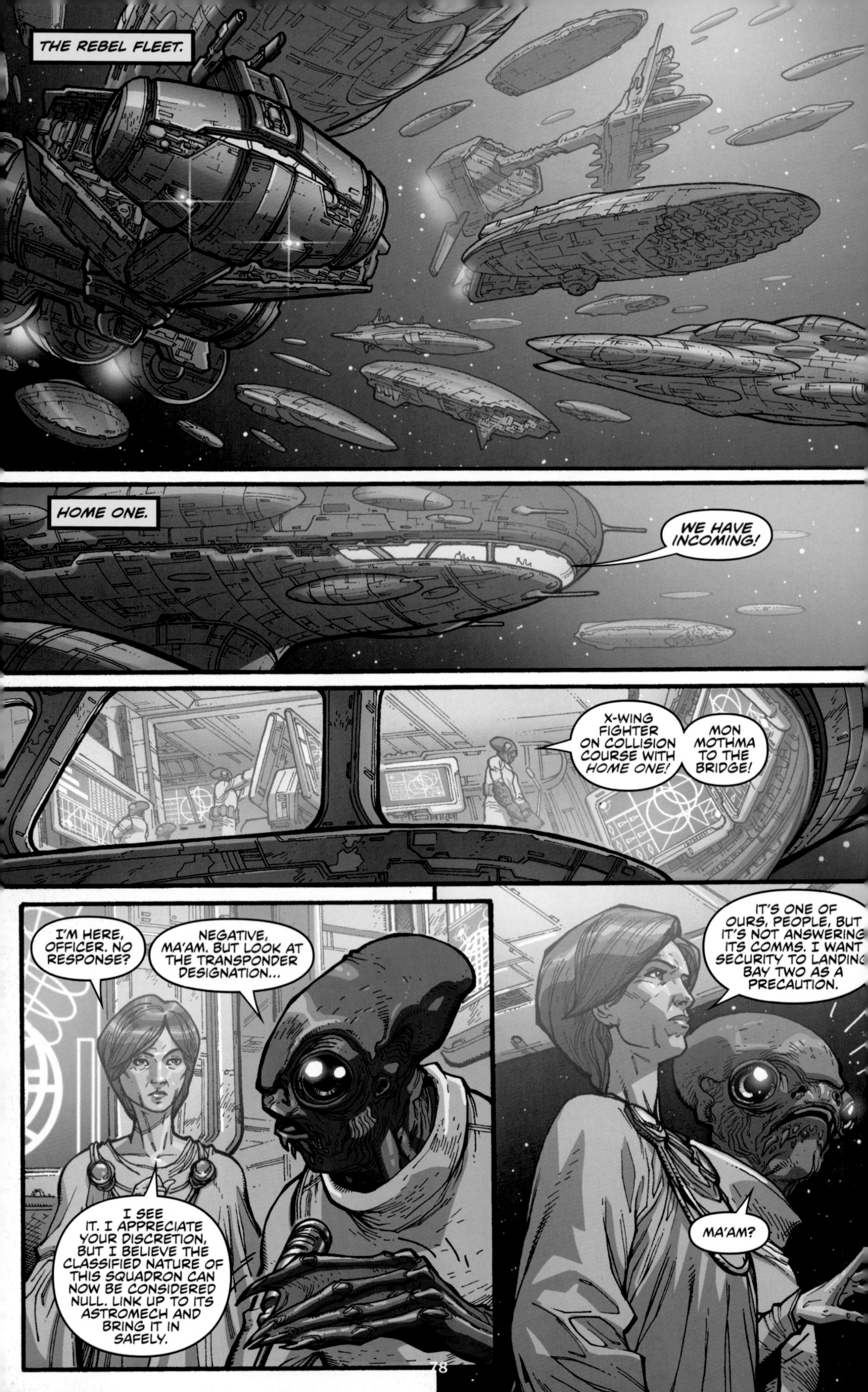
THE REBEL FLEET.
HOME ONE.
WE HAVE INCOMING!
X-WING FIGHTER ON COLLISION COURSE WITH HOME ONE!
MON MOTHMA TO THE BRIDGE!
I'M HERE, OFFICER. NO RESPONSE?
NEGATIVE, MA'AM. BUT LOOK AT THE TRANSPONDER DESIGNATION...
I SEE IT. I APPRECIATE YOUR DISCRETION, BUT I BELIEVE THE CLASSIFIED NATURE OF THIS SQUADRON CAN NOW BE CONSIDERED NULL. LINK UP TO ITS ASTROMECH AND BRING IT IN SAFELY.
IT'S ONE OF OURS, PEOPLE, BUT IT'S NOT ANSWERING ITS COMMS. I WANT SECURITY TO LANDING BAY TWO AS A PRECAUTION.
MA'AM?

MEDICAL TELEMETRY IS COMING BACK SUBNOMINAL. AND THE ASTROMECH IS REFUSING INQUIRIES FROM ANYONE BUT YOU.

FURTHER, ITS FLIGHT RECORDS INDICATE THE PILOT DEVIATED FROM HER ORDERS AND VIOLATED SECURITY PROTOCOLS IN THE PROCESS.

MEANING?

MEANING IF THAT FIGHTER WENT ANYWHERE *NEAR* AN IMPERIAL CAPITAL SHIP, MA'AM, IT'S A GOOD BET THE EMPIRE TRACKED IT BACK HERE.

UNDERSTOOD. KEEP SCANNING THE SYSTEM FOR ANY AND ALL TRAFFIC.

I'LL BE IN LANDING BAY TWO.

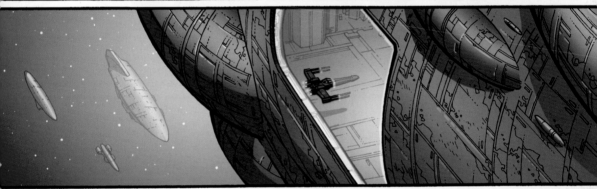

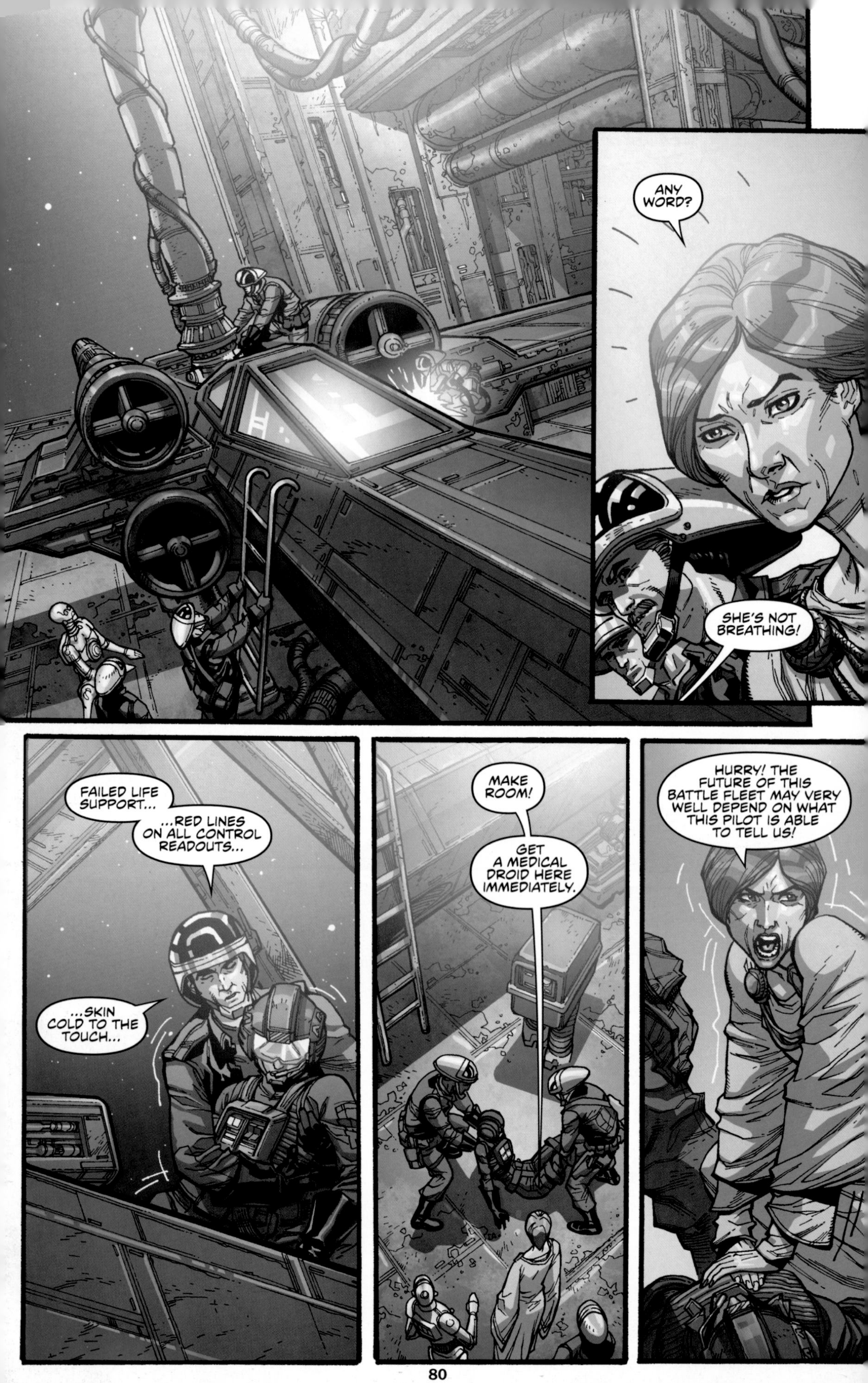
ANY WORD?
SHE'S NOT BREATHING!
FAILED LIFE SUPPORT...
...RED LINES ON ALL CONTROL READOUTS...
...SKIN COLD TO THE TOUCH...
MAKE ROOM!
GET A MEDICAL DROID HERE IMMEDIATELY.
HURRY! THE FUTURE OF THIS BATTLE FLEET MAY VERY WELL DEPEND ON WHAT THIS PILOT IS ABLE TO TELL US!

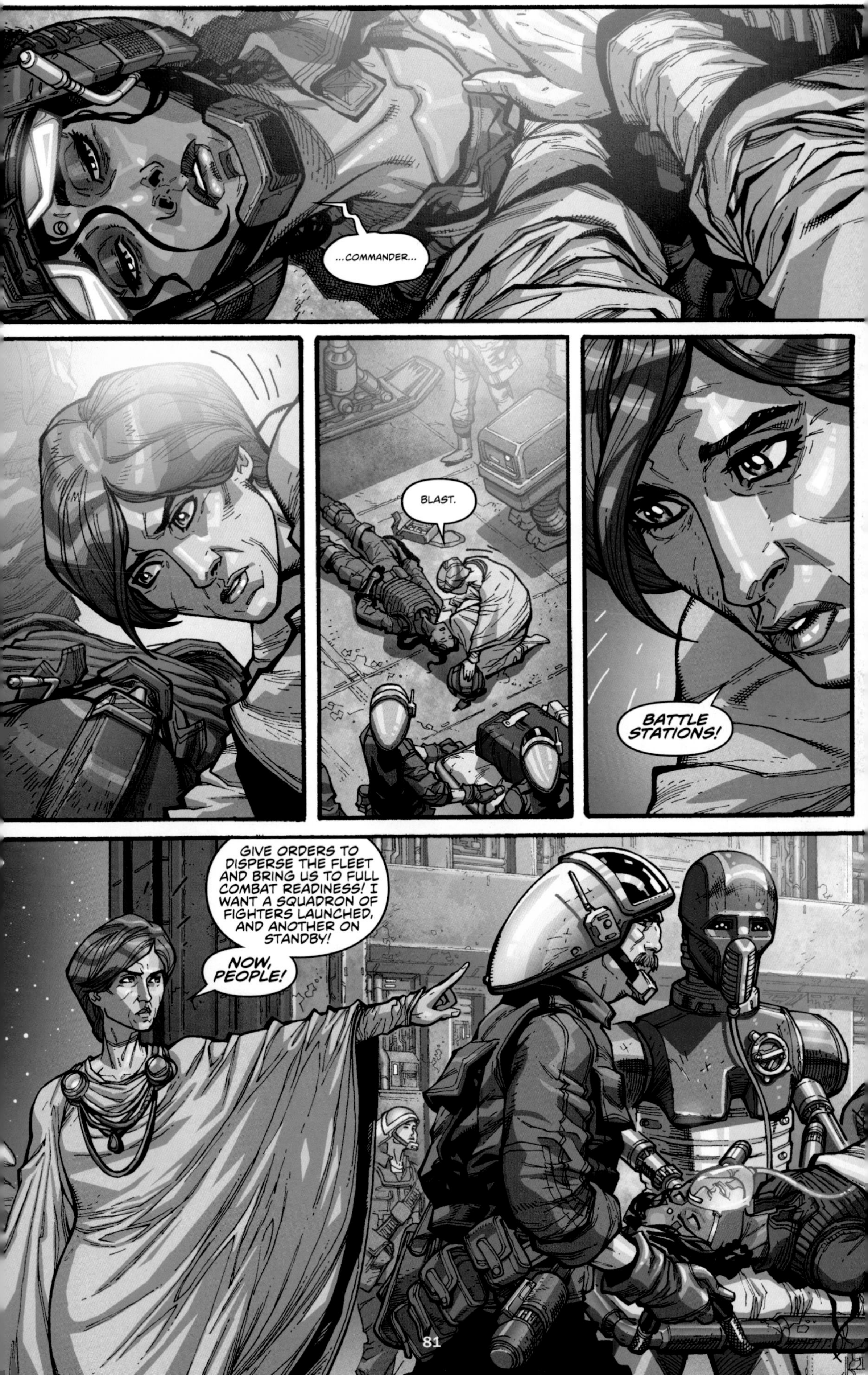
...COMMANDER...
BLAST.
BATTLE STATIONS!
GIVE ORDERS TO DISPERSE THE FLEET AND BRING US TO FULL COMBAT READINESS! I WANT A SQUADRON OF FIGHTERS LAUNCHED, AND ANOTHER ON STANDBY!
NOW, PEOPLE!

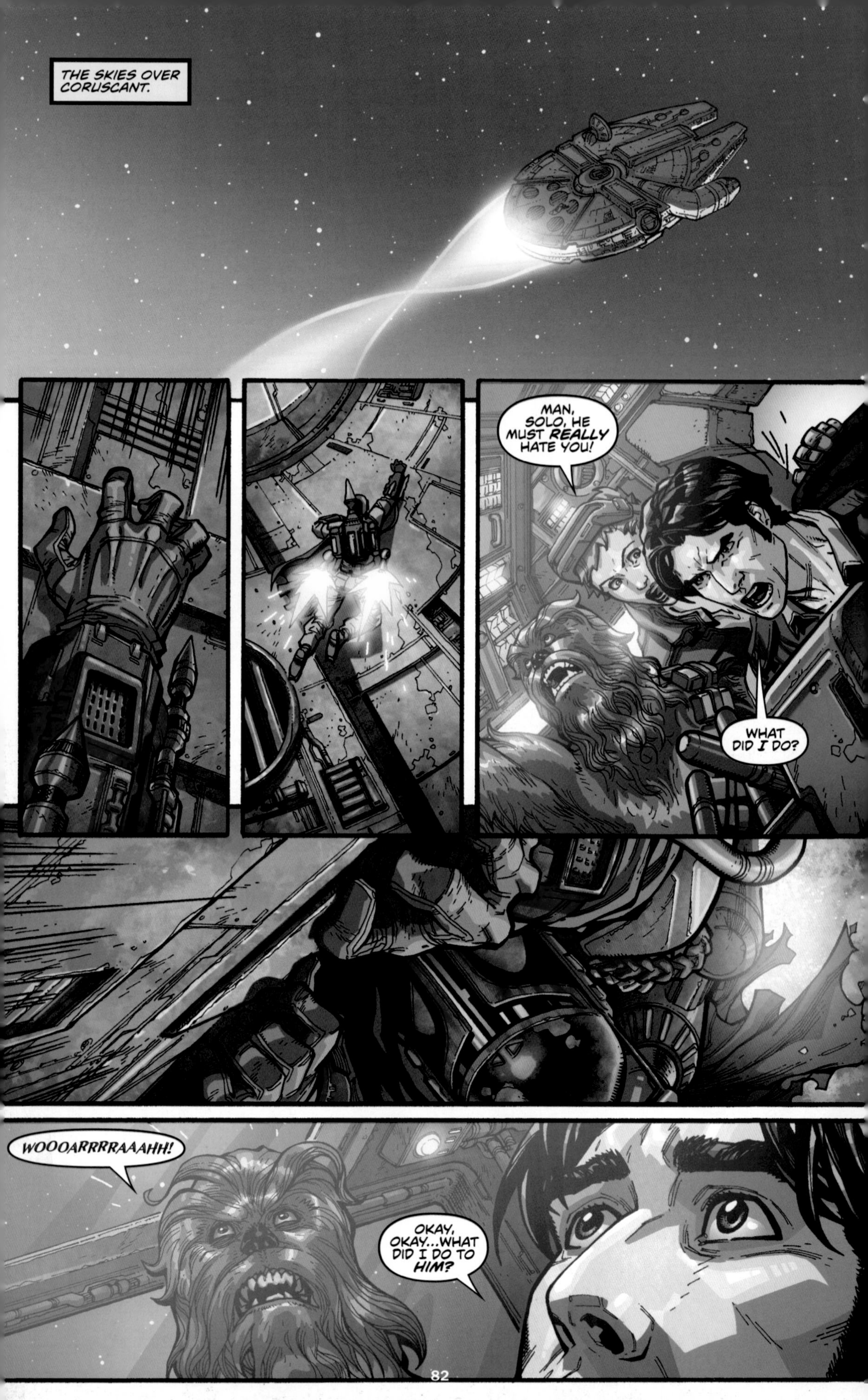

THE SKIES OVER CORUSCANT.
MAN, SOLO, HE MUST REALLY HATE YOU!
WHAT DID I DO?
WOOOARRRRAAAHH!
OKAY, OKAY...WHAT DID I DO TO HIM?

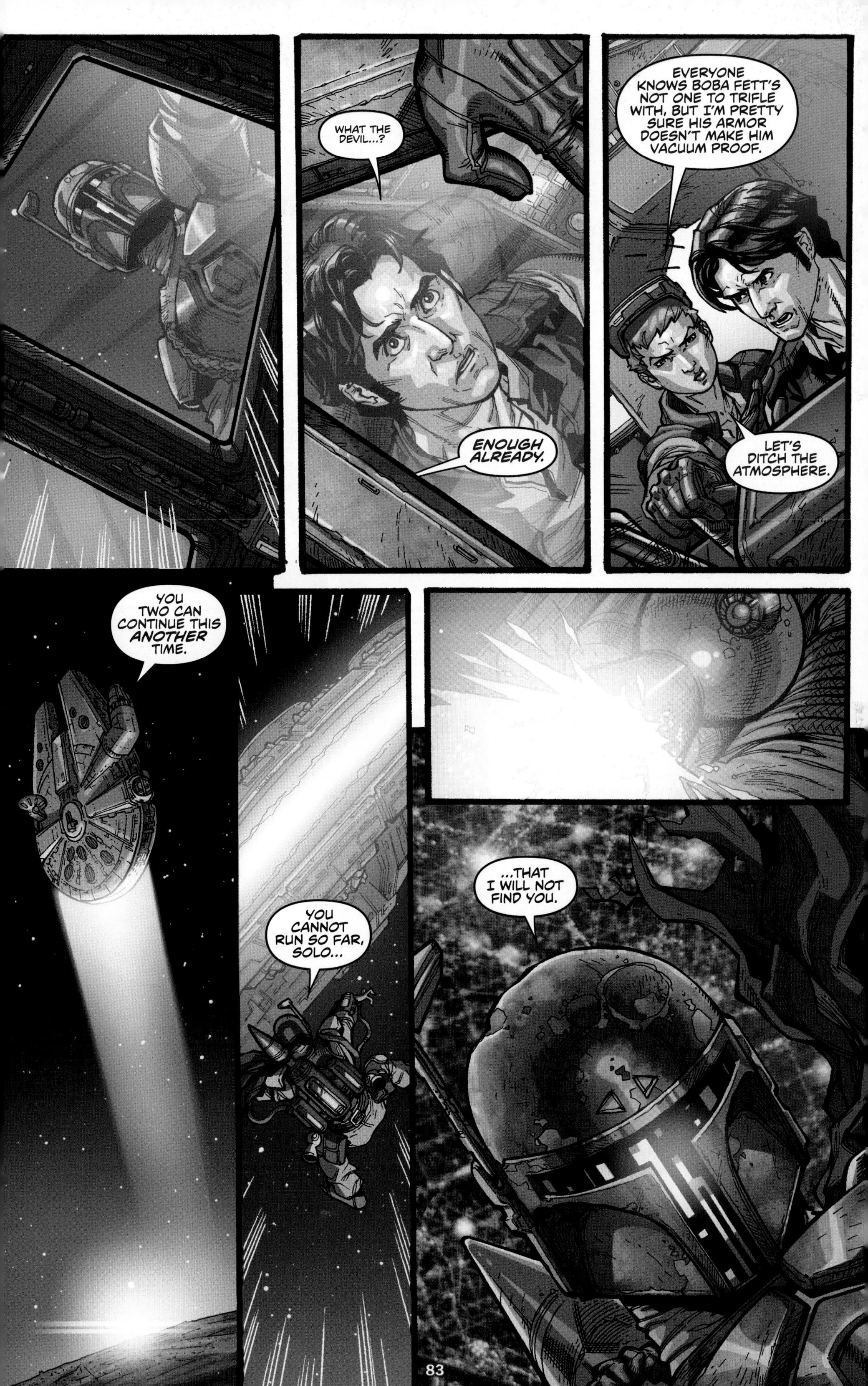

WHAT THE DEVIL...?
ENOUGH ALREADY.
EVERYONE KNOWS BOBA FETT'S NOT ONE TO TRIFLE WITH, BUT I'M PRETTY SURE HIS ARMOR DOESN'T MAKE HIM VACUUM PROOF.
LET'S DITCH THE ATMOSPHERE.
YOU TWO CAN CONTINUE THIS ANOTHER TIME.
YOU CANNOT RUN SO FAR, SOLO...
...THAT I WILL NOT FIND YOU.

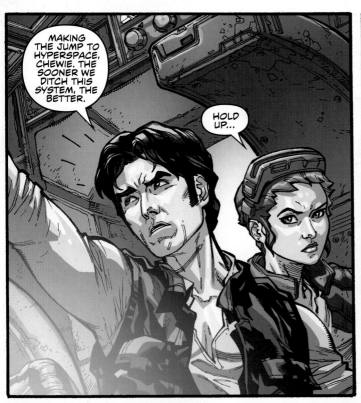

MAKING THE JUMP TO HYPERSPACE, CHEWIE. THE SOONER WE DITCH THIS SYSTEM, THE BETTER.

HOLD UP...

YOU'RE A HANDSOME GUY, HAN SOLO, BUT I'M NOT ABOUT TO LET YOU FLY ME ACROSS THE GALAXY JUST LIKE THAT. YOU AND I HAVE UNFINISHED BUSINESS.

MY MONEY?

A GIRL AFTER MY OWN HEART. BUT THINGS'RE STILL A LITTLE *BUSY* RIGHT NOW. THINK YOU CAN GIVE ME A SECOND?

I CAN DO BETTER...

HERE. COORDINATES. MAKE THE JUMP, CHEWBACCA.

AND WHERE WOULD THAT TAKE US?

SOMEPLACE SAFE AND QUIET. CALL IT A HIDEOUT IF YOU LIKE.

YOU AREN'T THE ONLY SMUGGLER IN THE GALAXY, SOLO.

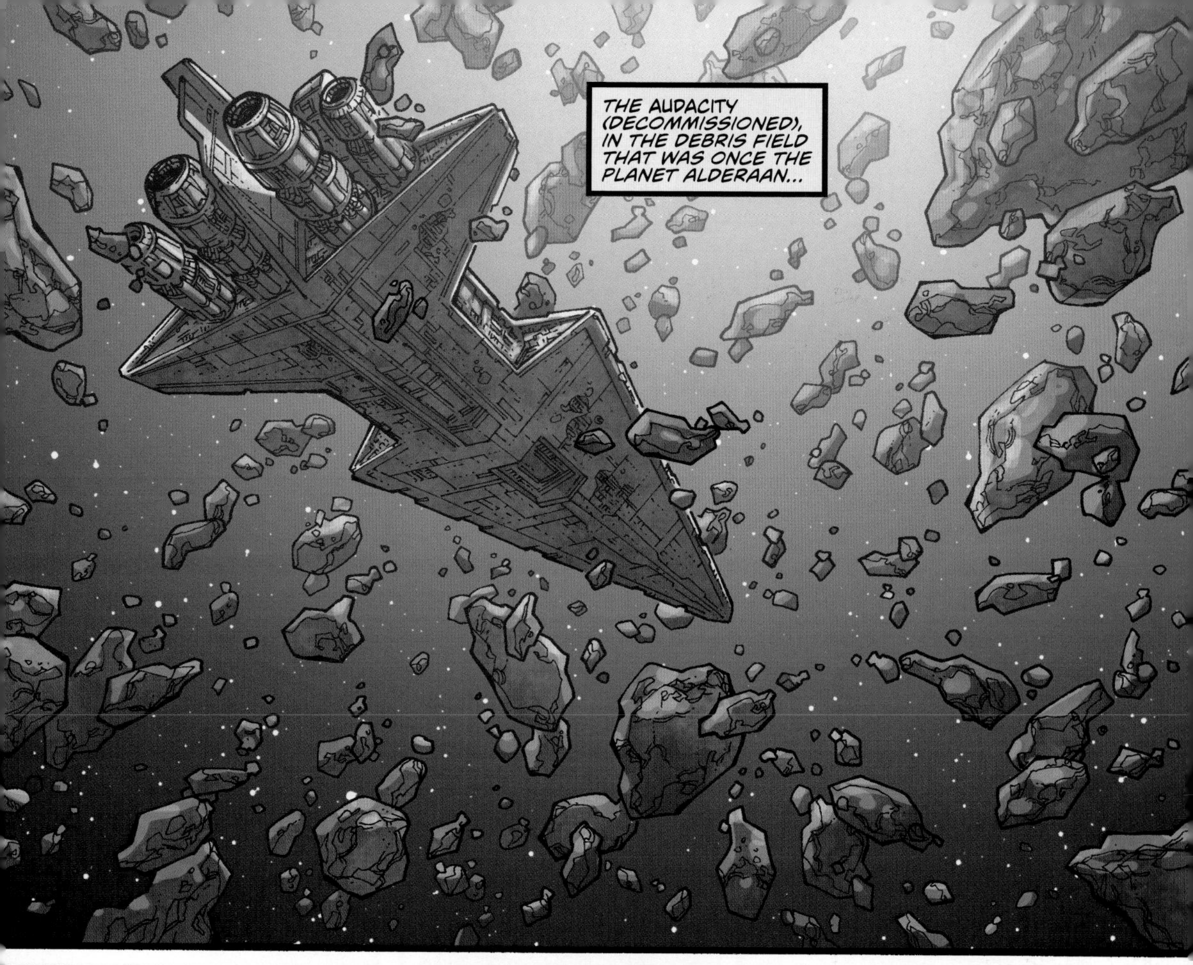
THE AUDACITY (DECOMMISSIONED), IN THE DEBRIS FIELD THAT WAS ONCE THE PLANET ALDERAAN...

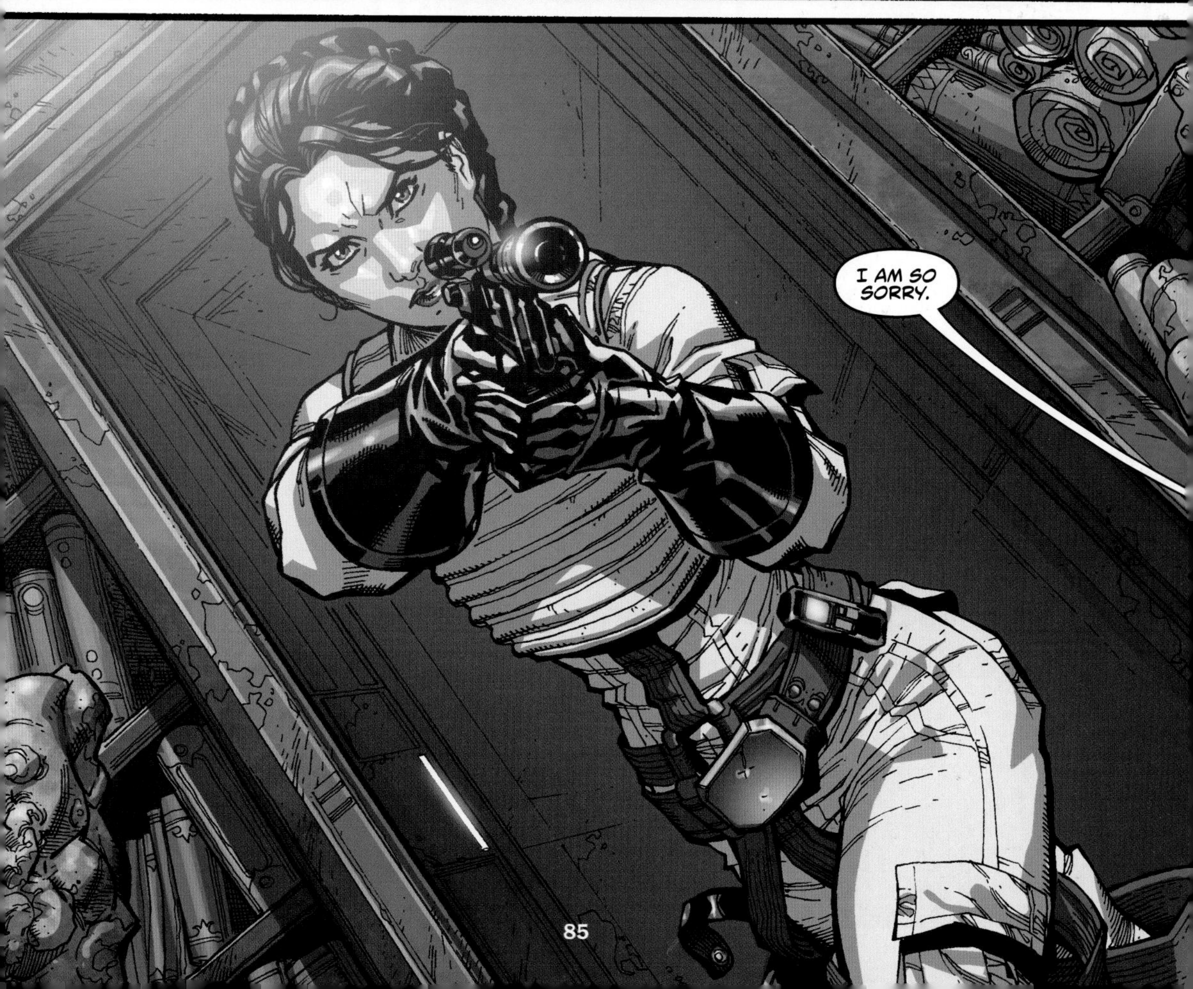
I AM SO SORRY.

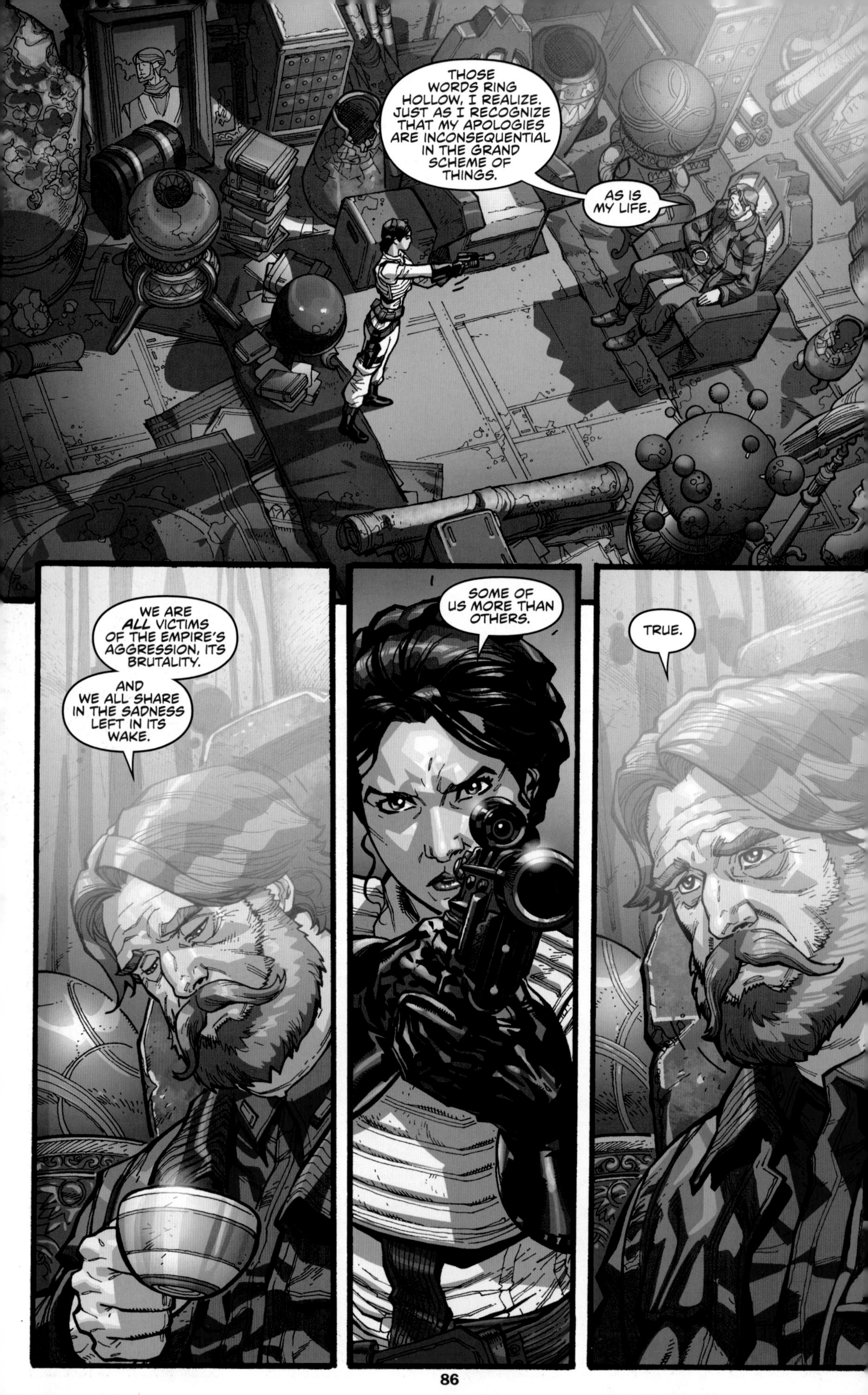
THOSE WORDS RING HOLLOW, I REALIZE. JUST AS I RECOGNIZE THAT MY APOLOGIES ARE INCONSEQUENTIAL IN THE GRAND SCHEME OF THINGS.
AS IS MY LIFE.
WE ARE ALL VICTIMS OF THE EMPIRE'S AGGRESSION, ITS BRUTALITY.
AND WE ALL SHARE IN THE SADNESS LEFT IN ITS WAKE.
SOME OF US MORE THAN OTHERS.
TRUE.

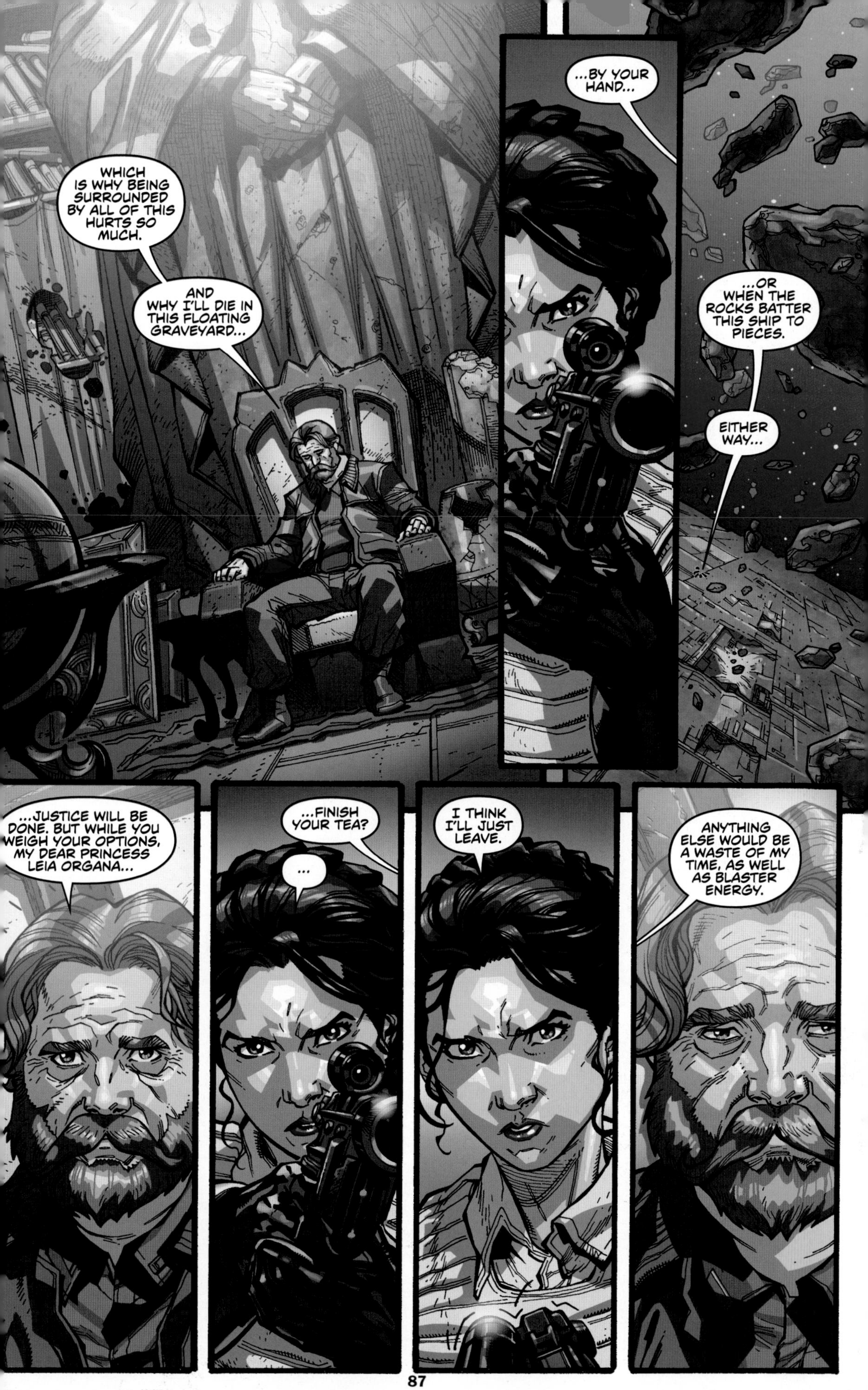
WHICH IS WHY BEING SURROUNDED BY ALL OF THIS HURTS SO MUCH.
AND WHY I'LL DIE IN THIS FLOATING GRAVEYARD...
...BY YOUR HAND...
...OR WHEN THE ROCKS BATTER THIS SHIP TO PIECES.
EITHER WAY...
...JUSTICE WILL BE DONE. BUT WHILE YOU WEIGH YOUR OPTIONS, MY DEAR PRINCESS LEIA ORGANA...
...FINISH YOUR TEA?
...
I THINK I'LL JUST LEAVE.
ANYTHING ELSE WOULD BE A WASTE OF MY TIME, AS WELL AS BLASTER ENERGY.

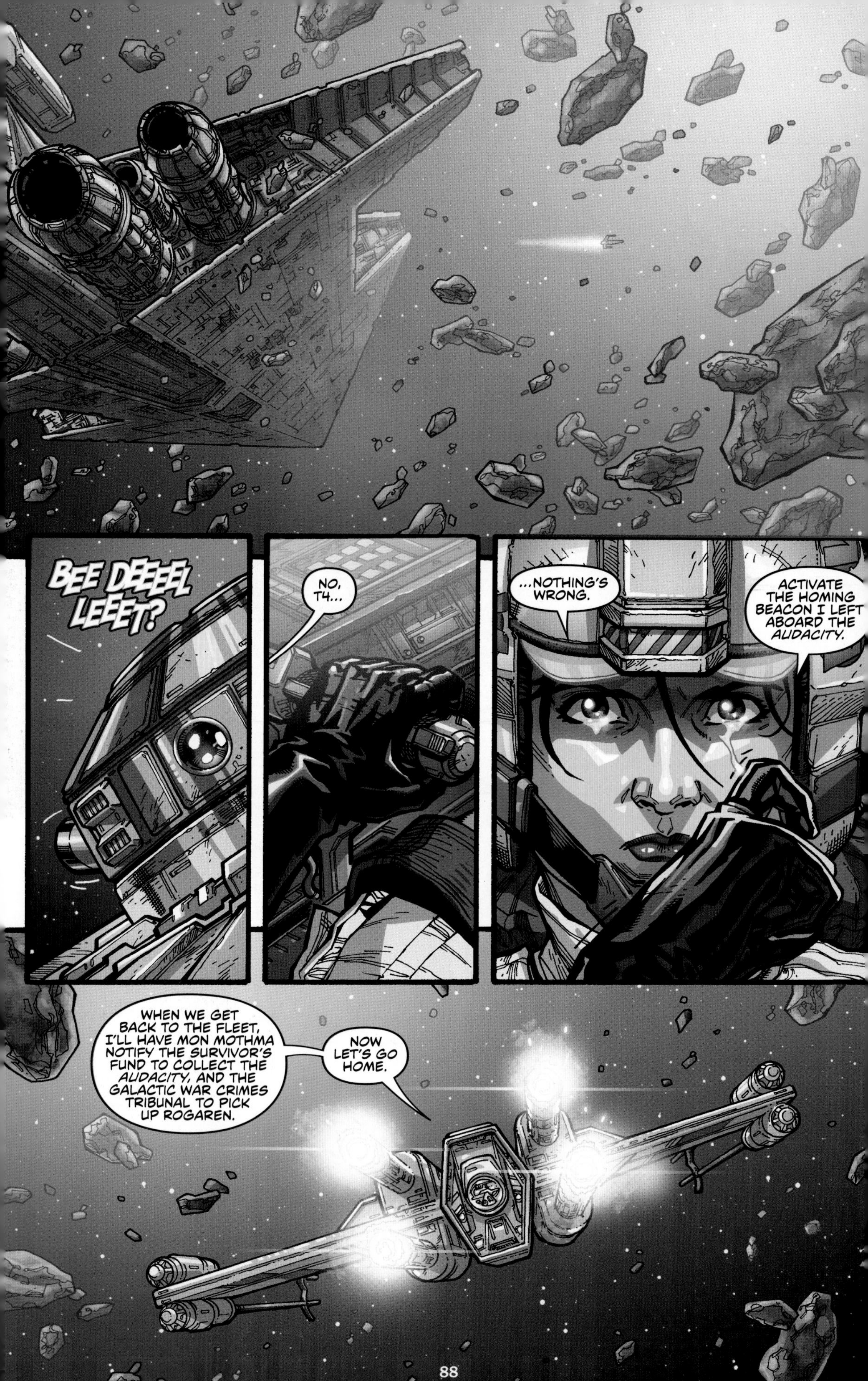
BEE DEEEEL LEEET?
NO, T4...
...NOTHING'S WRONG.
ACTIVATE THE HOMING BEACON I LEFT ABOARD THE *AUDACITY*.
WHEN WE GET BACK TO THE FLEET, I'LL HAVE MON MOTHMA NOTIFY THE SURVIVOR'S FUND TO COLLECT THE *AUDACITY*, AND THE GALACTIC WAR CRIMES TRIBUNAL TO PICK UP ROGAREN.
NOW LET'S GO HOME.

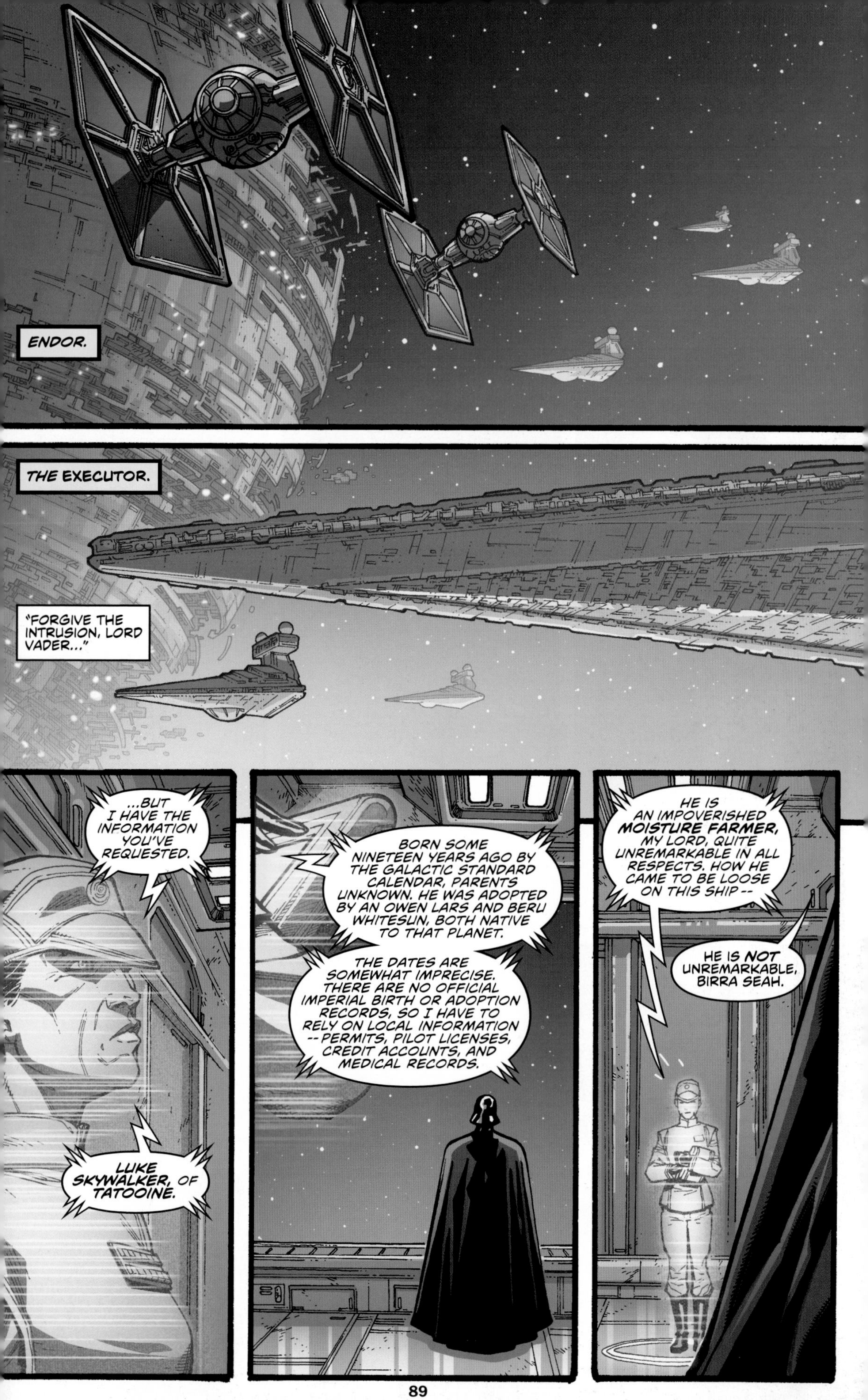
ENDOR.
THE EXECUTOR.
"FORGIVE THE INTRUSION, LORD VADER..."
...BUT I HAVE THE INFORMATION YOU'VE REQUESTED.
LUKE SKYWALKER, OF TATOOINE.
BORN SOME NINETEEN YEARS AGO BY THE GALACTIC STANDARD CALENDAR, PARENTS UNKNOWN. HE WAS ADOPTED BY AN OWEN LARS AND BERU WHITESUN, BOTH NATIVE TO THAT PLANET.
THE DATES ARE SOMEWHAT IMPRECISE. THERE ARE NO OFFICIAL IMPERIAL BIRTH OR ADOPTION RECORDS, SO I HAVE TO RELY ON LOCAL INFORMATION --PERMITS, PILOT LICENSES, CREDIT ACCOUNTS, AND MEDICAL RECORDS.
HE IS AN IMPOVERISHED MOISTURE FARMER, MY LORD, QUITE UNREMARKABLE IN ALL RESPECTS. HOW HE CAME TO BE LOOSE ON THIS SHIP --
HE IS NOT UNREMARKABLE, BIRRA SEAH.

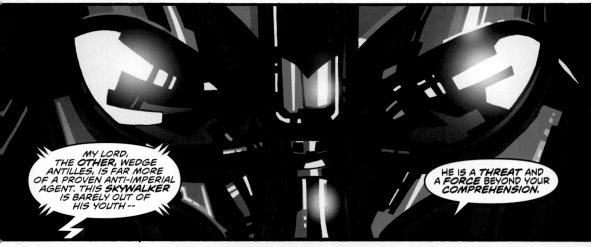

MY LORD, THE *OTHER*, WEDGE ANTILLES, IS FAR MORE OF A PROVEN ANTI-IMPERIAL AGENT. THIS *SKYWALKER* IS BARELY OUT OF HIS YOUTH --

HE IS A *THREAT* AND A *FORCE* BEYOND YOUR *COMPREHENSION.*

AH...

AM I BEING CLEAR?

NO, NO, QUITE CLEAR, MY LORD.

BY ALL MEANS, SEND A STORMTROOPER TO PUT A BOLT THROUGH ANTILLES'S FOREHEAD AND BE DONE WITH HIM.

BUT SKYWALKER?

IF IT TAKES HALF THE SHIP'S RESOURCES, YOU WILL LOCATE AND DETAIN THAT MAN. I AM TRUSTING NO ONE ELSE WITH THIS...

...DO NOT FAIL ME.

BY YOUR COMMAND, MY LORD.

WE'RE COMING OUT OF LIGHTSPEED NOW, COMMANDER.

LET ME SEE IT.

WE'RE SOME THIRTY KILOMETERS AWAY, BUT IT SEEMS AS THOUGH THEY'VE BEEN ALERTED TO OUR PRESENCE. THEIR FLEET IS DISPERSING AND AN ENERGY BARRIER HAS BEEN RAISED AROUND THEIR PRIMARY SHIP.

I HAD NO IDEA THEY WERE USING SUCH ANTIQUATED VESSELS.

THIS WILL BE AN EASY VICTORY.

MIGHT I REMIND YOU, SIR --

OH, YES, YES...

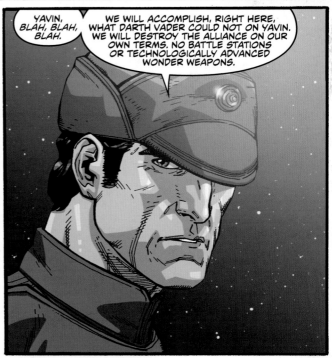

YAVIN, BLAH, BLAH, BLAH.

WE WILL ACCOMPLISH, RIGHT HERE, WHAT DARTH VADER COULD NOT ON YAVIN. WE WILL DESTROY THE ALLIANCE ON OUR OWN TERMS. NO BATTLE STATIONS OR TECHNOLOGICALLY ADVANCED WONDER WEAPONS.

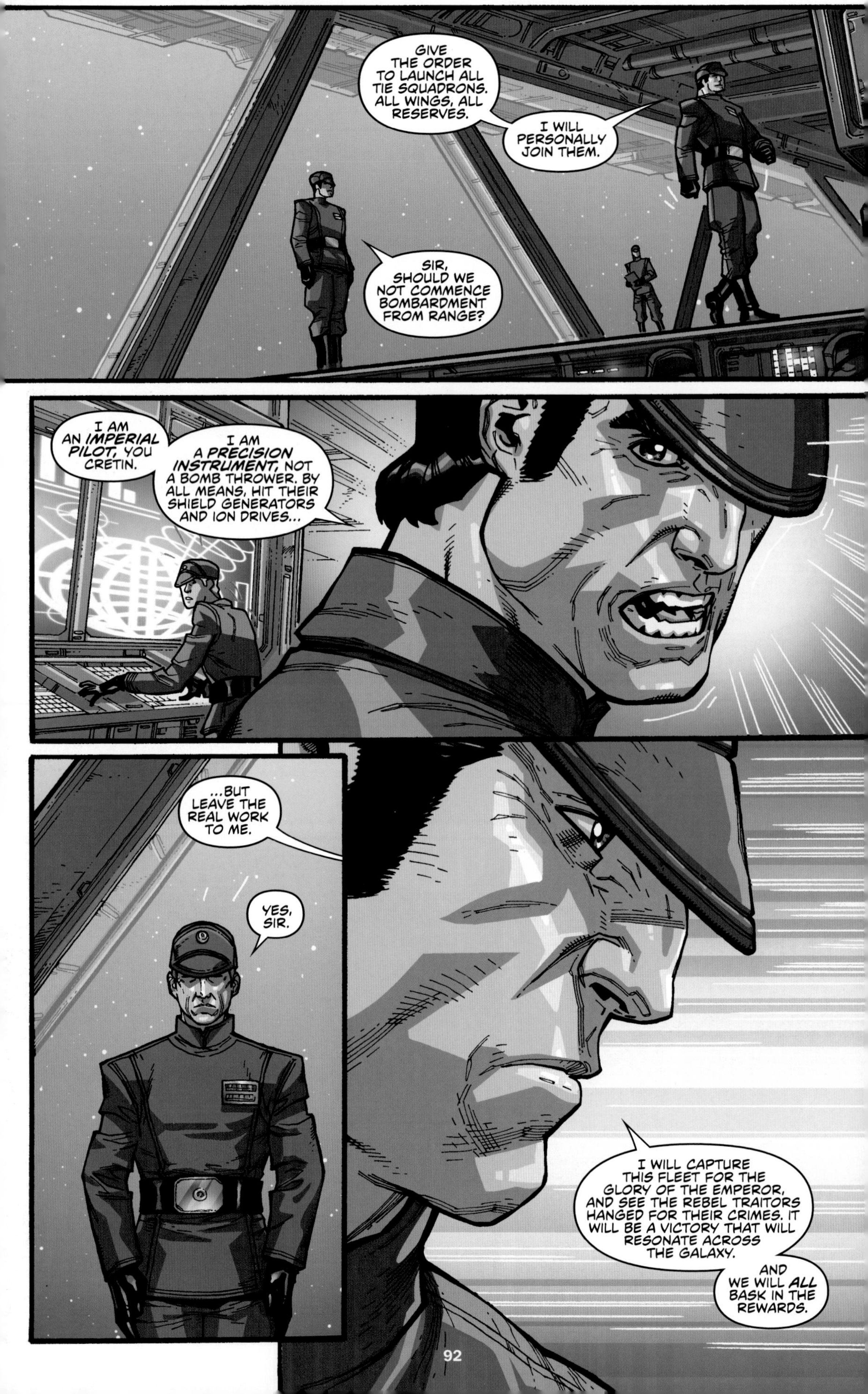
GIVE THE ORDER TO LAUNCH ALL TIE SQUADRONS. ALL WINGS, ALL RESERVES.
I WILL PERSONALLY JOIN THEM.
SIR, SHOULD WE NOT COMMENCE BOMBARDMENT FROM RANGE?
I AM AN *IMPERIAL PILOT,* YOU CRETIN.
I AM A *PRECISION INSTRUMENT,* NOT A BOMB THROWER. BY ALL MEANS, HIT THEIR SHIELD GENERATORS AND ION DRIVES...
...BUT LEAVE THE REAL WORK TO ME.
YES, SIR.
I WILL CAPTURE THIS FLEET FOR THE GLORY OF THE EMPEROR, AND SEE THE REBEL TRAITORS HANGED FOR THEIR CRIMES. IT WILL BE A VICTORY THAT WILL RESONATE ACROSS THE GALAXY.
AND WE WILL *ALL* BASK IN THE REWARDS.

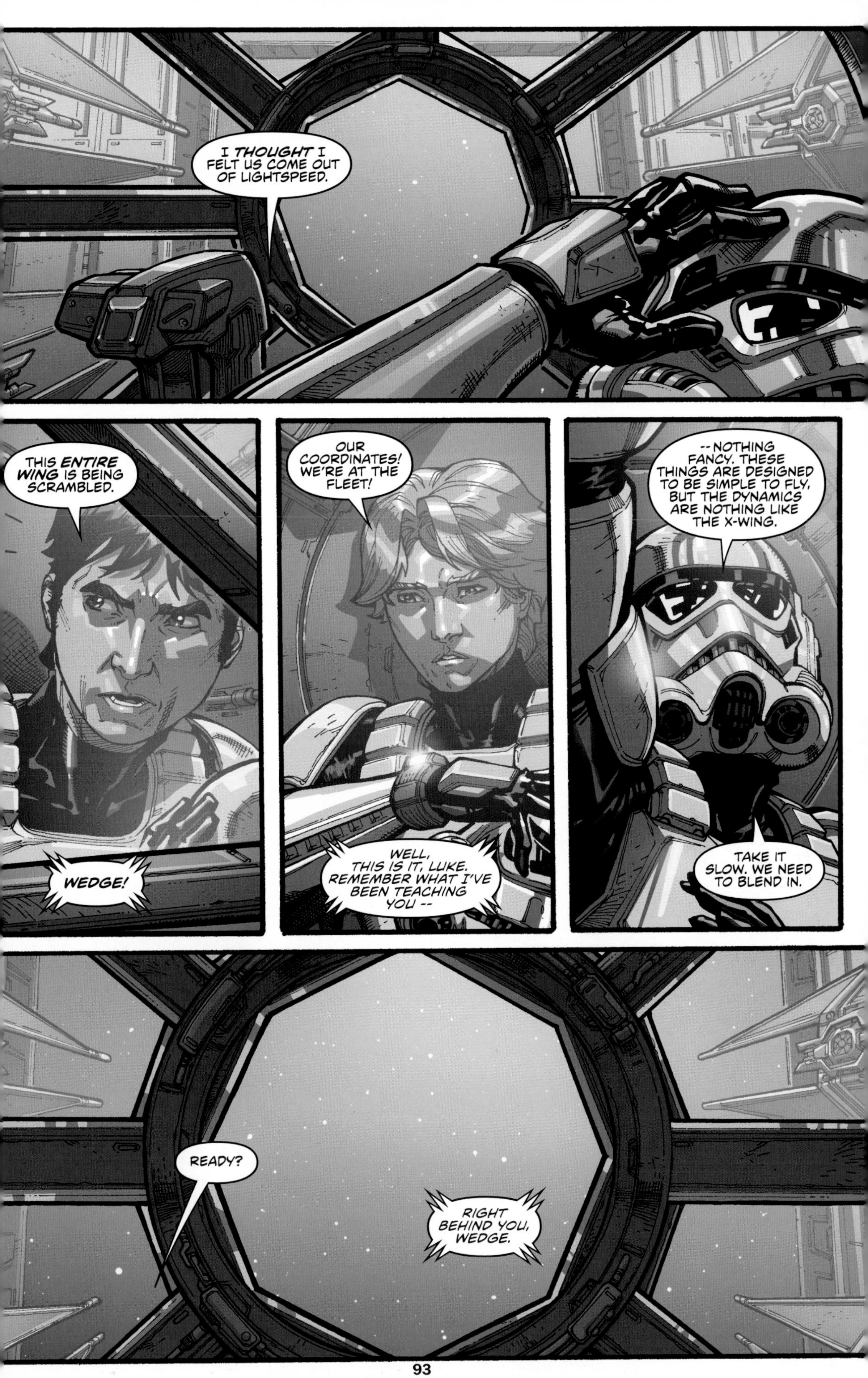
I THOUGHT I FELT US COME OUT OF LIGHTSPEED.
THIS ENTIRE WING IS BEING SCRAMBLED.
WEDGE!
OUR COORDINATES! WE'RE AT THE FLEET!
WELL, THIS IS IT, LUKE. REMEMBER WHAT I'VE BEEN TEACHING YOU --
--NOTHING FANCY. THESE THINGS ARE DESIGNED TO BE SIMPLE TO FLY, BUT THE DYNAMICS ARE NOTHING LIKE THE X-WING.
TAKE IT SLOW. WE NEED TO BLEND IN.
READY?
RIGHT BEHIND YOU, WEDGE.

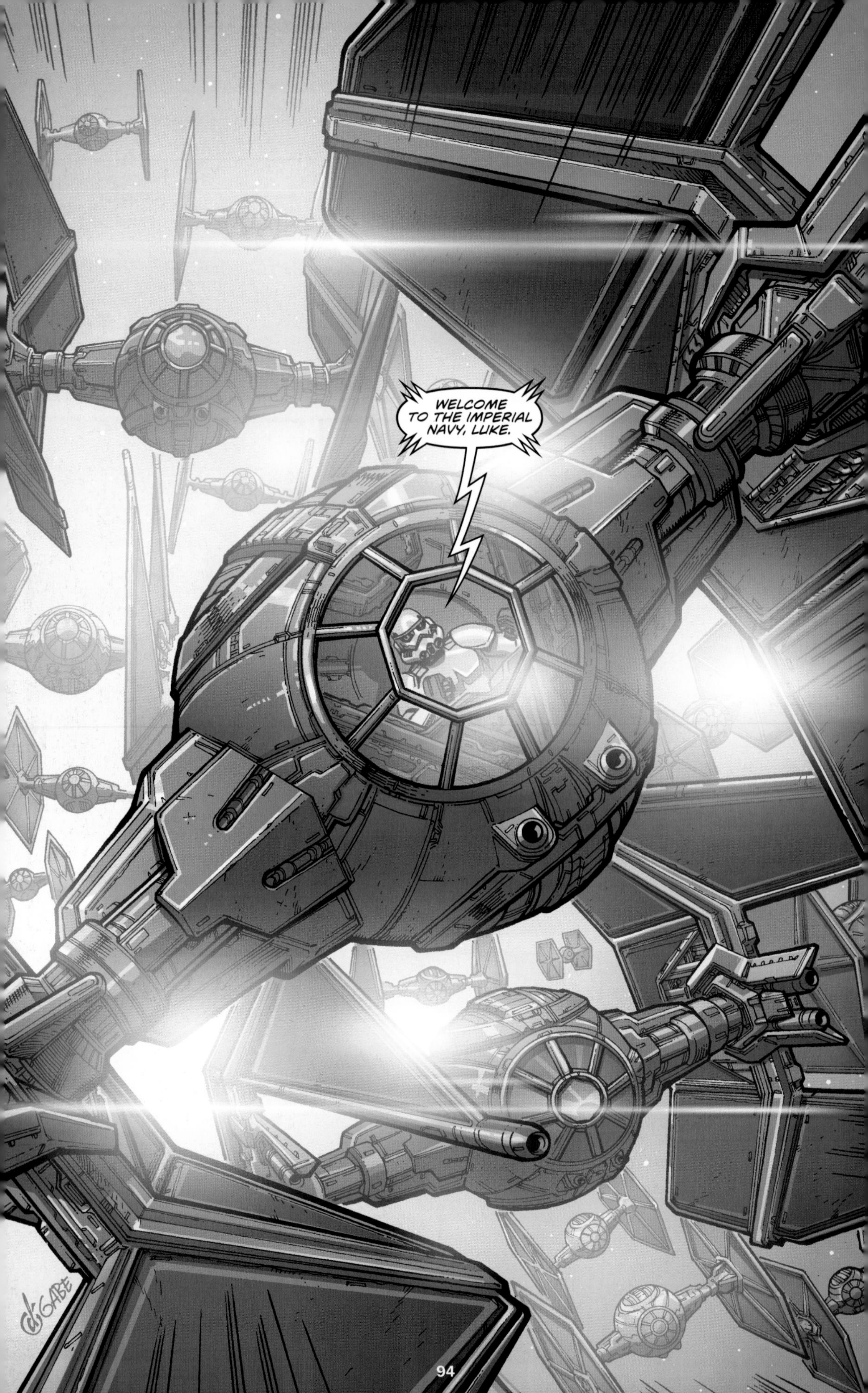
WELCOME TO THE IMPERIAL NAVY, LUKE.
GABE

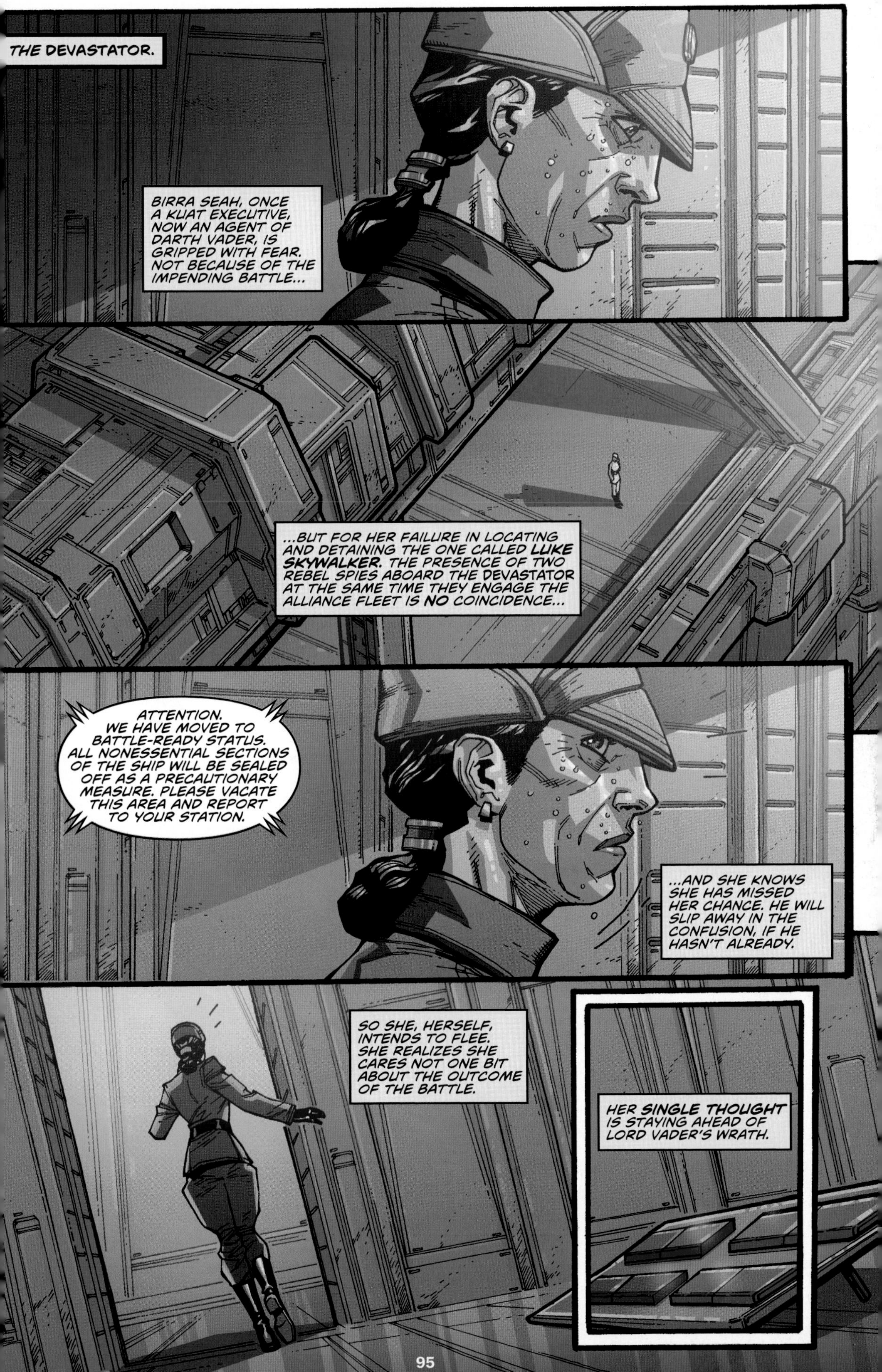
THE DEVASTATOR.
BIRRA SEAH, ONCE A KUAT EXECUTIVE, NOW AN AGENT OF DARTH VADER, IS GRIPPED WITH FEAR. NOT BECAUSE OF THE IMPENDING BATTLE...
...BUT FOR HER FAILURE IN LOCATING AND DETAINING THE ONE CALLED **LUKE SKYWALKER.** THE PRESENCE OF TWO REBEL SPIES ABOARD THE DEVASTATOR AT THE SAME TIME THEY ENGAGE THE ALLIANCE FLEET IS **NO** COINCIDENCE...
ATTENTION. WE HAVE MOVED TO BATTLE-READY STATUS. ALL NONESSENTIAL SECTIONS OF THE SHIP WILL BE SEALED OFF AS A PRECAUTIONARY MEASURE. PLEASE VACATE THIS AREA AND REPORT TO YOUR STATION.
...AND SHE KNOWS SHE HAS MISSED HER CHANCE. HE WILL SLIP AWAY IN THE CONFUSION, IF HE HASN'T ALREADY.
SO SHE, HERSELF, INTENDS TO FLEE. SHE REALIZES SHE CARES NOT ONE BIT ABOUT THE OUTCOME OF THE BATTLE.
HER **SINGLE THOUGHT** IS STAYING AHEAD OF LORD VADER'S WRATH.

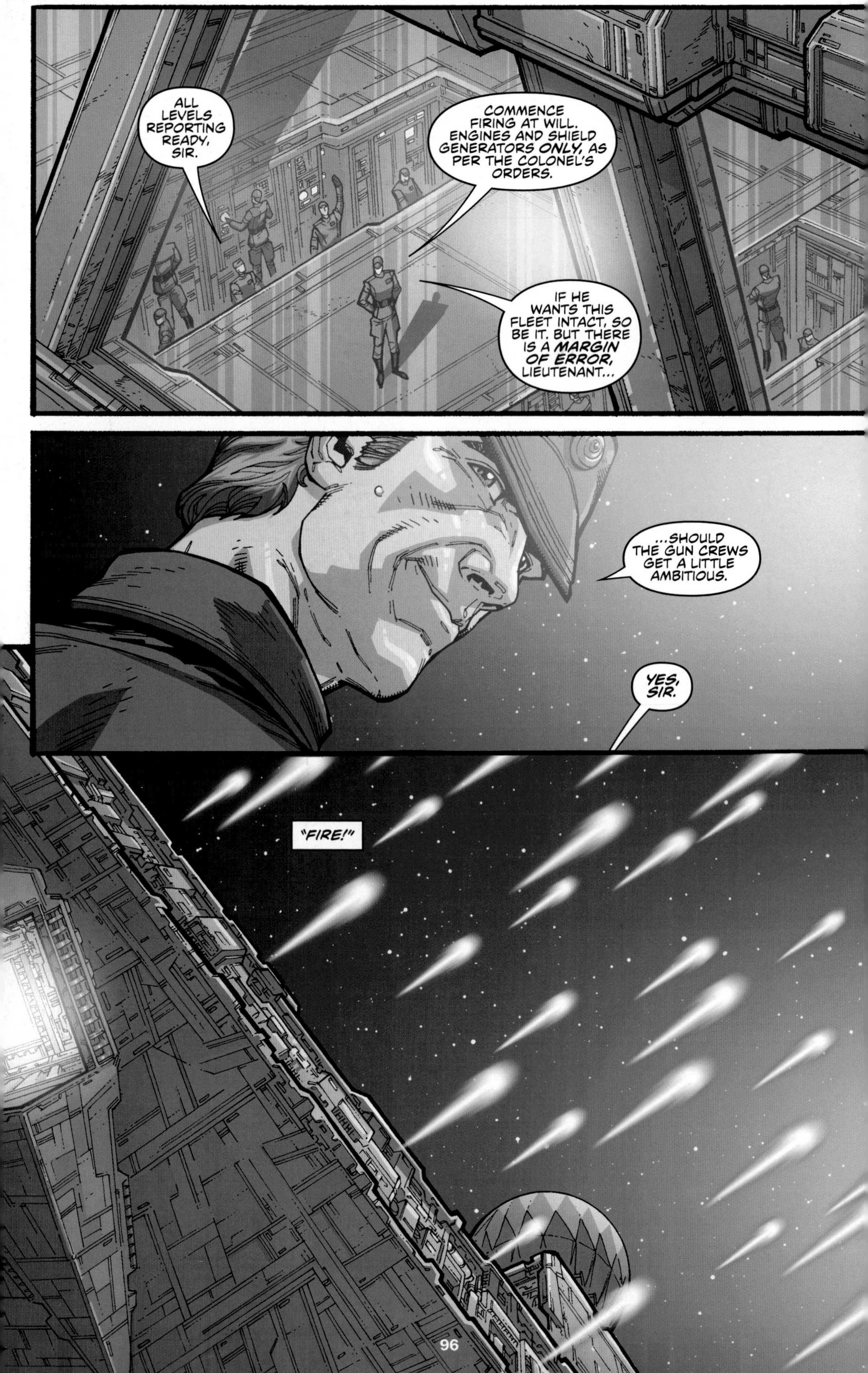
ALL LEVELS REPORTING READY, SIR.
COMMENCE FIRING AT WILL. ENGINES AND SHIELD GENERATORS ONLY, AS PER THE COLONEL'S ORDERS.
IF HE WANTS THIS FLEET INTACT, SO BE IT. BUT THERE IS A MARGIN OF ERROR, LIEUTENANT...
...SHOULD THE GUN CREWS GET A LITTLE AMBITIOUS.
YES, SIR.
"FIRE!"

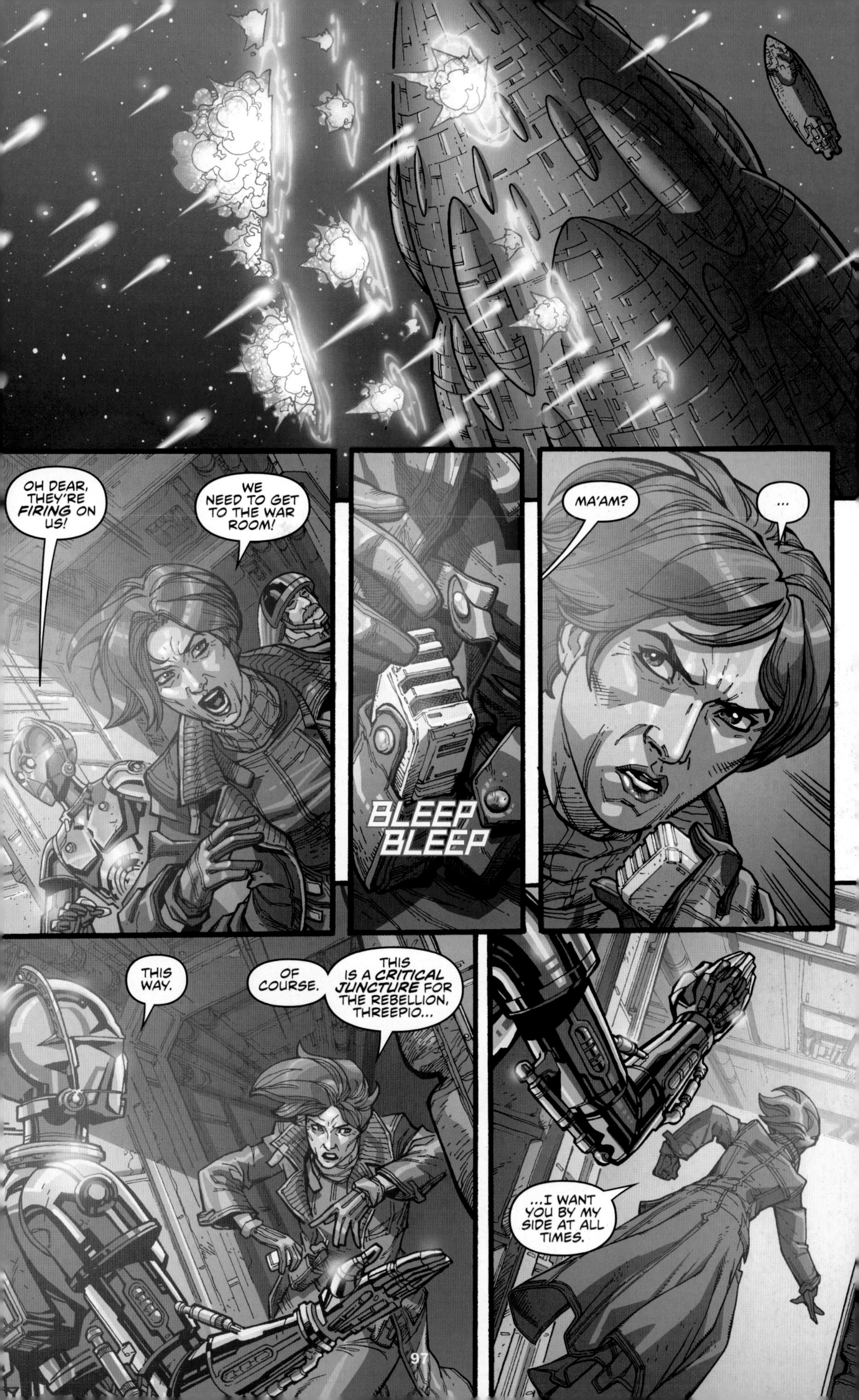
OH DEAR, THEY'RE FIRING ON US!
WE NEED TO GET TO THE WAR ROOM!
BLEEP BLEEP
MA'AM?
...
THIS WAY.
OF COURSE.
THIS IS A CRITICAL JUNCTURE FOR THE REBELLION, THREEPIO...
...I WANT YOU BY MY SIDE AT ALL TIMES.

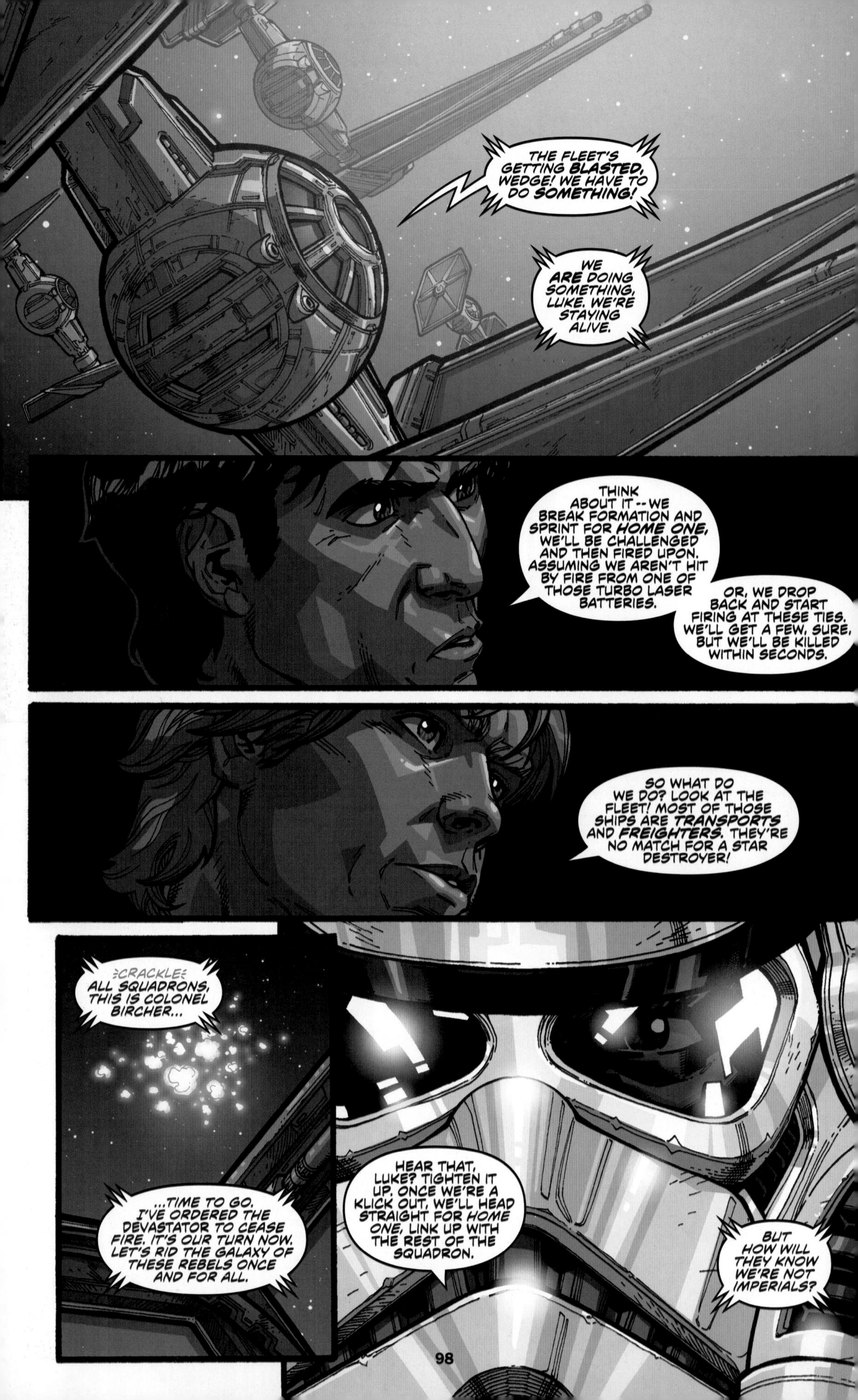
THE FLEET'S GETTING BLASTED, WEDGE! WE HAVE TO DO SOMETHING!
WE ARE DOING SOMETHING, LUKE. WE'RE STAYING ALIVE.
THINK ABOUT IT -- WE BREAK FORMATION AND SPRINT FOR HOME ONE, WE'LL BE CHALLENGED AND THEN FIRED UPON. ASSUMING WE AREN'T HIT BY FIRE FROM ONE OF THOSE TURBO LASER BATTERIES.
OR, WE DROP BACK AND START FIRING AT THESE TIES. WE'LL GET A FEW, SURE, BUT WE'LL BE KILLED WITHIN SECONDS.
SO WHAT DO WE DO? LOOK AT THE FLEET! MOST OF THOSE SHIPS ARE TRANSPORTS AND FREIGHTERS. THEY'RE NO MATCH FOR A STAR DESTROYER!
CRACKLE ALL SQUADRONS, THIS IS COLONEL BIRCHER...
...TIME TO GO. I'VE ORDERED THE DEVASTATOR TO CEASE FIRE. IT'S OUR TURN NOW. LET'S RID THE GALAXY OF THESE REBELS ONCE AND FOR ALL.
HEAR THAT, LUKE? TIGHTEN IT UP. ONCE WE'RE A KLICK OUT, WE'LL HEAD STRAIGHT FOR HOME ONE, LINK UP WITH THE REST OF THE SQUADRON.
BUT HOW WILL THEY KNOW WE'RE NOT IMPERIALS?

THEY WON'T. NOT UNTIL WE SET DOWN IN HOME ONE'S HANGAR AND POP THE HATCH.

THIS IS WHERE WE FIND OUT WHAT KIND OF PILOTS WE *BOTH* ARE.

COPY THAT, WEDGE, YOU CAN COUNT ON ME.

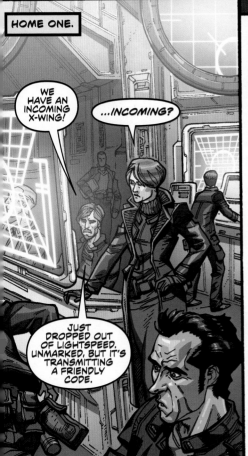

HOME ONE.

WE HAVE AN INCOMING X-WING!

...INCOMING?

JUST DROPPED OUT OF LIGHTSPEED. UNMARKED, BUT IT'S TRANSMITTING A FRIENDLY CODE.

LET IT THROUGH.

DAMAGE REPORT: WE LOST NINE SMALLER CRAFT, HEAVY DAMAGE TO TWO CRUISERS, ALL OTHERS REPORTING LIGHT DAMAGE. HOME ONE'S SHIELDS ARE HOLDING.

BUT, MA'AM?

OUR ENGINES TOOK AN ION HIT. WE HAVE ZERO PRO-PULSION.

ONE WAY OR THE OTHER...

...WE MAKE OUR STAND HERE, YES.

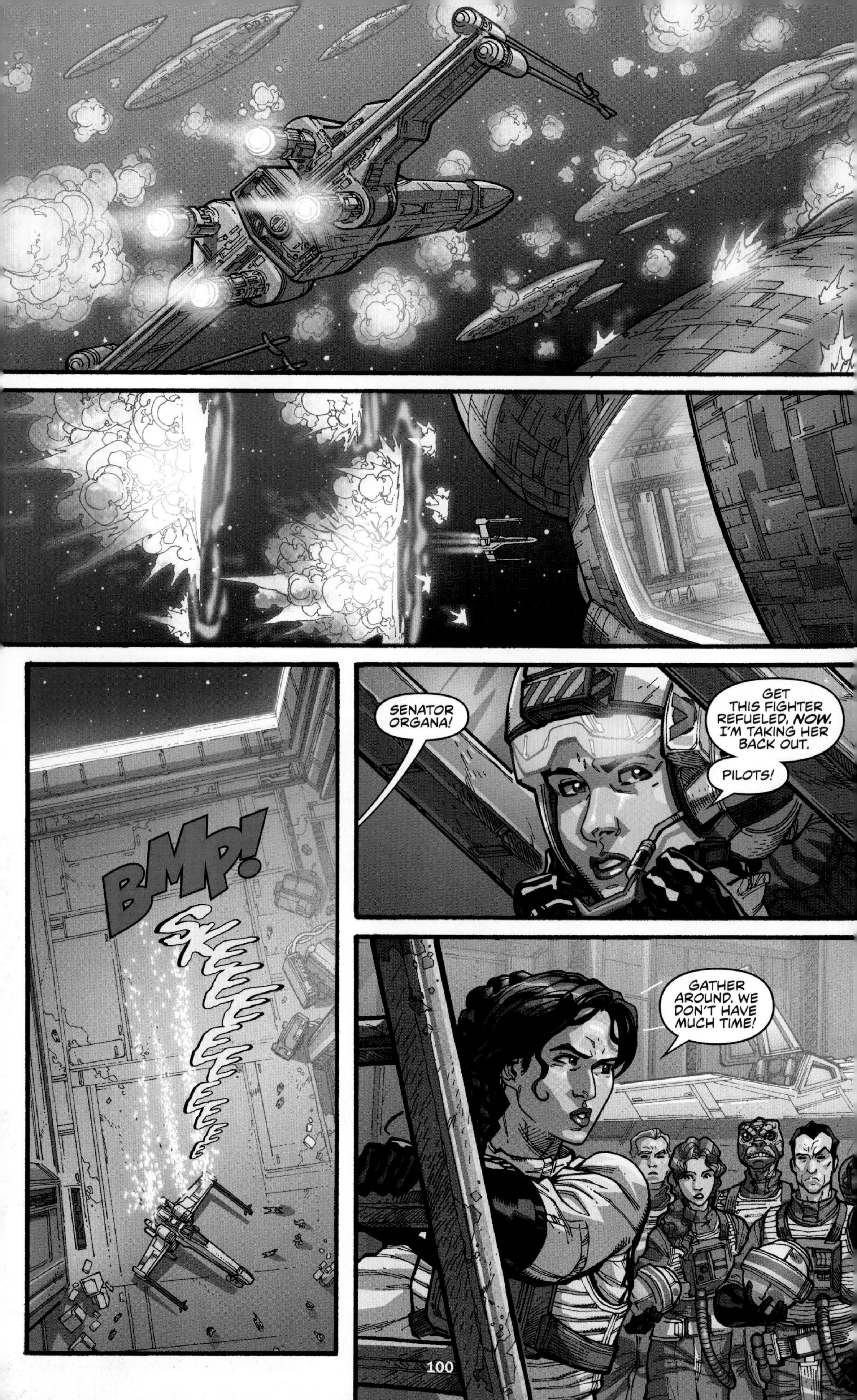
BMP!
SKEEEEEEEEEEE
SENATOR ORGANA!
GET THIS FIGHTER REFUELED, NOW. I'M TAKING HER BACK OUT.
PILOTS!
GATHER AROUND. WE DON'T HAVE MUCH TIME!

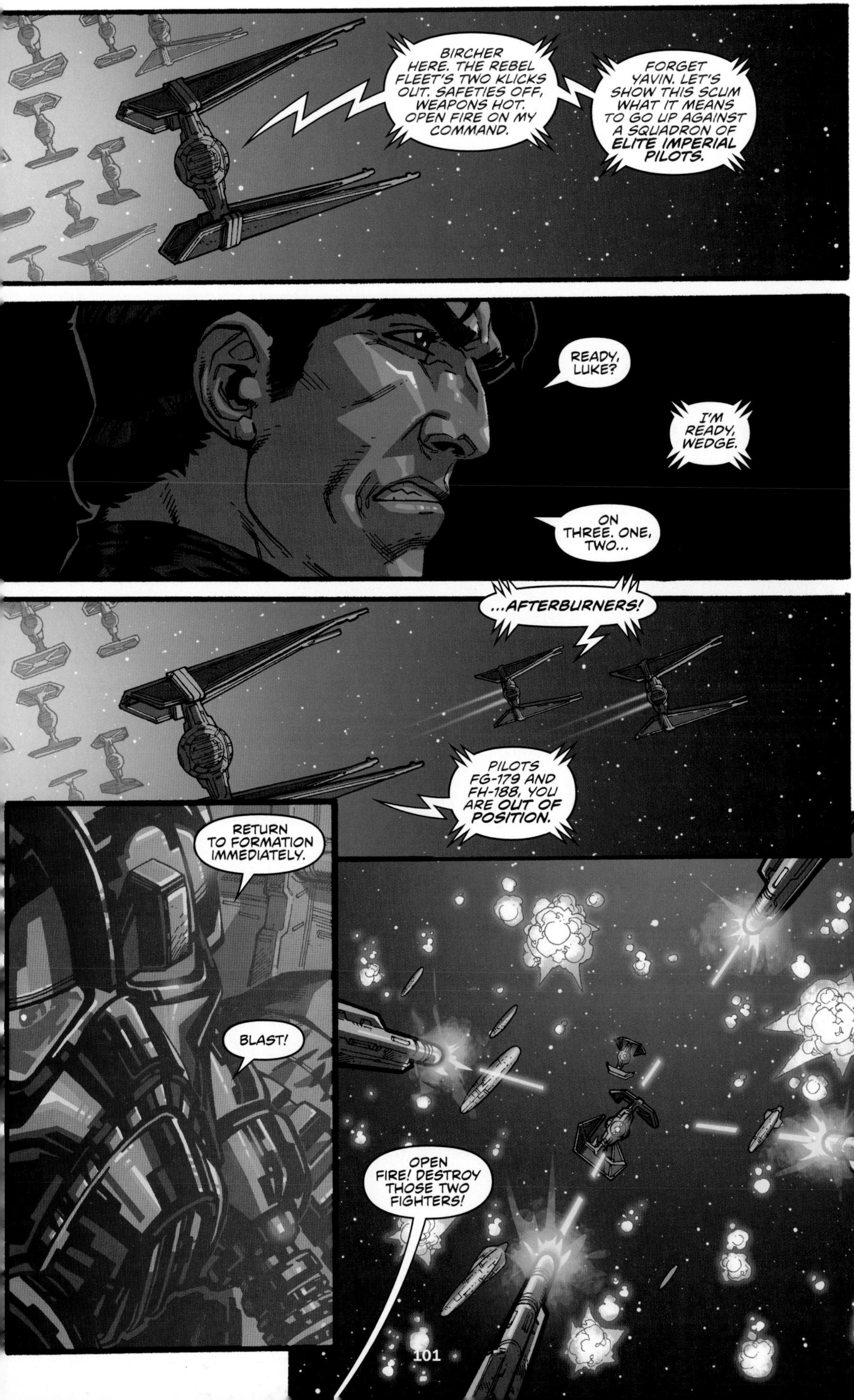
BIRCHER HERE. THE REBEL FLEET'S TWO KLICKS OUT. SAFETIES OFF, WEAPONS HOT. OPEN FIRE ON MY COMMAND.
FORGET YAVIN. LET'S SHOW THIS SCUM WHAT IT MEANS TO GO UP AGAINST A SQUADRON OF ELITE IMPERIAL PILOTS.
READY, LUKE?
I'M READY, WEDGE.
ON THREE. ONE, TWO...
...AFTERBURNERS!
PILOTS FG-179 AND FH-188, YOU ARE OUT OF POSITION.
RETURN TO FORMATION IMMEDIATELY.
BLAST!
OPEN FIRE! DESTROY THOSE TWO FIGHTERS!

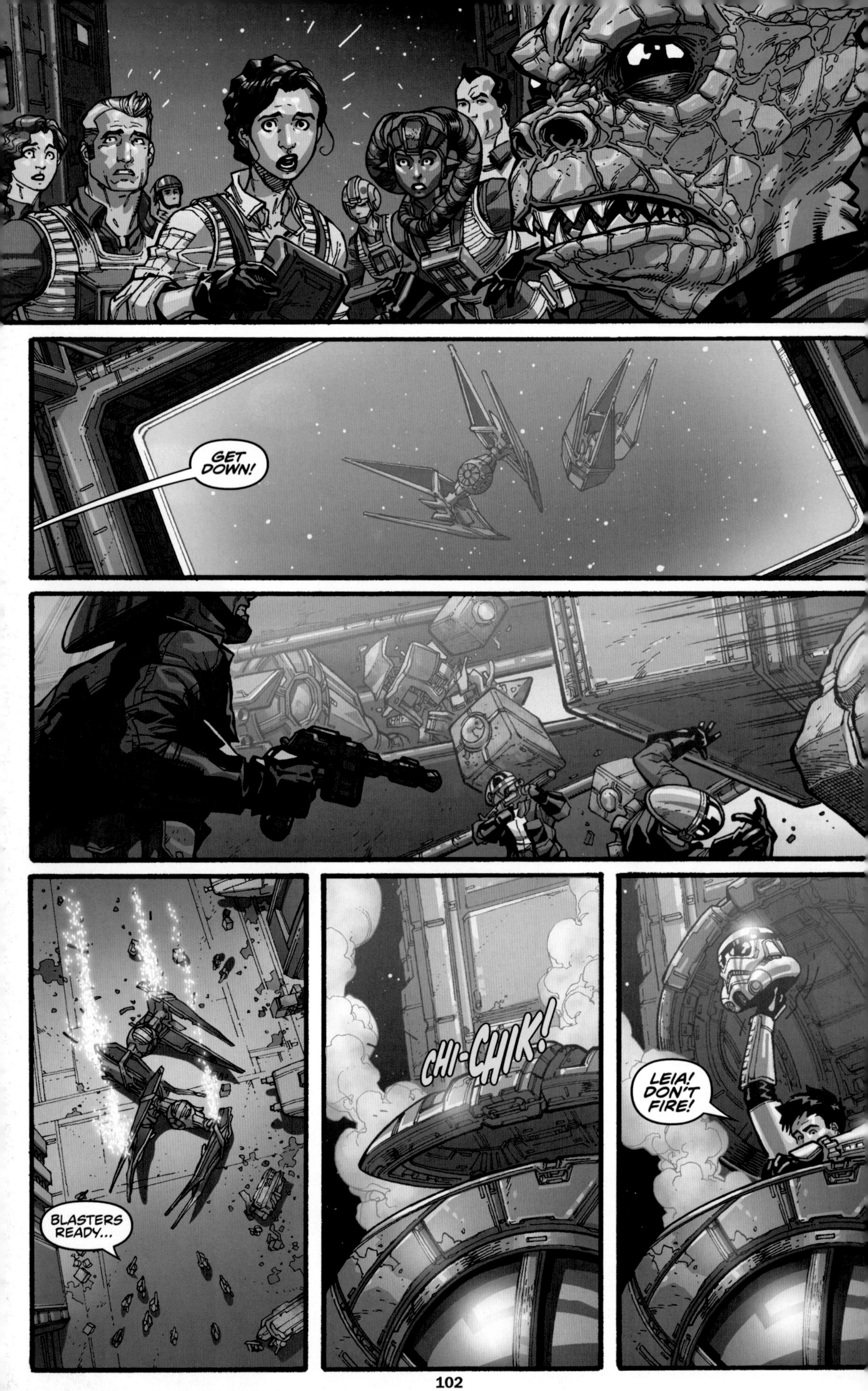
GET DOWN!
BLASTERS READY...
CHI-CHIK!
LEIA! DON'T FIRE!

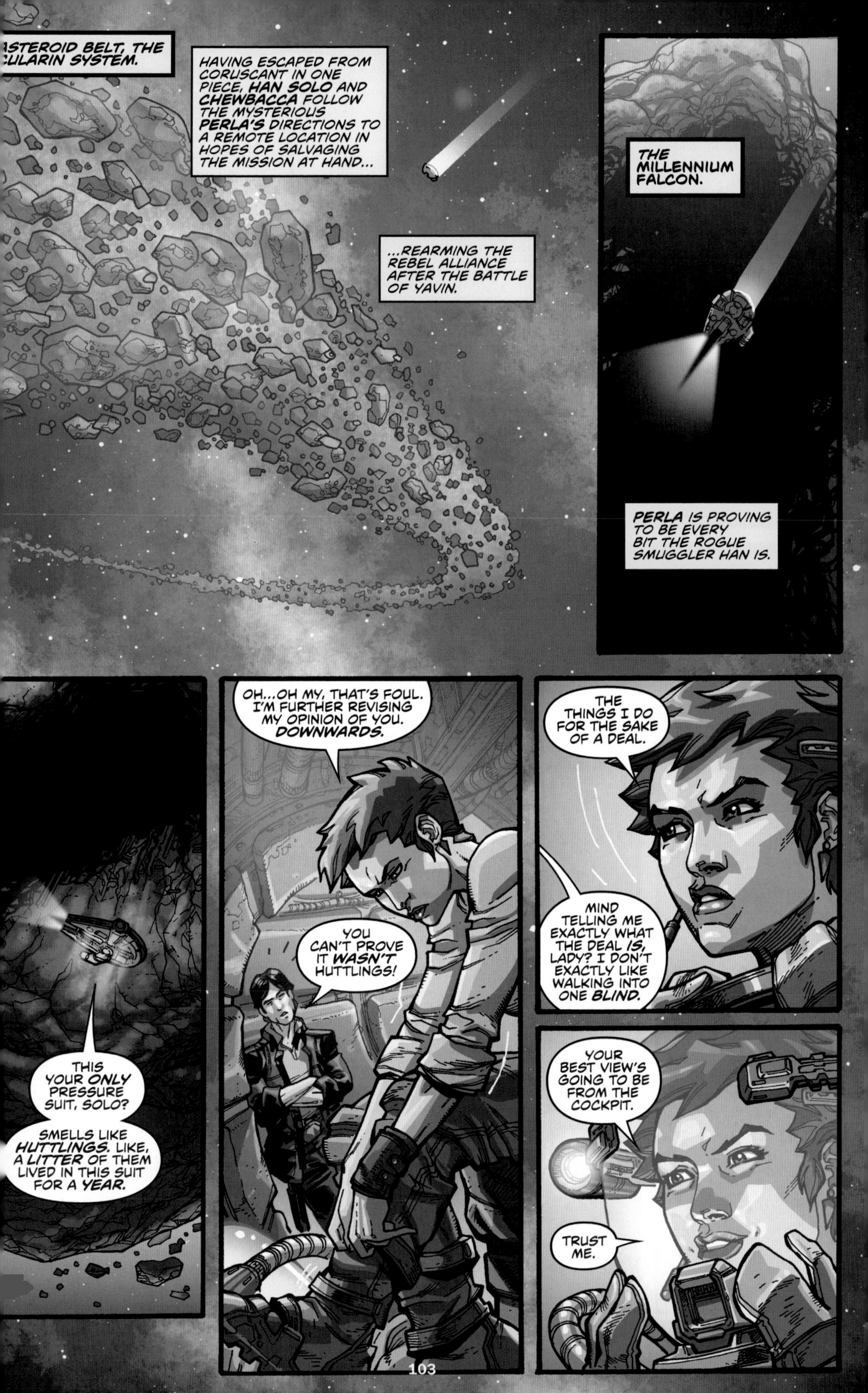
ASTEROID BELT, THE CULARIN SYSTEM.
HAVING ESCAPED FROM CORUSCANT IN ONE PIECE, HAN SOLO AND CHEWBACCA FOLLOW THE MYSTERIOUS PERLA'S DIRECTIONS TO A REMOTE LOCATION IN HOPES OF SALVAGING THE MISSION AT HAND...
...REARMING THE REBEL ALLIANCE AFTER THE BATTLE OF YAVIN.
THE MILLENNIUM FALCON.
PERLA IS PROVING TO BE EVERY BIT THE ROGUE SMUGGLER HAN IS.
THIS YOUR ONLY PRESSURE SUIT, SOLO?
SMELLS LIKE HUTTLINGS. LIKE, A LITTER OF THEM LIVED IN THIS SUIT FOR A YEAR.
YOU CAN'T PROVE IT WASN'T HUTTLINGS!
OH...OH MY, THAT'S FOUL. I'M FURTHER REVISING MY OPINION OF YOU. DOWNWARDS.
THE THINGS I DO FOR THE SAKE OF A DEAL.
MIND TELLING ME EXACTLY WHAT THE DEAL IS, LADY? I DON'T EXACTLY LIKE WALKING INTO ONE BLIND.
YOUR BEST VIEW'S GOING TO BE FROM THE COCKPIT.
TRUST ME.

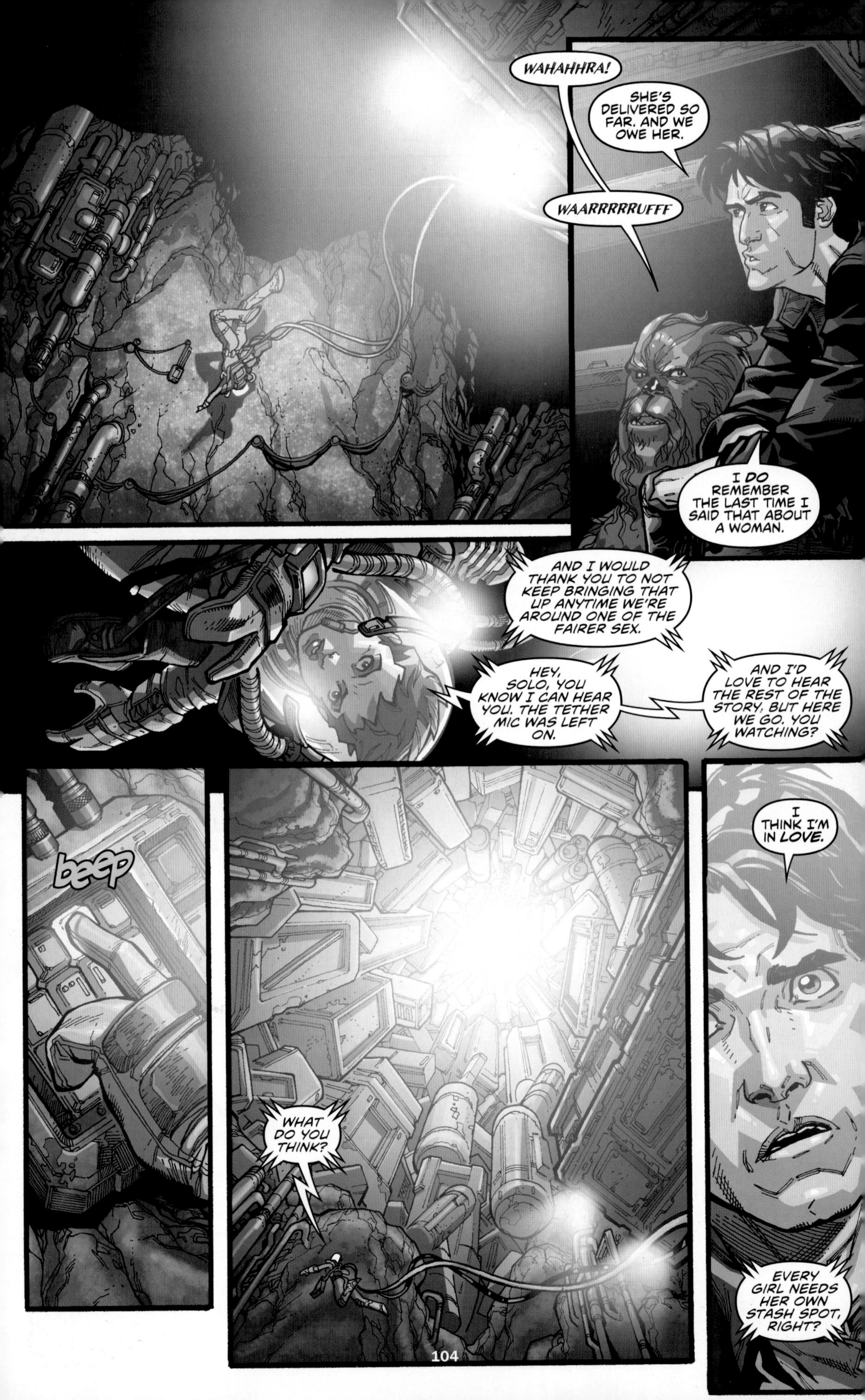
WAHAHHRA!
SHE'S DELIVERED SO FAR. AND WE OWE HER.
WAARRRRRUFFF
I DO REMEMBER THE LAST TIME I SAID THAT ABOUT A WOMAN.
AND I WOULD THANK YOU TO NOT KEEP BRINGING THAT UP ANYTIME WE'RE AROUND ONE OF THE FAIRER SEX.
HEY, SOLO, YOU KNOW I CAN HEAR YOU. THE TETHER MIC WAS LEFT ON.
AND I'D LOVE TO HEAR THE REST OF THE STORY, BUT HERE WE GO. YOU WATCHING?
beep
WHAT DO YOU THINK?
I THINK I'M IN LOVE.
EVERY GIRL NEEDS HER OWN STASH SPOT, RIGHT?

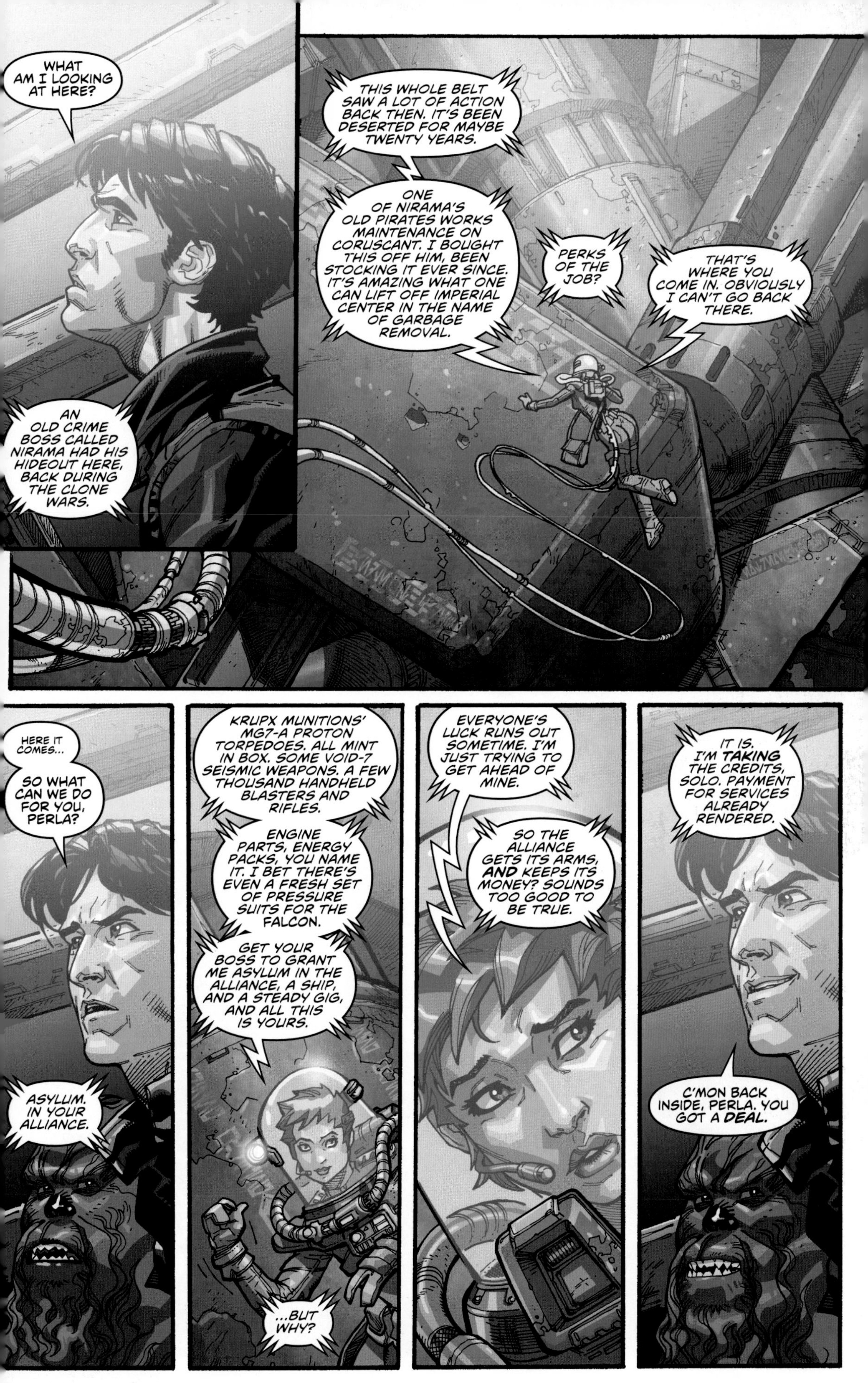
WHAT AM I LOOKING AT HERE?
AN OLD CRIME BOSS CALLED NIRAMA HAD HIS HIDEOUT HERE, BACK DURING THE CLONE WARS.
THIS WHOLE BELT SAW A LOT OF ACTION BACK THEN. IT'S BEEN DESERTED FOR MAYBE TWENTY YEARS.
ONE OF NIRAMA'S OLD PIRATES WORKS MAINTENANCE ON CORUSCANT. I BOUGHT THIS OFF HIM, BEEN STOCKING IT EVER SINCE. IT'S AMAZING WHAT ONE CAN LIFT OFF IMPERIAL CENTER IN THE NAME OF GARBAGE REMOVAL.
PERKS OF THE JOB?
THAT'S WHERE YOU COME IN. OBVIOUSLY I CAN'T GO BACK THERE.
HERE IT COMES...
SO WHAT CAN WE DO FOR YOU, PERLA?
ASYLUM. IN YOUR ALLIANCE.
KRUPX MUNITIONS' MG7-A PROTON TORPEDOES. ALL MINT IN BOX. SOME VOID-7 SEISMIC WEAPONS. A FEW THOUSAND HANDHELD BLASTERS AND RIFLES.
ENGINE PARTS, ENERGY PACKS, YOU NAME IT. I BET THERE'S EVEN A FRESH SET OF PRESSURE SUITS FOR THE FALCON.
GET YOUR BOSS TO GRANT ME ASYLUM IN THE ALLIANCE, A SHIP, AND A STEADY GIG, AND ALL THIS IS YOURS.
...BUT WHY?
EVERYONE'S LUCK RUNS OUT SOMETIME. I'M JUST TRYING TO GET AHEAD OF MINE.
SO THE ALLIANCE GETS ITS ARMS, AND KEEPS ITS MONEY? SOUNDS TOO GOOD TO BE TRUE.
IT IS. I'M TAKING THE CREDITS, SOLO. PAYMENT FOR SERVICES ALREADY RENDERED.
C'MON BACK INSIDE, PERLA. YOU GOT A DEAL.

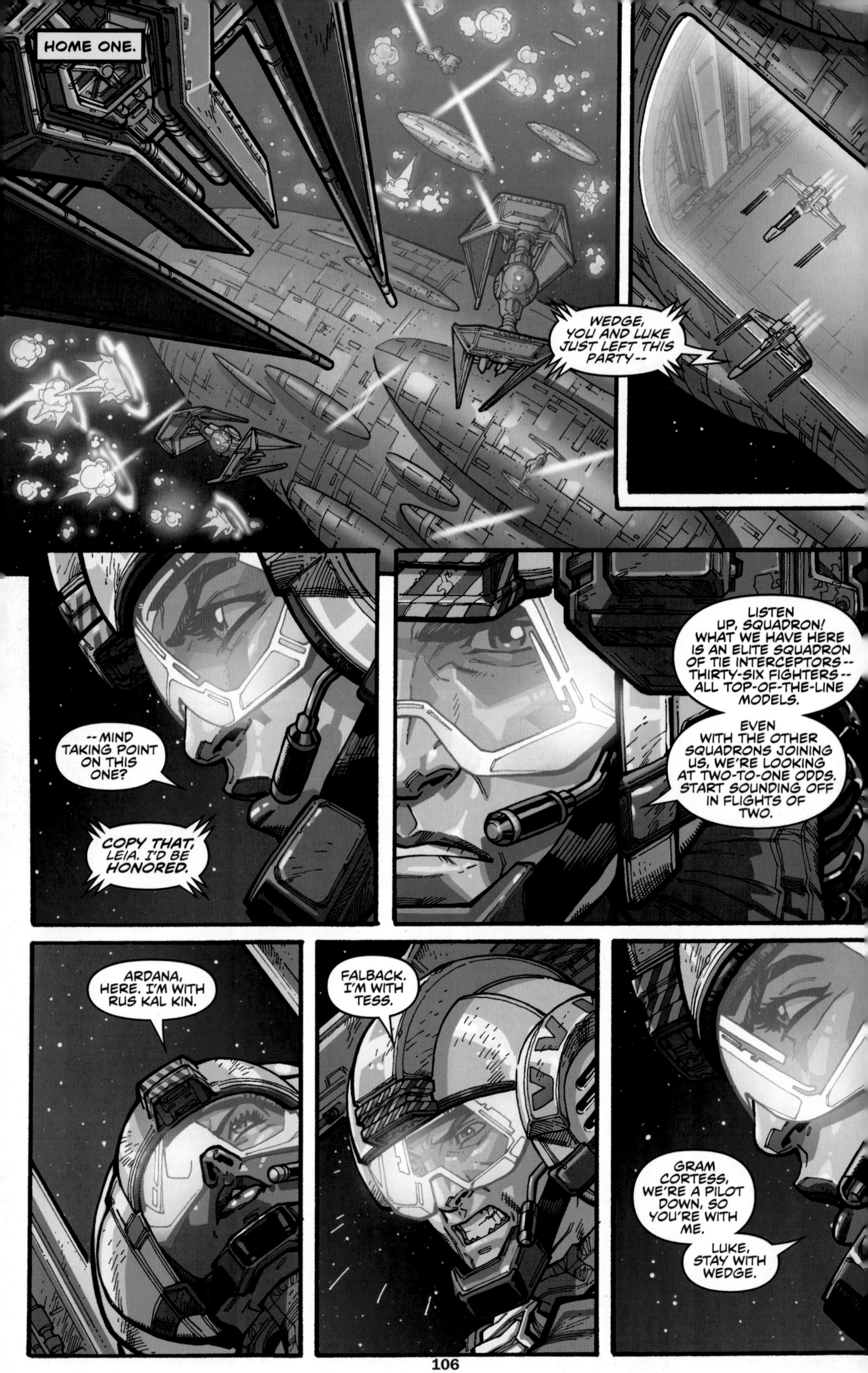
HOME ONE.
WEDGE, YOU AND LUKE JUST LEFT THIS PARTY--
--MIND TAKING POINT ON THIS ONE?
COPY THAT, LEIA. I'D BE HONORED.
LISTEN UP, SQUADRON! WHAT WE HAVE HERE IS AN ELITE SQUADRON OF TIE INTERCEPTORS-- THIRTY-SIX FIGHTERS-- ALL TOP-OF-THE-LINE MODELS.
EVEN WITH THE OTHER SQUADRONS JOINING US, WE'RE LOOKING AT TWO-TO-ONE ODDS. START SOUNDING OFF IN FLIGHTS OF TWO.
ARDANA, HERE. I'M WITH RUS KAL KIN.
FALBACK. I'M WITH TESS.
GRAM CORTESS, WE'RE A PILOT DOWN, SO YOU'RE WITH ME.
LUKE, STAY WITH WEDGE.

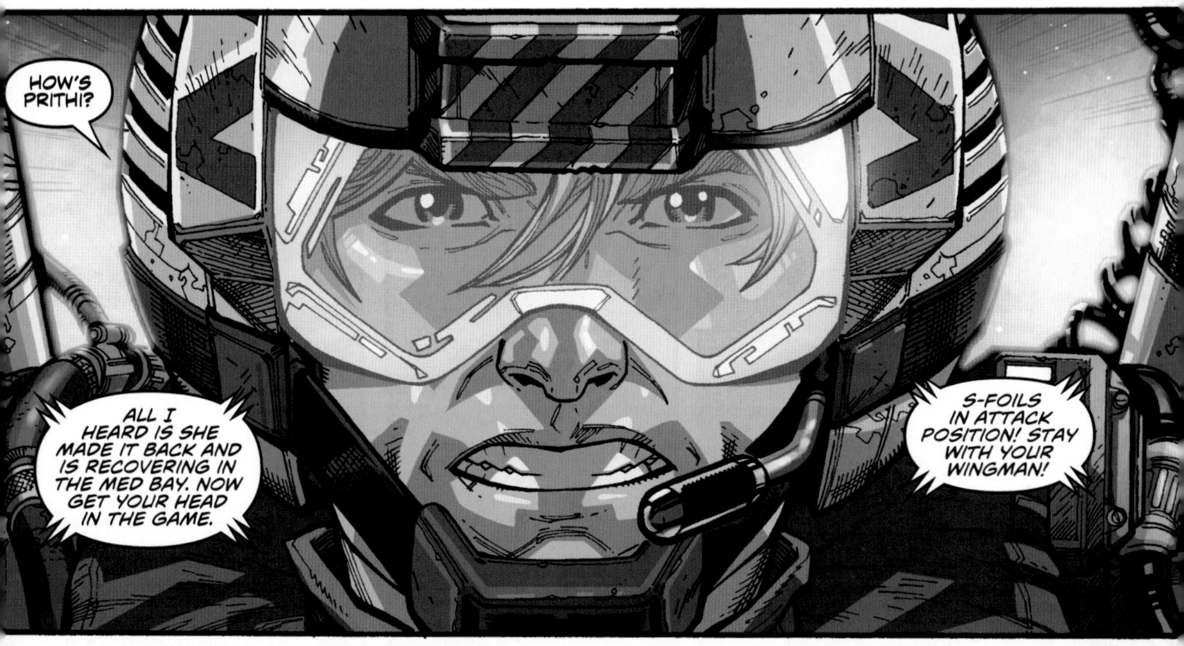
HOW'S PRITHI?
ALL I HEARD IS SHE MADE IT BACK AND IS RECOVERING IN THE MED BAY. NOW GET YOUR HEAD IN THE GAME.
S-FOILS IN ATTACK POSITION! STAY WITH YOUR WINGMAN!

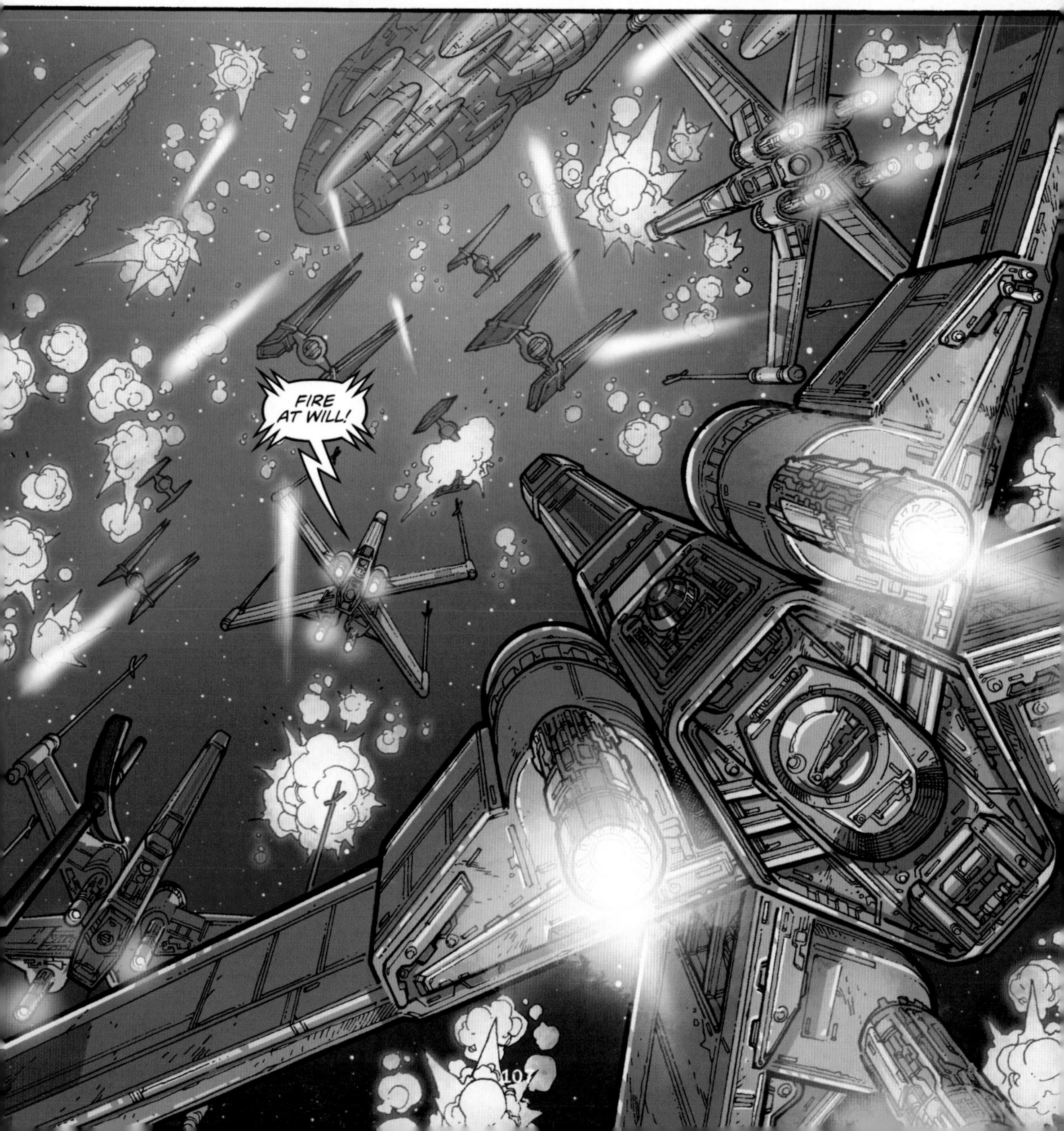
FIRE AT WILL!

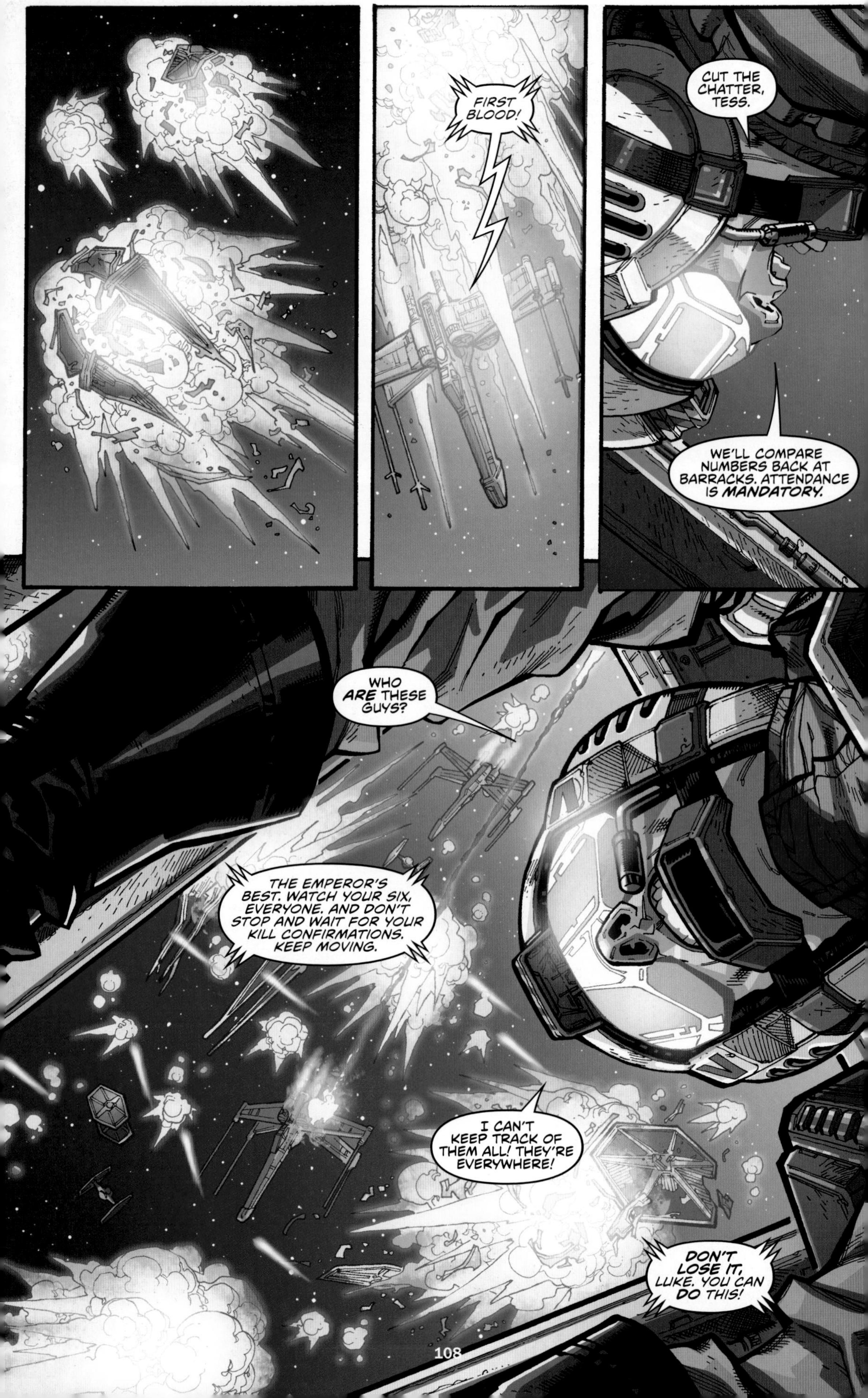
FIRST BLOOD!
CUT THE CHATTER, TESS.
WE'LL COMPARE NUMBERS BACK AT BARRACKS. ATTENDANCE IS MANDATORY.
WHO ARE THESE GUYS?
THE EMPEROR'S BEST. WATCH YOUR SIX, EVERYONE. AND DON'T STOP AND WAIT FOR YOUR KILL CONFIRMATIONS. KEEP MOVING.
I CAN'T KEEP TRACK OF THEM ALL! THEY'RE EVERYWHERE!
DON'T LOSE IT, LUKE. YOU CAN DO THIS!

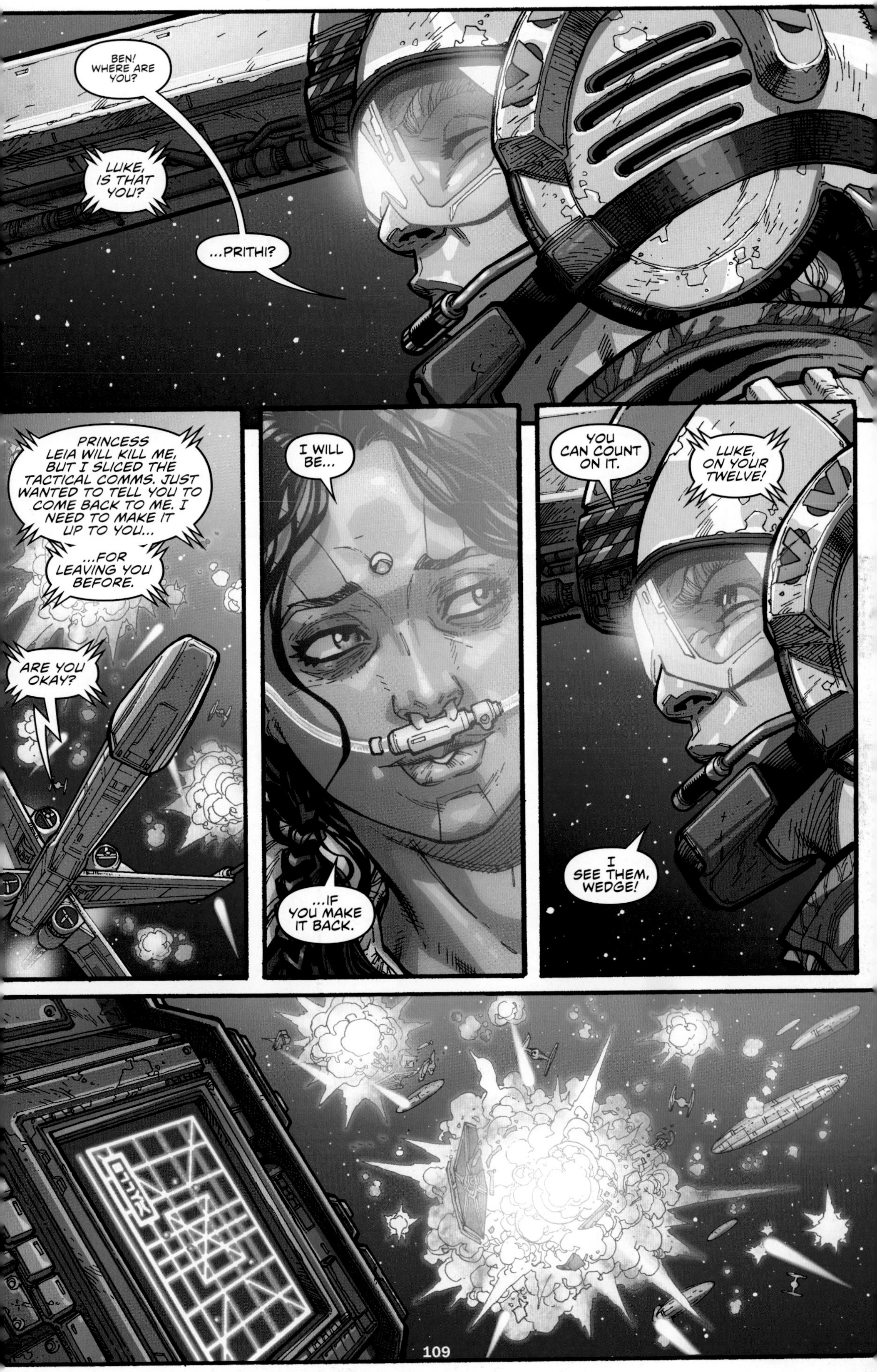

BEN! WHERE ARE YOU?
LUKE, IS THAT YOU?
...PRITHI?
PRINCESS LEIA WILL KILL ME, BUT I SLICED THE TACTICAL COMMS. JUST WANTED TO TELL YOU TO COME BACK TO ME. I NEED TO MAKE IT UP TO YOU...
...FOR LEAVING YOU BEFORE.
ARE YOU OKAY?
I WILL BE...
...IF YOU MAKE IT BACK.
YOU CAN COUNT ON IT.
LUKE, ON YOUR TWELVE!
I SEE THEM, WEDGE!

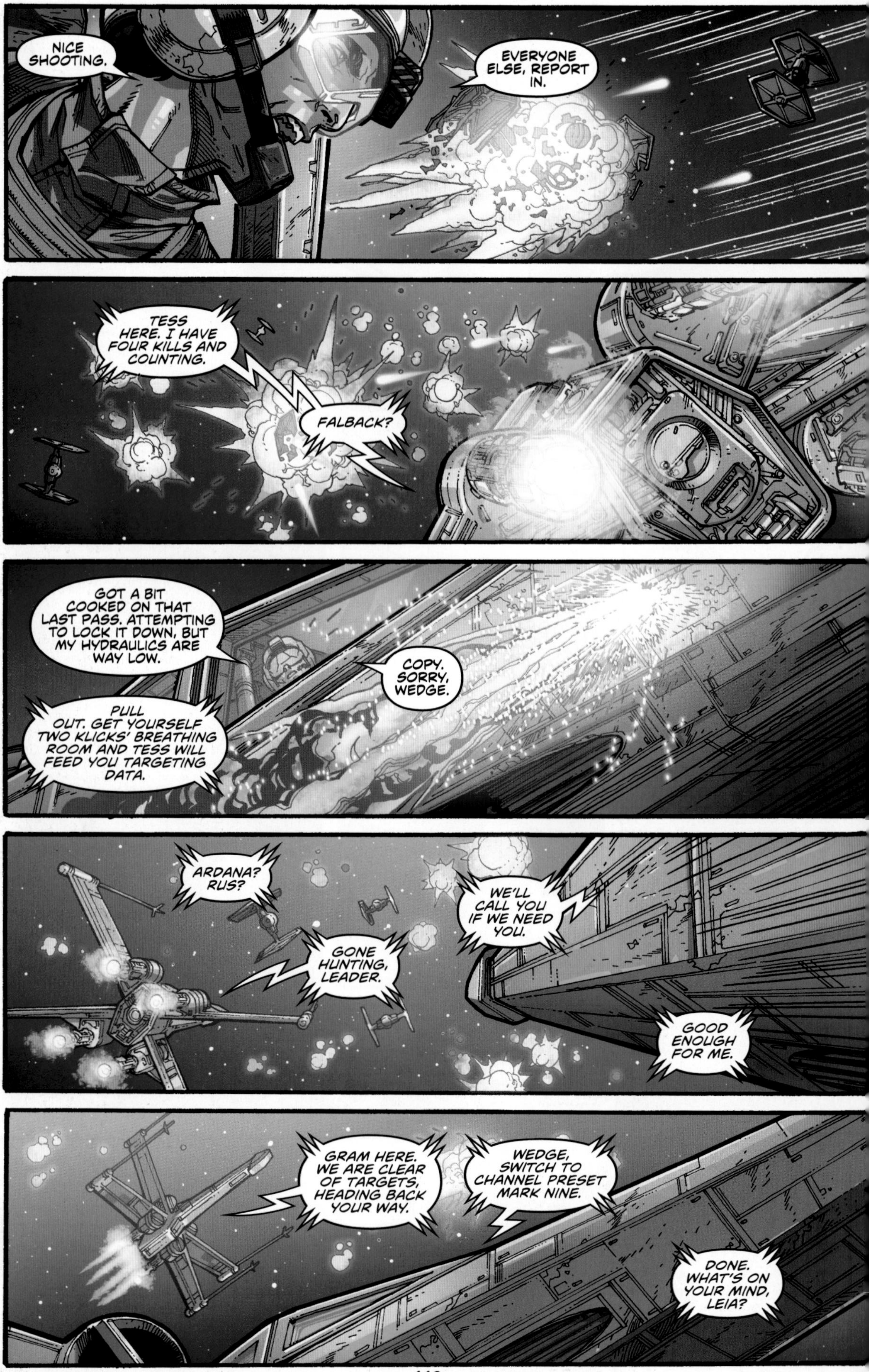
NICE SHOOTING.
EVERYONE ELSE, REPORT IN.
TESS HERE. I HAVE FOUR KILLS AND COUNTING.
FALBACK?
GOT A BIT COOKED ON THAT LAST PASS. ATTEMPTING TO LOCK IT DOWN, BUT MY HYDRAULICS ARE WAY LOW.
COPY. SORRY, WEDGE.
PULL OUT. GET YOURSELF TWO KLICKS' BREATHING ROOM AND TESS WILL FEED YOU TARGETING DATA.
ARDANA? RUS?
GONE HUNTING, LEADER.
WE'LL CALL YOU IF WE NEED YOU.
GOOD ENOUGH FOR ME.
GRAM HERE. WE ARE CLEAR OF TARGETS, HEADING BACK YOUR WAY.
WEDGE, SWITCH TO CHANNEL PRESET MARK NINE.
DONE. WHAT'S ON YOUR MIND, LEIA?

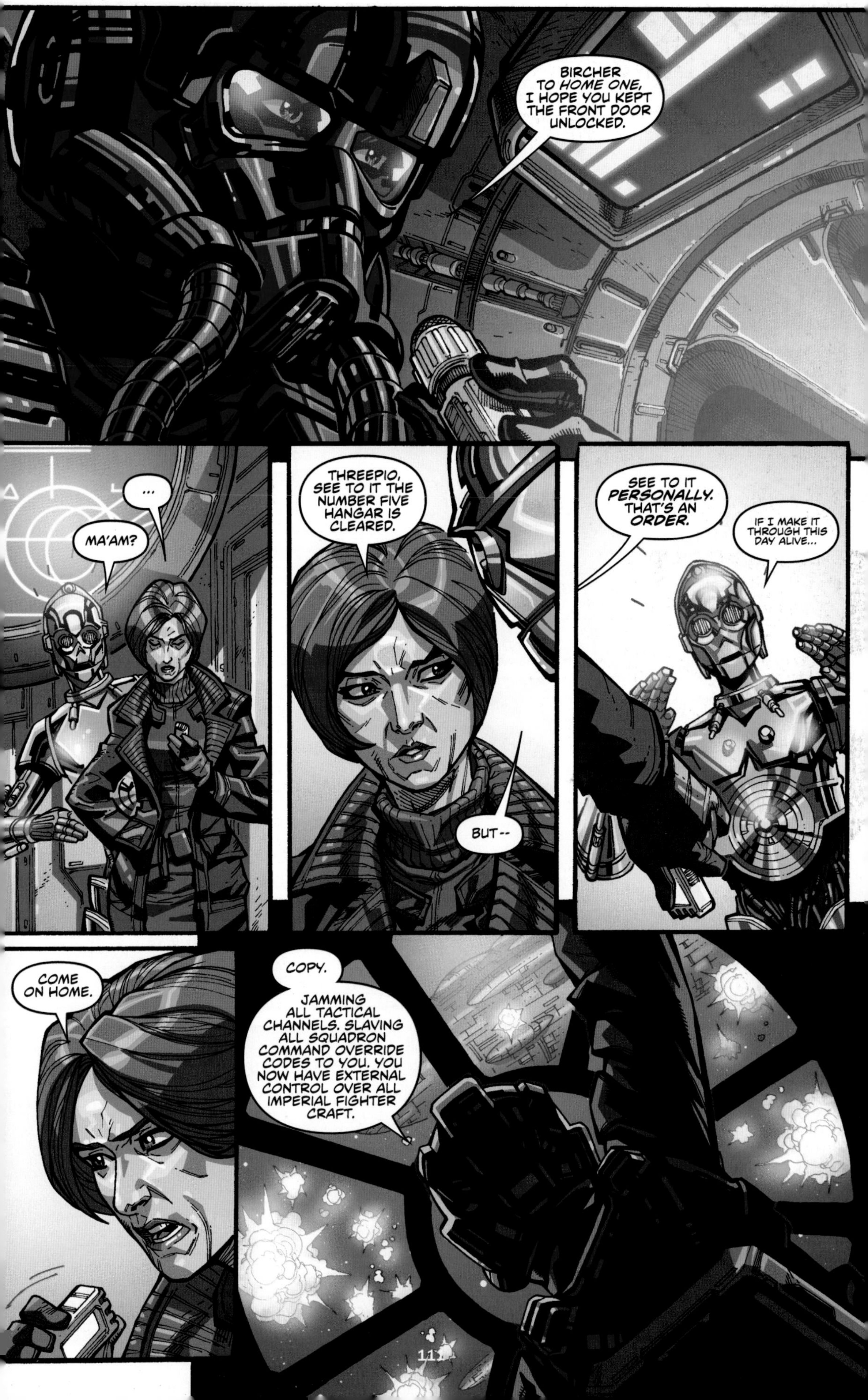
BIRCHER TO HOME ONE, I HOPE YOU KEPT THE FRONT DOOR UNLOCKED.
...
MA'AM?
THREEPIO, SEE TO IT THE NUMBER FIVE HANGAR IS CLEARED.
BUT--
SEE TO IT PERSONALLY. THAT'S AN ORDER.
IF I MAKE IT THROUGH THIS DAY ALIVE...
COME ON HOME.
COPY.
JAMMING ALL TACTICAL CHANNELS. SLAVING ALL SQUADRON COMMAND OVERRIDE CODES TO YOU. YOU NOW HAVE EXTERNAL CONTROL OVER ALL IMPERIAL FIGHTER CRAFT.

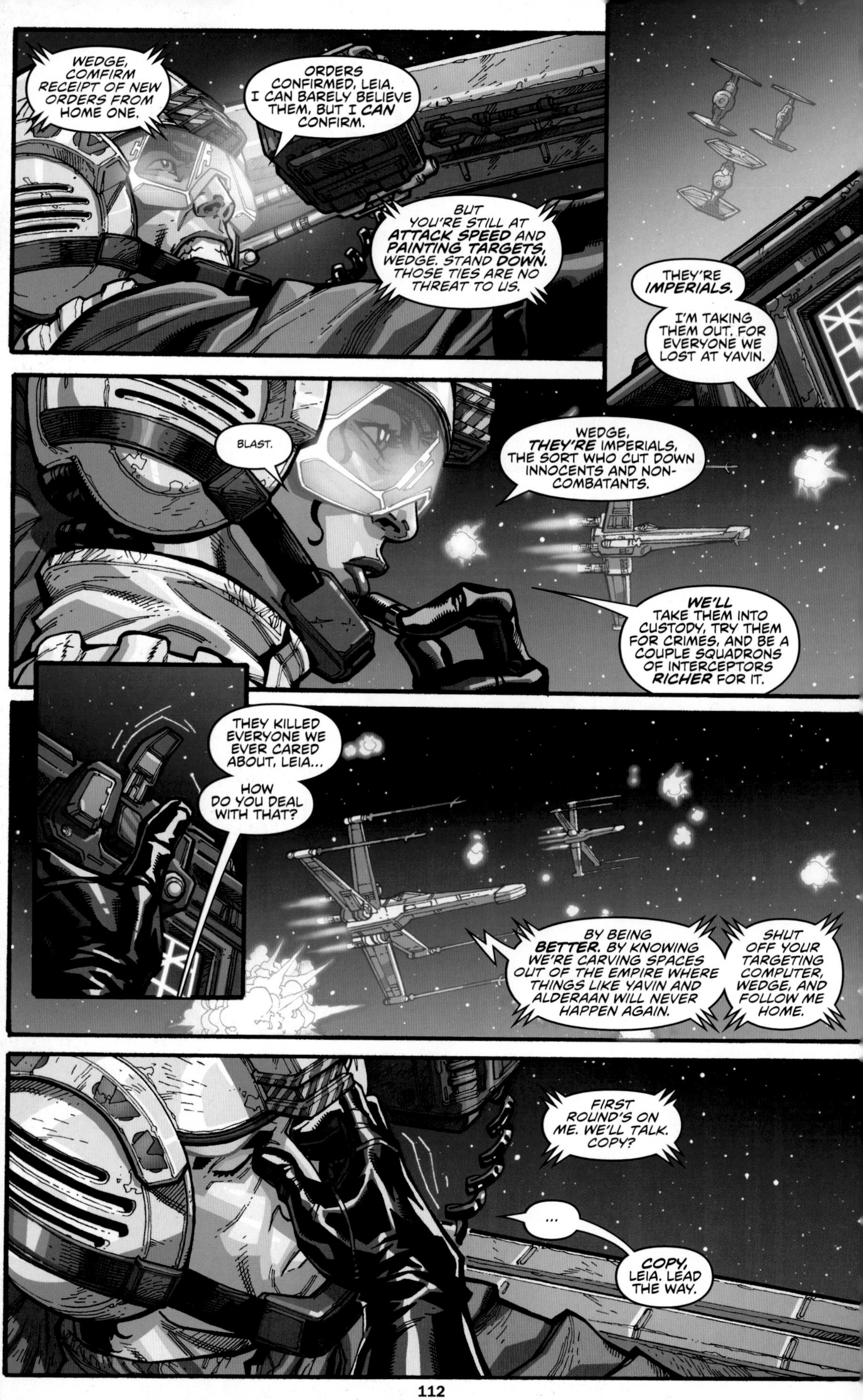
WEDGE, COMFIRM RECEIPT OF NEW ORDERS FROM HOME ONE.
ORDERS CONFIRMED, LEIA. I CAN BARELY BELIEVE THEM, BUT I CAN CONFIRM.
BUT YOU'RE STILL AT ATTACK SPEED AND PAINTING TARGETS, WEDGE. STAND DOWN. THOSE TIES ARE NO THREAT TO US.
THEY'RE IMPERIALS.
I'M TAKING THEM OUT. FOR EVERYONE WE LOST AT YAVIN.
BLAST.
WEDGE, THEY'RE IMPERIALS, THE SORT WHO CUT DOWN INNOCENTS AND NON-COMBATANTS.
WE'LL TAKE THEM INTO CUSTODY, TRY THEM FOR CRIMES, AND BE A COUPLE SQUADRONS OF INTERCEPTORS RICHER FOR IT.
THEY KILLED EVERYONE WE EVER CARED ABOUT, LEIA...
HOW DO YOU DEAL WITH THAT?
BY BEING BETTER. BY KNOWING WE'RE CARVING SPACES OUT OF THE EMPIRE WHERE THINGS LIKE YAVIN AND ALDERAAN WILL NEVER HAPPEN AGAIN.
SHUT OFF YOUR TARGETING COMPUTER, WEDGE, AND FOLLOW ME HOME.
FIRST ROUND'S ON ME. WE'LL TALK. COPY?
...
COPY, LEIA. LEAD THE WAY.

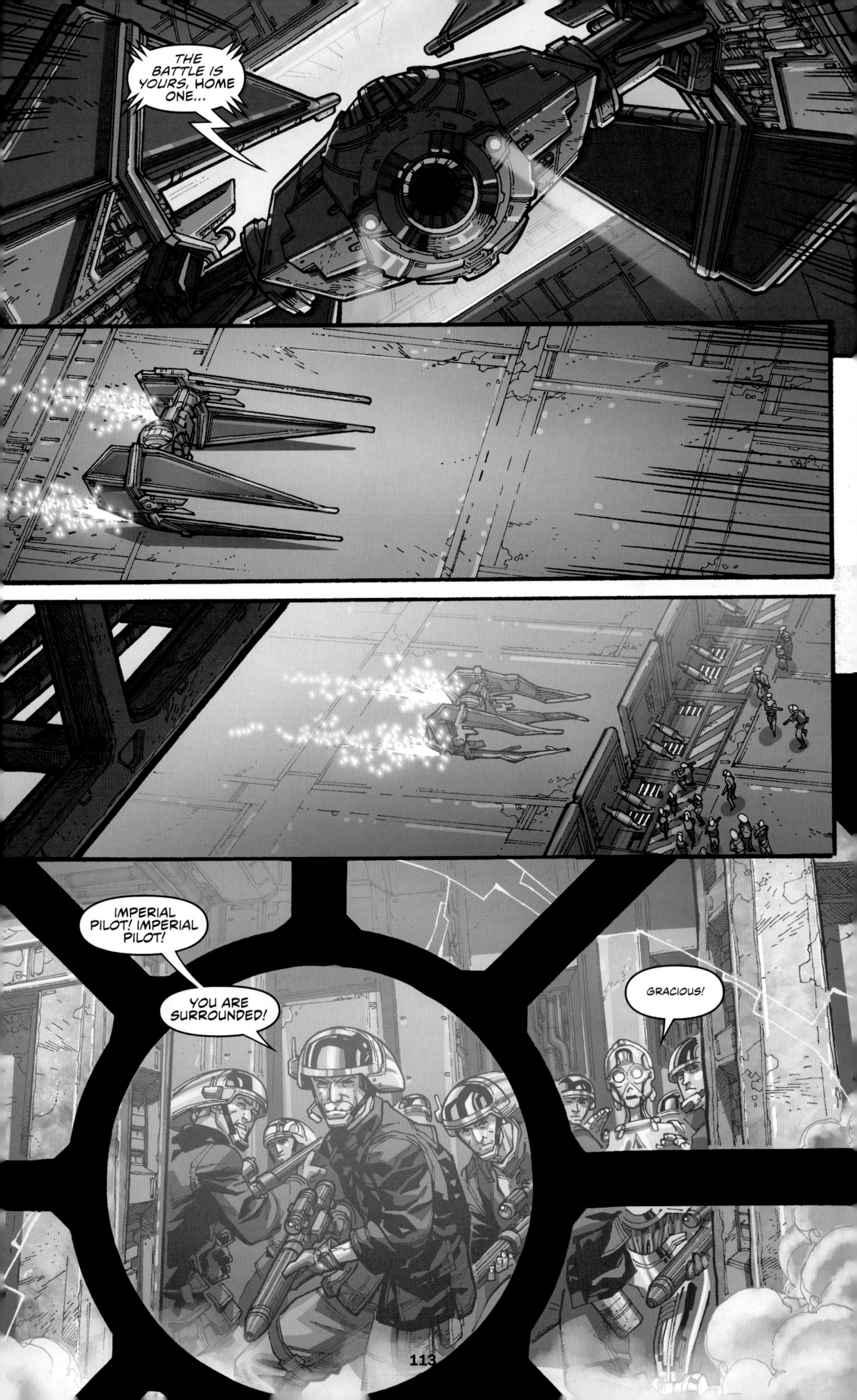
THE BATTLE IS YOURS, HOME ONE...
IMPERIAL PILOT! IMPERIAL PILOT!
YOU ARE SURROUNDED!
GRACIOUS!

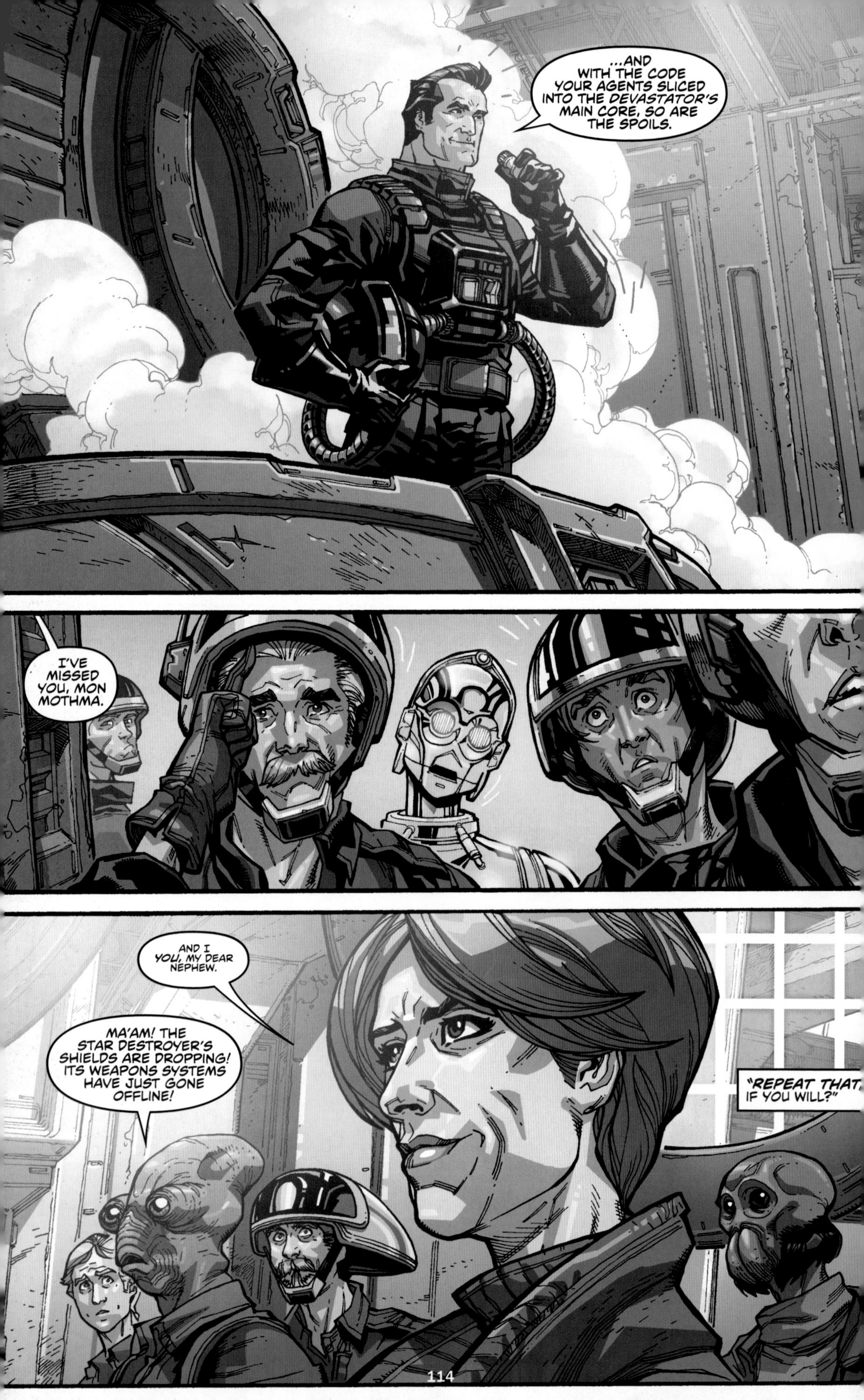
...AND WITH THE CODE YOUR AGENTS SLICED INTO THE DEVASTATOR'S MAIN CORE, SO ARE THE SPOILS.
I'VE MISSED YOU, MON MOTHMA.
AND I YOU, MY DEAR NEPHEW.
MA'AM! THE STAR DESTROYER'S SHIELDS ARE DROPPING! ITS WEAPONS SYSTEMS HAVE JUST GONE OFFLINE!
"REPEAT THAT, IF YOU WILL?"

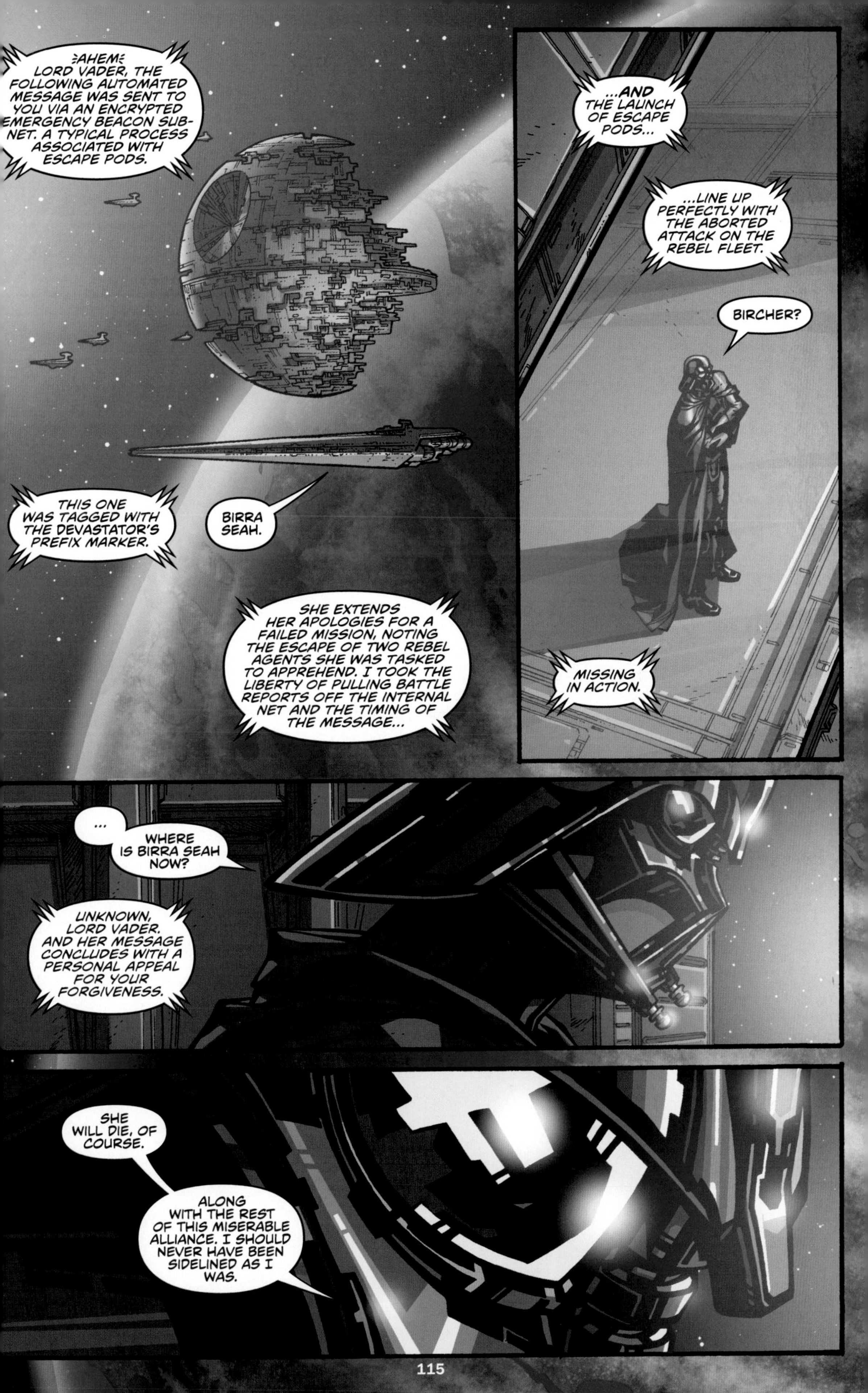
AHEM
LORD VADER, THE FOLLOWING AUTOMATED MESSAGE WAS SENT TO YOU VIA AN ENCRYPTED EMERGENCY BEACON SUB-NET. A TYPICAL PROCESS ASSOCIATED WITH ESCAPE PODS.
THIS ONE WAS TAGGED WITH THE DEVASTATOR'S PREFIX MARKER.
BIRRA SEAH.
SHE EXTENDS HER APOLOGIES FOR A FAILED MISSION, NOTING THE ESCAPE OF TWO REBEL AGENTS SHE WAS TASKED TO APPREHEND. I TOOK THE LIBERTY OF PULLING BATTLE REPORTS OFF THE INTERNAL NET AND THE TIMING OF THE MESSAGE...
...AND THE LAUNCH OF ESCAPE PODS...
...LINE UP PERFECTLY WITH THE ABORTED ATTACK ON THE REBEL FLEET.
BIRCHER?
MISSING IN ACTION.
...
WHERE IS BIRRA SEAH NOW?
UNKNOWN, LORD VADER. AND HER MESSAGE CONCLUDES WITH A PERSONAL APPEAL FOR YOUR FORGIVENESS.
SHE WILL DIE, OF COURSE.
ALONG WITH THE REST OF THIS MISERABLE ALLIANCE. I SHOULD NEVER HAVE BEEN SIDELINED AS I WAS.

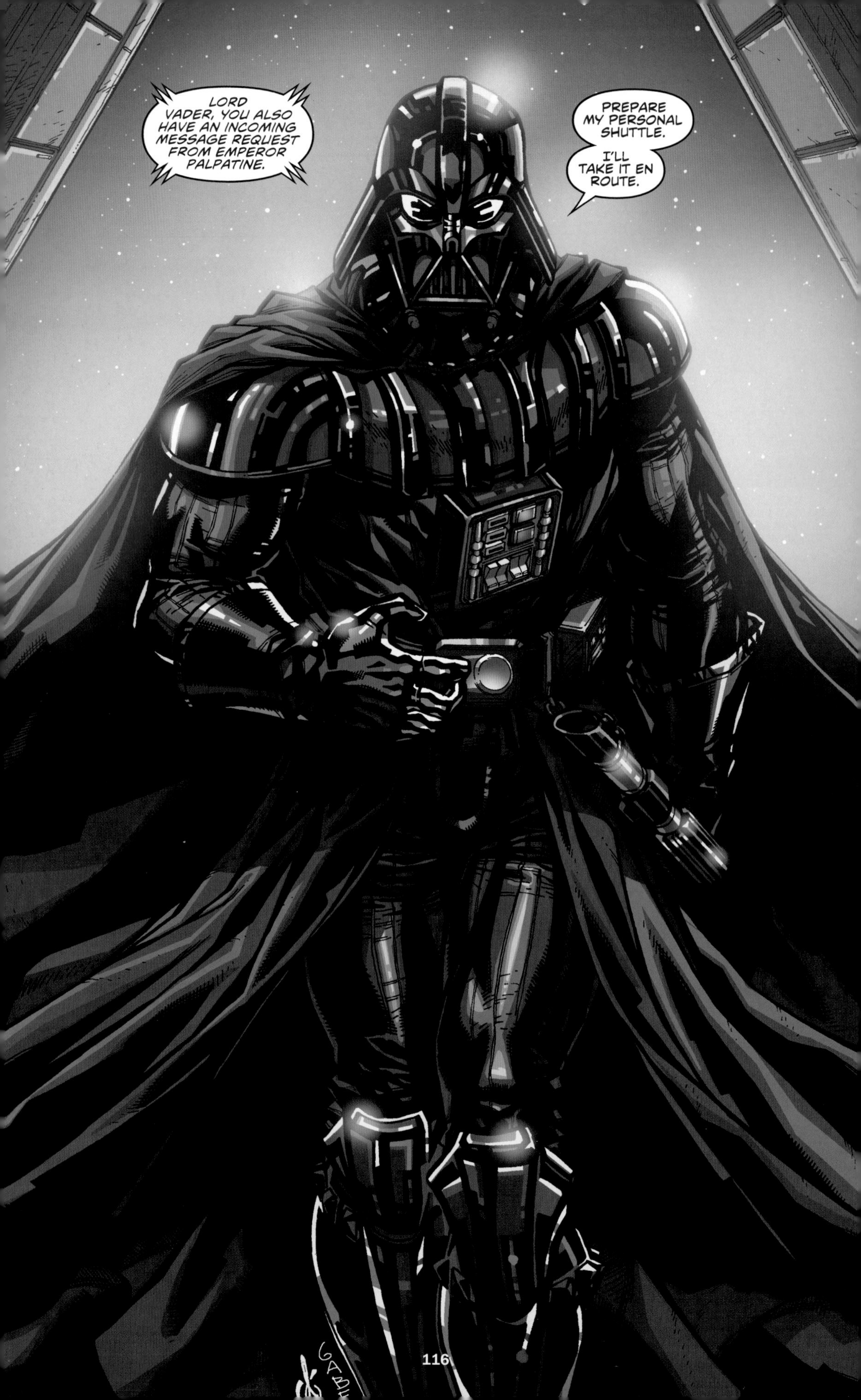
LORD VADER, YOU ALSO HAVE AN INCOMING MESSAGE REQUEST FROM EMPEROR PALPATINE.
PREPARE MY PERSONAL SHUTTLE.
I'LL TAKE IT EN ROUTE.
GABE

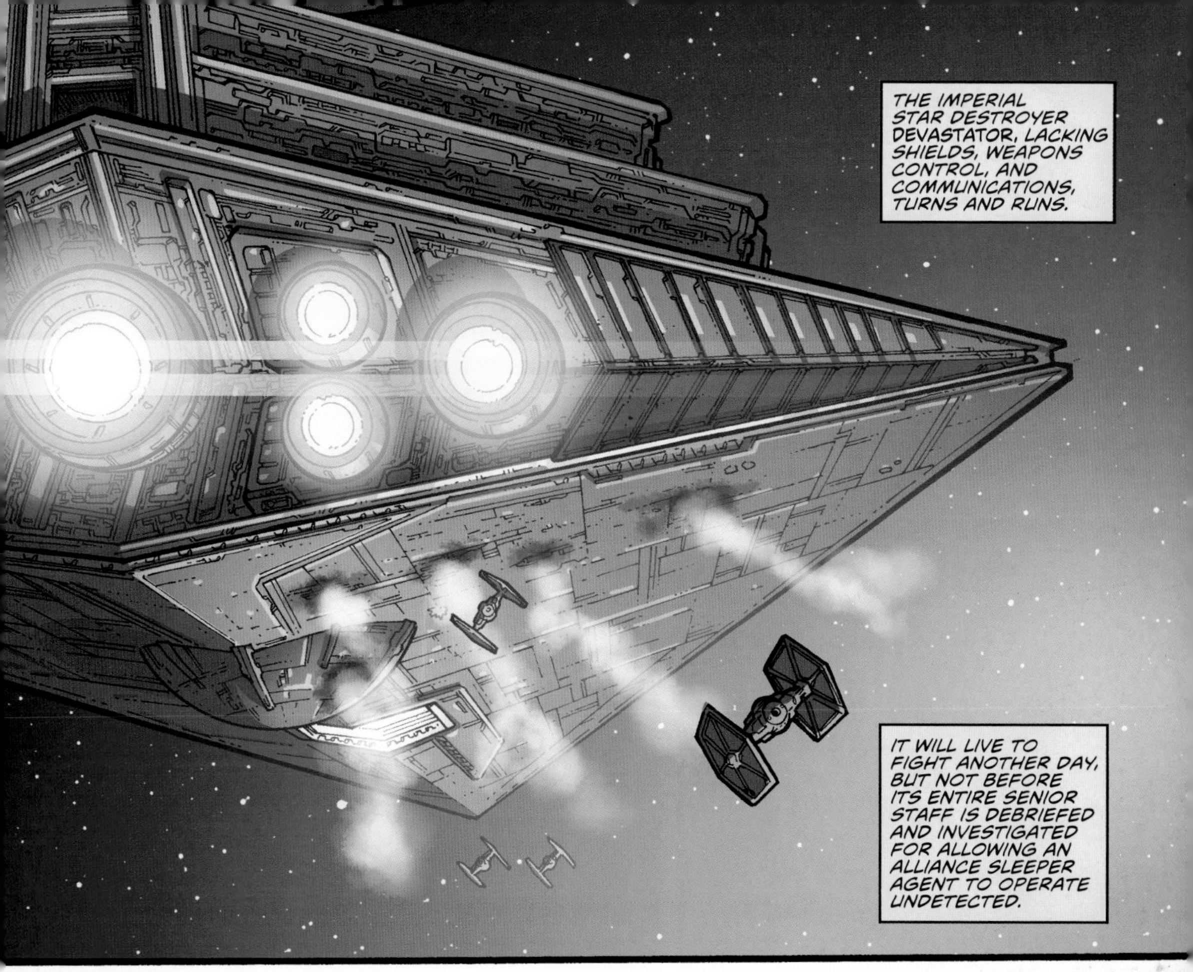
THE IMPERIAL STAR DESTROYER DEVASTATOR, LACKING SHIELDS, WEAPONS CONTROL, AND COMMUNICATIONS, TURNS AND RUNS.
IT WILL LIVE TO FIGHT ANOTHER DAY, BUT NOT BEFORE ITS ENTIRE SENIOR STAFF IS DEBRIEFED AND INVESTIGATED FOR ALLOWING AN ALLIANCE SLEEPER AGENT TO OPERATE UNDETECTED.

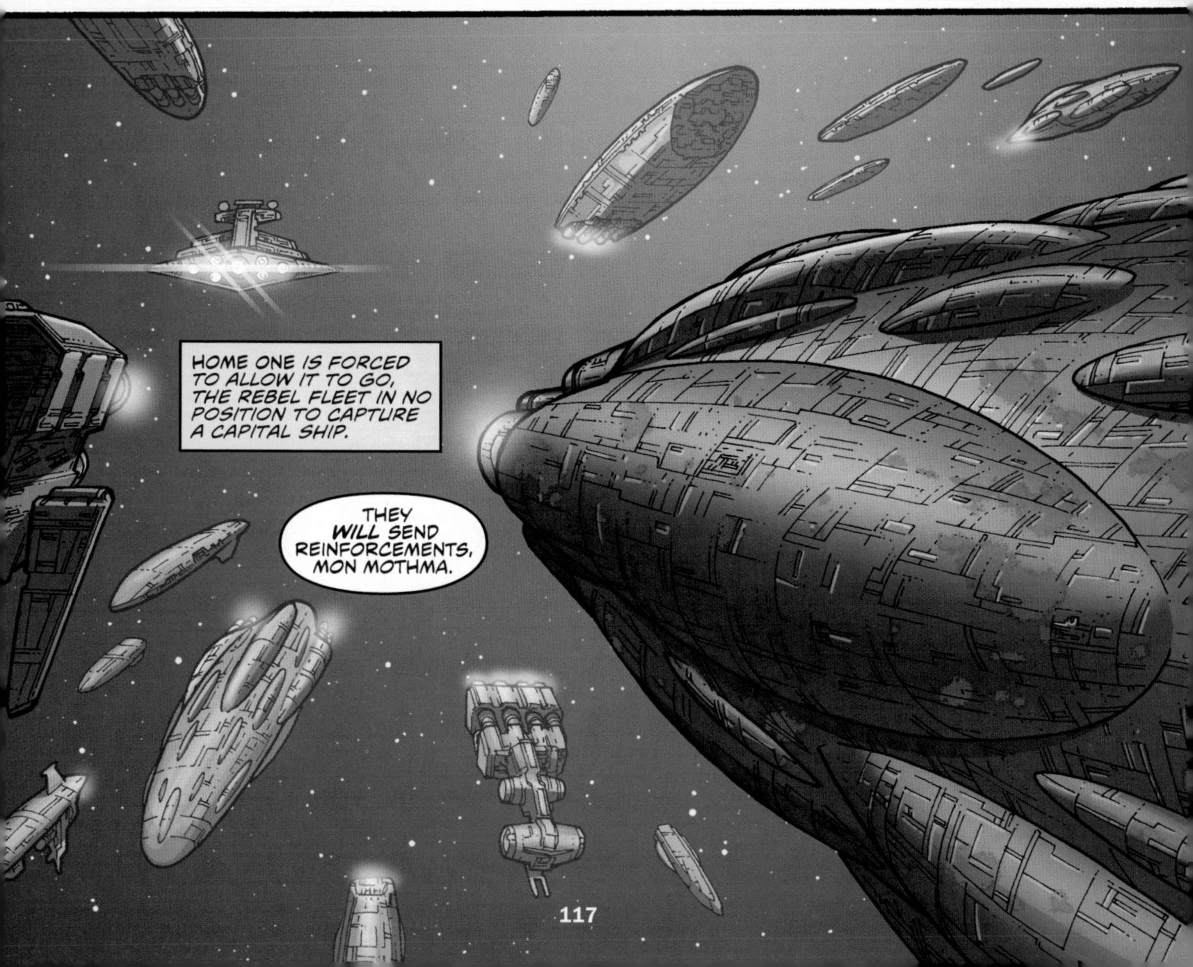
HOME ONE IS FORCED TO ALLOW IT TO GO, THE REBEL FLEET IN NO POSITION TO CAPTURE A CAPITAL SHIP.
THEY **WILL** SEND REINFORCEMENTS, MON MOTHMA.

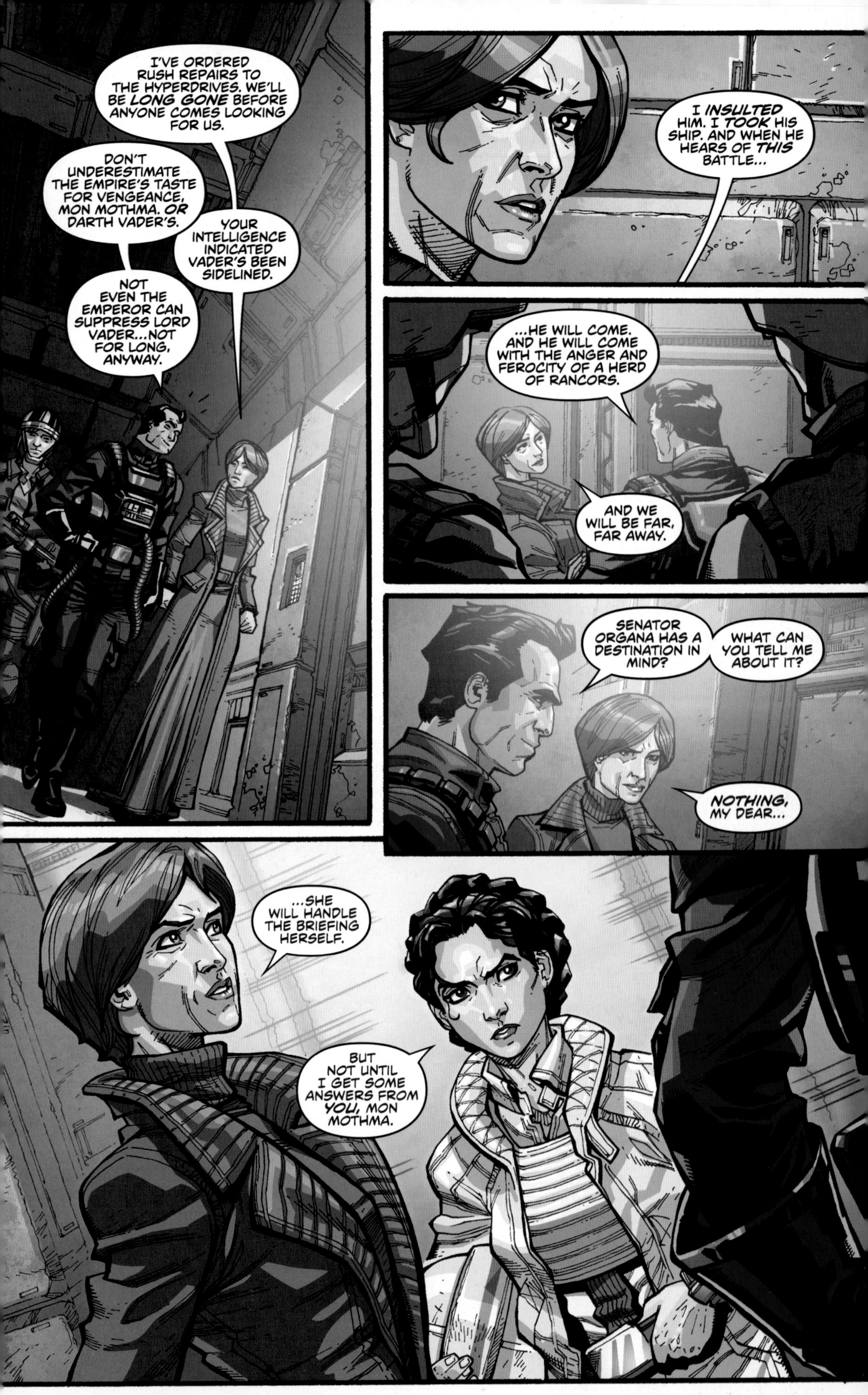

I'VE ORDERED RUSH REPAIRS TO THE HYPERDRIVES. WE'LL BE LONG GONE BEFORE ANYONE COMES LOOKING FOR US.
DON'T UNDERESTIMATE THE EMPIRE'S TASTE FOR VENGEANCE, MON MOTHMA. OR DARTH VADER'S.
YOUR INTELLIGENCE INDICATED VADER'S BEEN SIDELINED.
NOT EVEN THE EMPEROR CAN SUPPRESS LORD VADER...NOT FOR LONG, ANYWAY.
I INSULTED HIM. I TOOK HIS SHIP. AND WHEN HE HEARS OF THIS BATTLE...
...HE WILL COME. AND HE WILL COME WITH THE ANGER AND FEROCITY OF A HERD OF RANCORS.
AND WE WILL BE FAR, FAR AWAY.
SENATOR ORGANA HAS A DESTINATION IN MIND?
WHAT CAN YOU TELL ME ABOUT IT?
NOTHING, MY DEAR...
...SHE WILL HANDLE THE BRIEFING HERSELF.
BUT NOT UNTIL I GET SOME ANSWERS FROM YOU, MON MOTHMA.

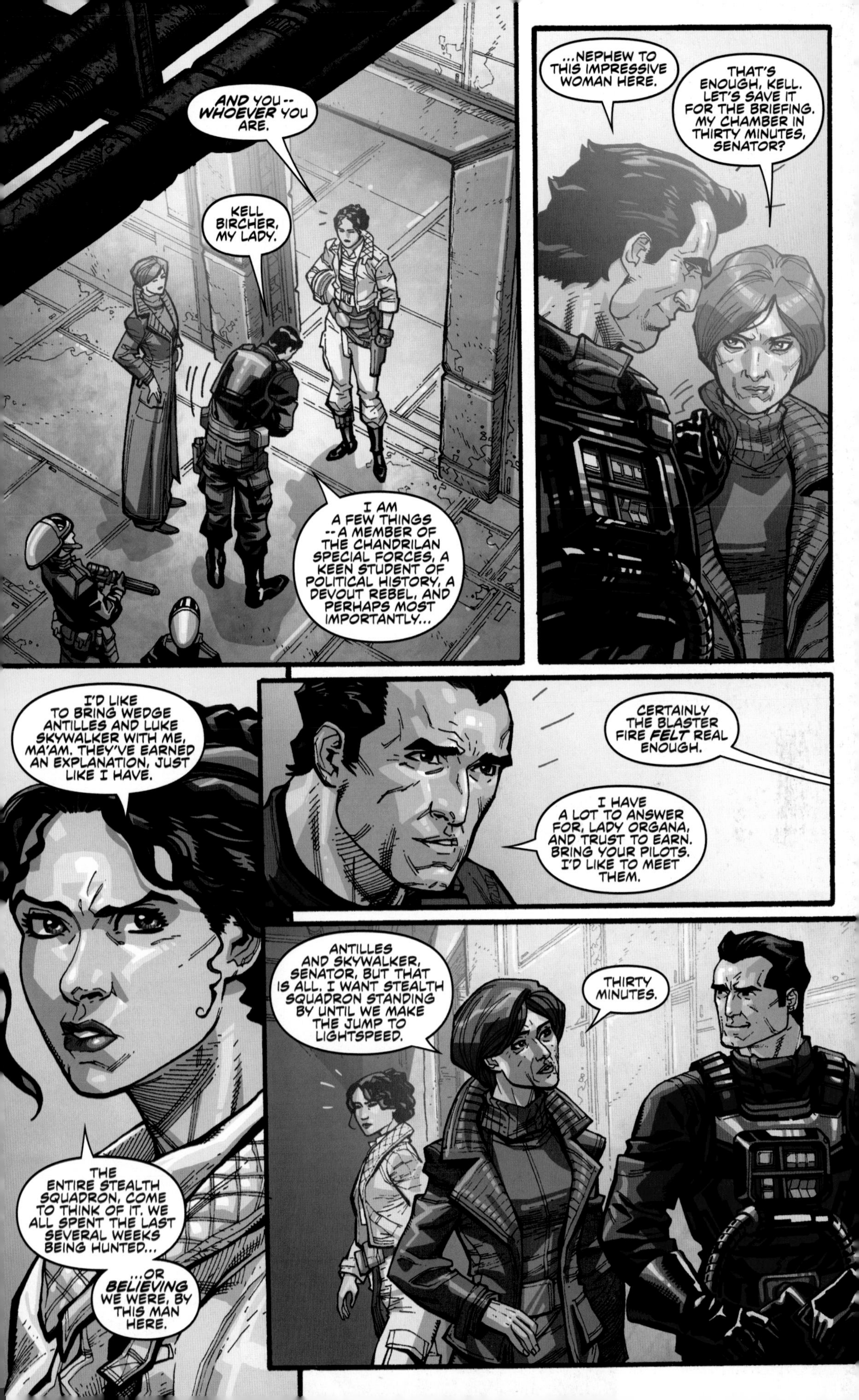
AND YOU -- WHOEVER YOU ARE.
KELL BIRCHER, MY LADY.
I AM A FEW THINGS -- A MEMBER OF THE CHANDRILAN SPECIAL FORCES, A KEEN STUDENT OF POLITICAL HISTORY, A DEVOUT REBEL, AND PERHAPS MOST IMPORTANTLY...
...NEPHEW TO THIS IMPRESSIVE WOMAN HERE.
THAT'S ENOUGH, KELL. LET'S SAVE IT FOR THE BRIEFING. MY CHAMBER IN THIRTY MINUTES, SENATOR?
I'D LIKE TO BRING WEDGE ANTILLES AND LUKE SKYWALKER WITH ME, MA'AM. THEY'VE EARNED AN EXPLANATION, JUST LIKE I HAVE.
THE ENTIRE STEALTH SQUADRON, COME TO THINK OF IT. WE ALL SPENT THE LAST SEVERAL WEEKS BEING HUNTED...
...OR BELIEVING WE WERE, BY THIS MAN HERE.
CERTAINLY THE BLASTER FIRE FELT REAL ENOUGH.
I HAVE A LOT TO ANSWER FOR, LADY ORGANA, AND TRUST TO EARN. BRING YOUR PILOTS. I'D LIKE TO MEET THEM.
ANTILLES AND SKYWALKER, SENATOR, BUT THAT IS ALL. I WANT STEALTH SQUADRON STANDING BY UNTIL WE MAKE THE JUMP TO LIGHTSPEED.
THIRTY MINUTES.

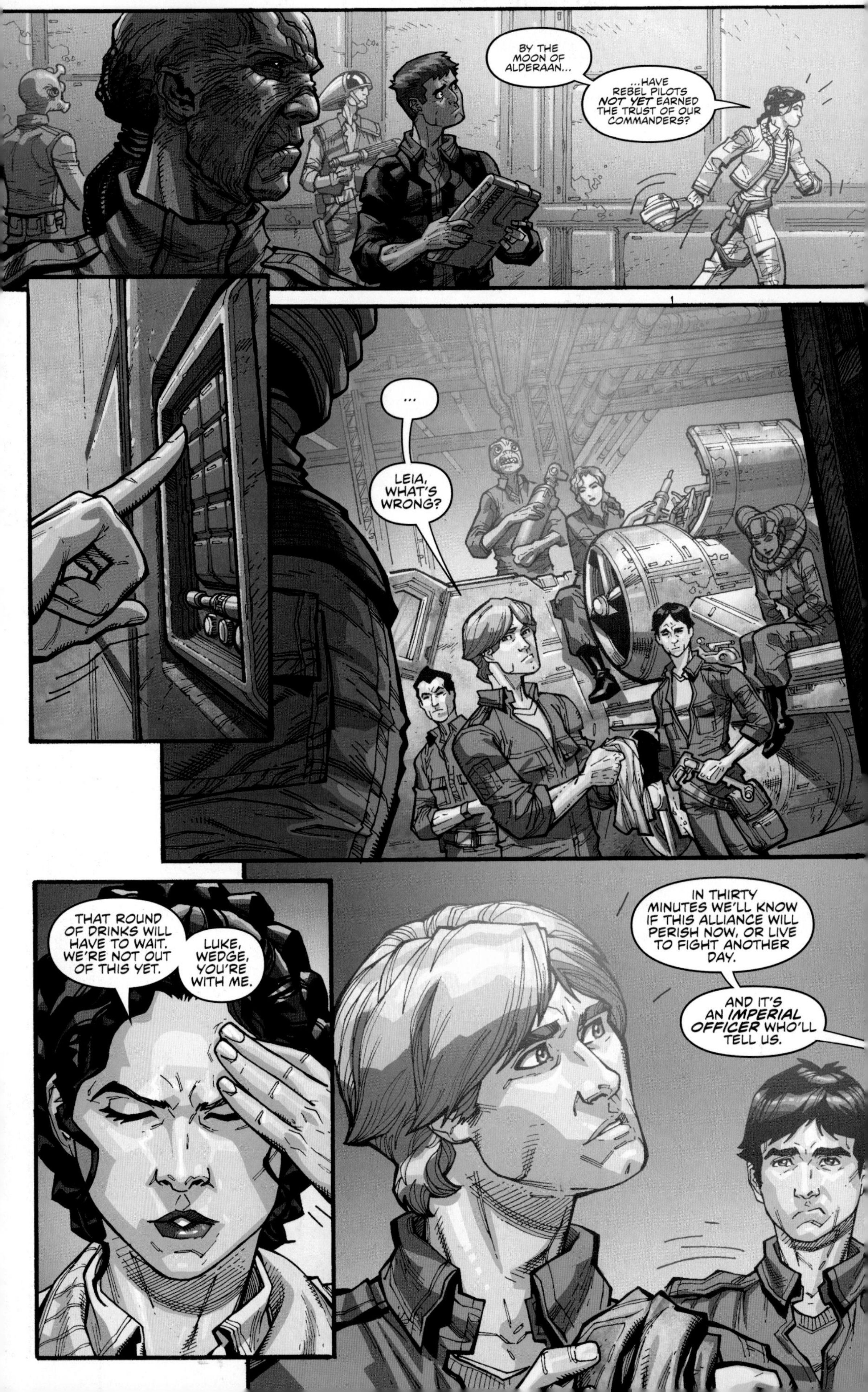

BY THE MOON OF ALDERAAN...
...HAVE REBEL PILOTS NOT YET EARNED THE TRUST OF OUR COMMANDERS?
...
LEIA, WHAT'S WRONG?
THAT ROUND OF DRINKS WILL HAVE TO WAIT. WE'RE NOT OUT OF THIS YET.
LUKE, WEDGE, YOU'RE WITH ME.
IN THIRTY MINUTES WE'LL KNOW IF THIS ALLIANCE WILL PERISH NOW, OR LIVE TO FIGHT ANOTHER DAY.
AND IT'S AN IMPERIAL OFFICER WHO'LL TELL US.

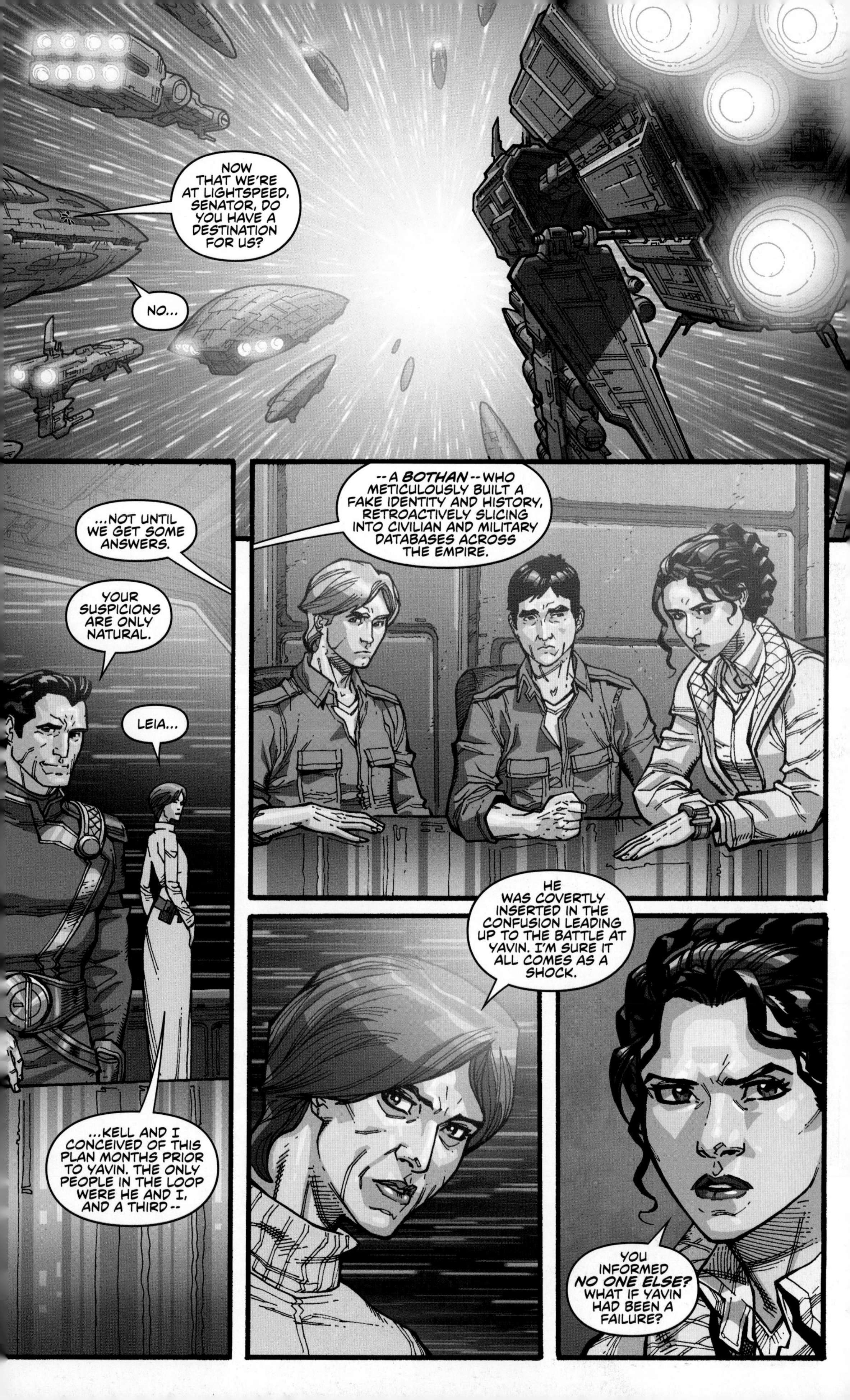
NOW THAT WE'RE AT LIGHTSPEED, SENATOR, DO YOU HAVE A DESTINATION FOR US?
NO...
...NOT UNTIL WE GET SOME ANSWERS.
YOUR SUSPICIONS ARE ONLY NATURAL.
LEIA...
...KELL AND I CONCEIVED OF THIS PLAN MONTHS PRIOR TO YAVIN. THE ONLY PEOPLE IN THE LOOP WERE HE AND I, AND A THIRD --
-- A BOTHAN -- WHO METICULOUSLY BUILT A FAKE IDENTITY AND HISTORY, RETROACTIVELY SLICING INTO CIVILIAN AND MILITARY DATABASES ACROSS THE EMPIRE.
HE WAS COVERTLY INSERTED IN THE CONFUSION LEADING UP TO THE BATTLE AT YAVIN. I'M SURE IT ALL COMES AS A SHOCK.
YOU INFORMED NO ONE ELSE? WHAT IF YAVIN HAD BEEN A FAILURE?

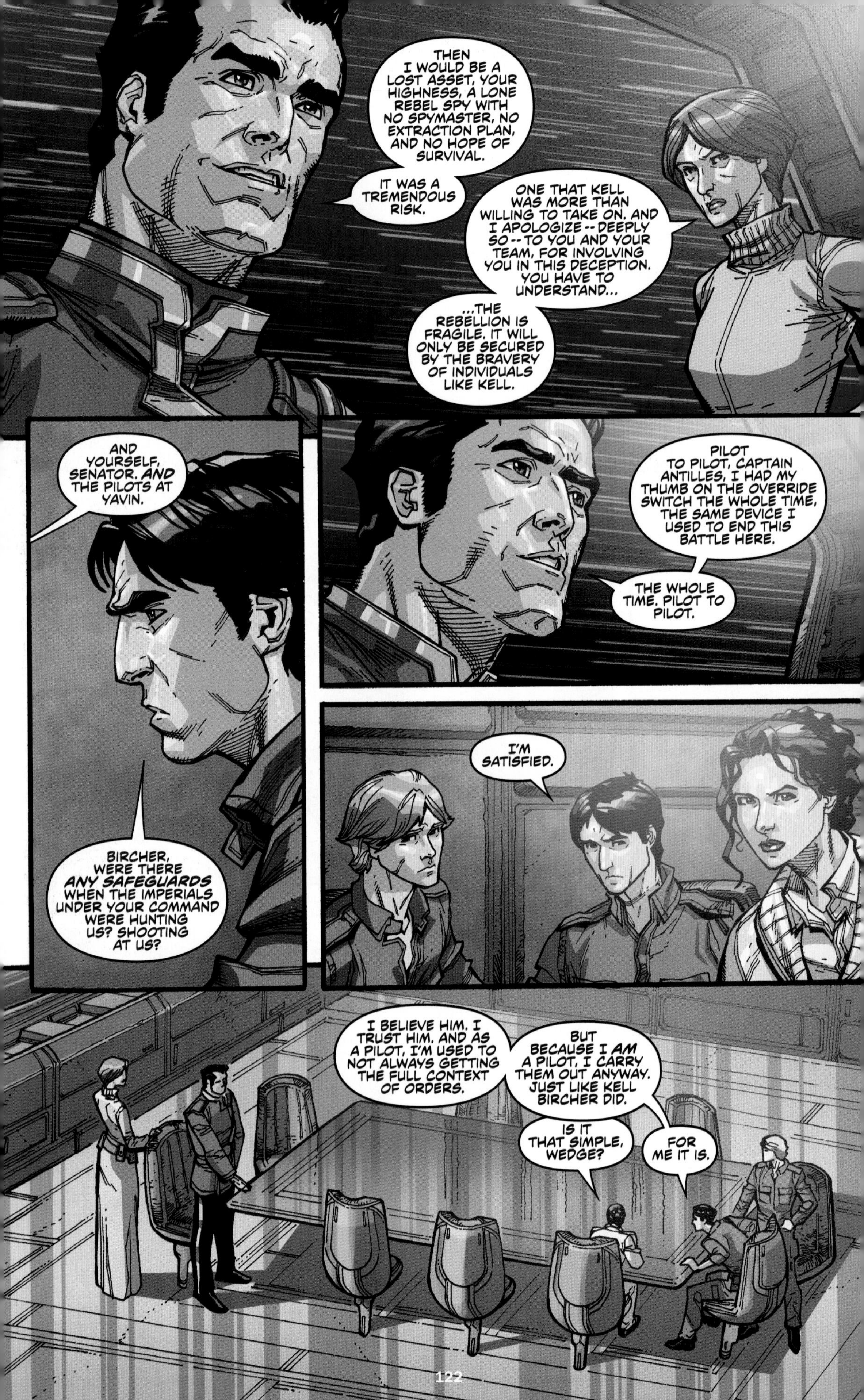
THEN I WOULD BE A LOST ASSET, YOUR HIGHNESS, A LONE REBEL SPY WITH NO SPYMASTER, NO EXTRACTION PLAN, AND NO HOPE OF SURVIVAL.
IT WAS A TREMENDOUS RISK.
ONE THAT KELL WAS MORE THAN WILLING TO TAKE ON. AND I APOLOGIZE -- DEEPLY SO -- TO YOU AND YOUR TEAM, FOR INVOLVING YOU IN THIS DECEPTION. YOU HAVE TO UNDERSTAND...
...THE REBELLION IS FRAGILE. IT WILL ONLY BE SECURED BY THE BRAVERY OF INDIVIDUALS LIKE KELL.
AND YOURSELF, SENATOR. AND THE PILOTS AT YAVIN.
BIRCHER, WERE THERE ANY SAFEGUARDS WHEN THE IMPERIALS UNDER YOUR COMMAND WERE HUNTING US? SHOOTING AT US?
PILOT TO PILOT, CAPTAIN ANTILLES, I HAD MY THUMB ON THE OVERRIDE SWITCH THE WHOLE TIME, THE SAME DEVICE I USED TO END THIS BATTLE HERE.
THE WHOLE TIME. PILOT TO PILOT.
I'M SATISFIED.
I BELIEVE HIM. I TRUST HIM. AND AS A PILOT, I'M USED TO NOT ALWAYS GETTING THE FULL CONTEXT OF ORDERS.
BUT BECAUSE I AM A PILOT, I CARRY THEM OUT ANYWAY. JUST LIKE KELL BIRCHER DID.
IS IT THAT SIMPLE, WEDGE?
FOR ME IT IS.

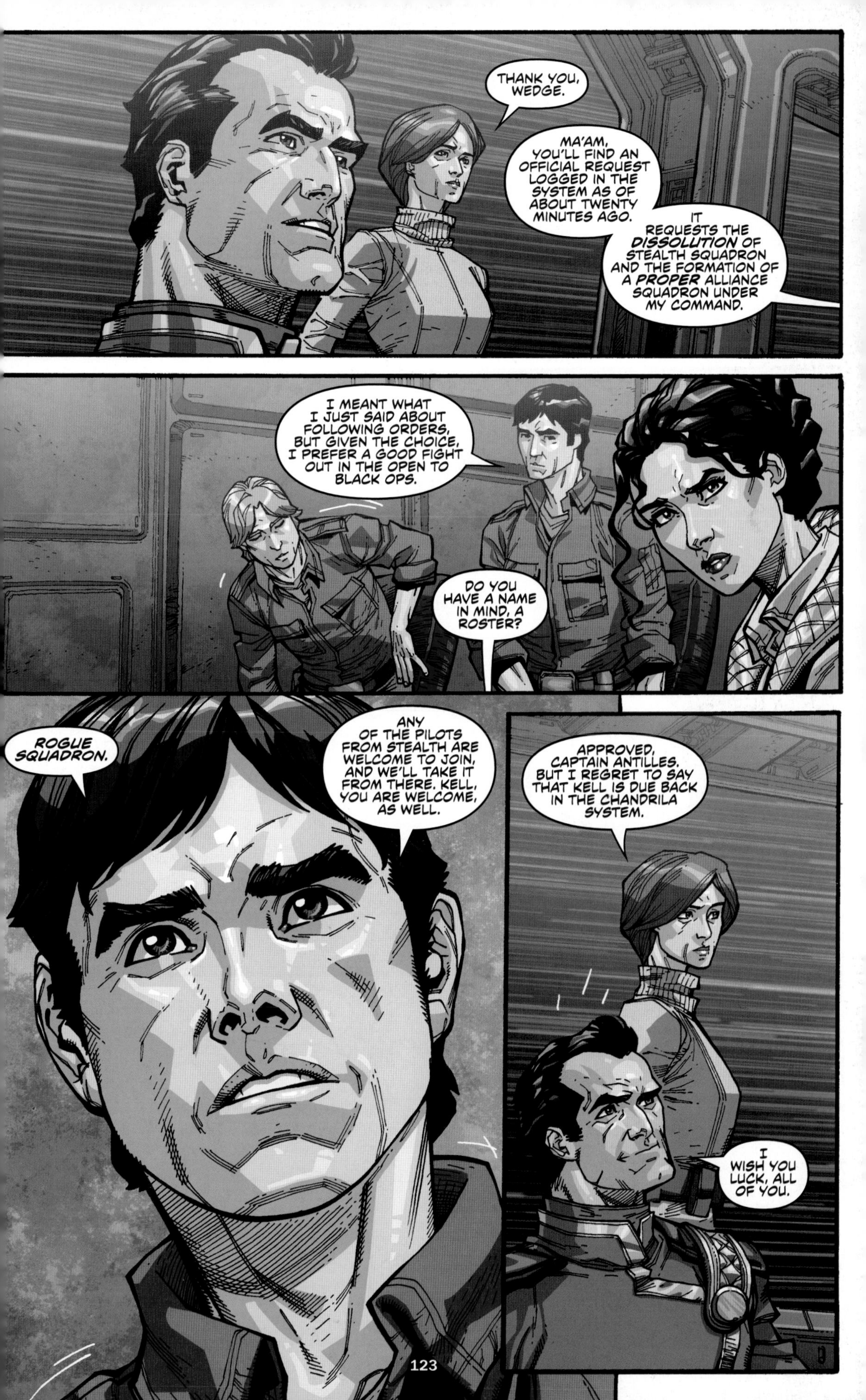
THANK YOU, WEDGE.
MA'AM, YOU'LL FIND AN OFFICIAL REQUEST LOGGED IN THE SYSTEM AS OF ABOUT TWENTY MINUTES AGO.
IT REQUESTS THE DISSOLUTION OF STEALTH SQUADRON AND THE FORMATION OF A PROPER ALLIANCE SQUADRON UNDER MY COMMAND.
I MEANT WHAT I JUST SAID ABOUT FOLLOWING ORDERS, BUT GIVEN THE CHOICE, I PREFER A GOOD FIGHT OUT IN THE OPEN TO BLACK OPS.
DO YOU HAVE A NAME IN MIND, A ROSTER?
ROGUE SQUADRON.
ANY OF THE PILOTS FROM STEALTH ARE WELCOME TO JOIN, AND WE'LL TAKE IT FROM THERE. KELL, YOU ARE WELCOME, AS WELL.
APPROVED, CAPTAIN ANTILLES. BUT I REGRET TO SAY THAT KELL IS DUE BACK IN THE CHANDRILA SYSTEM.
I WISH YOU LUCK, ALL OF YOU.

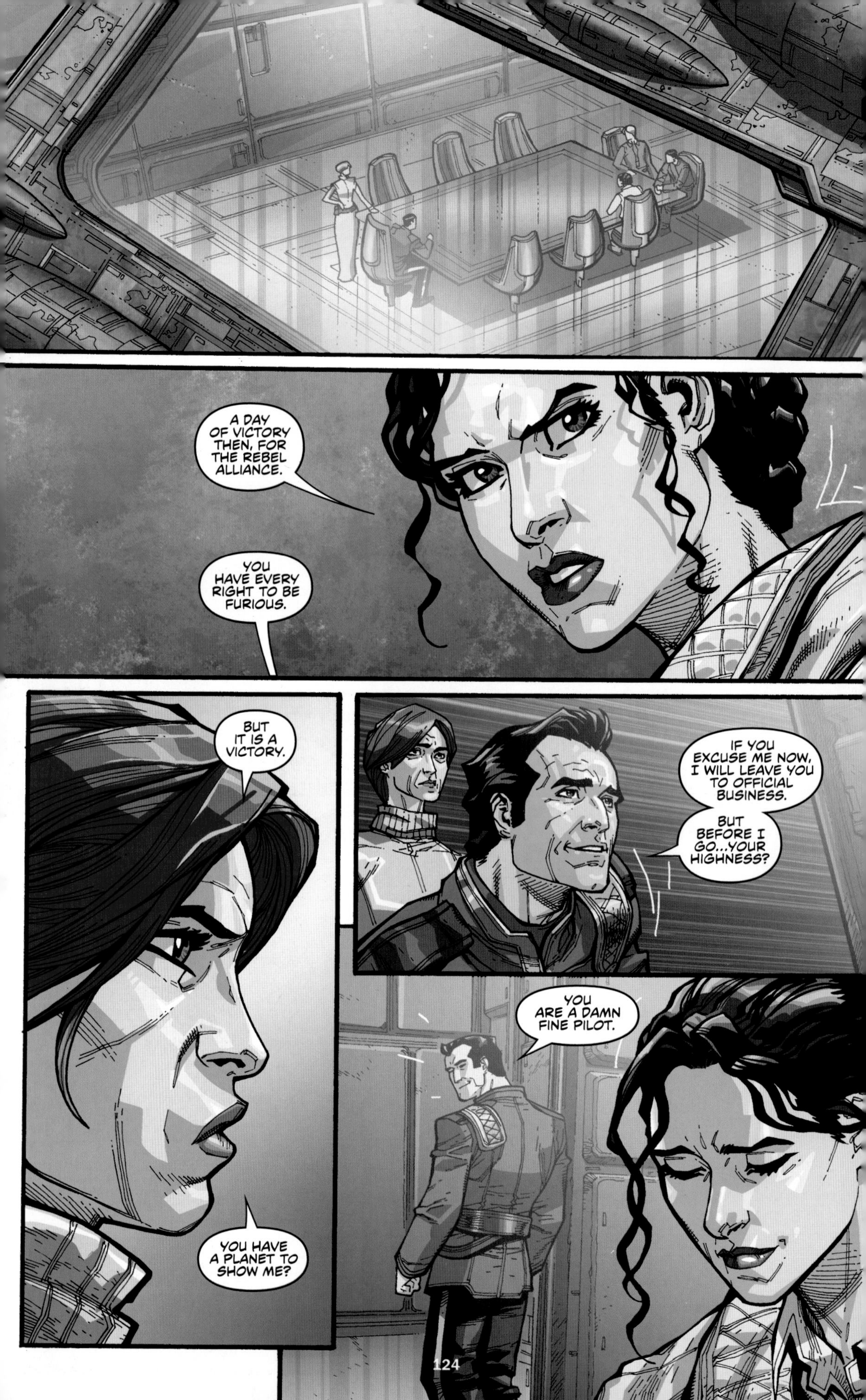

A DAY OF VICTORY THEN, FOR THE REBEL ALLIANCE.
YOU HAVE EVERY RIGHT TO BE FURIOUS.
BUT IT IS A VICTORY.
IF YOU EXCUSE ME NOW, I WILL LEAVE YOU TO OFFICIAL BUSINESS.
BUT BEFORE I GO...YOUR HIGHNESS?
YOU ARE A DAMN FINE PILOT.
YOU HAVE A PLANET TO SHOW ME?

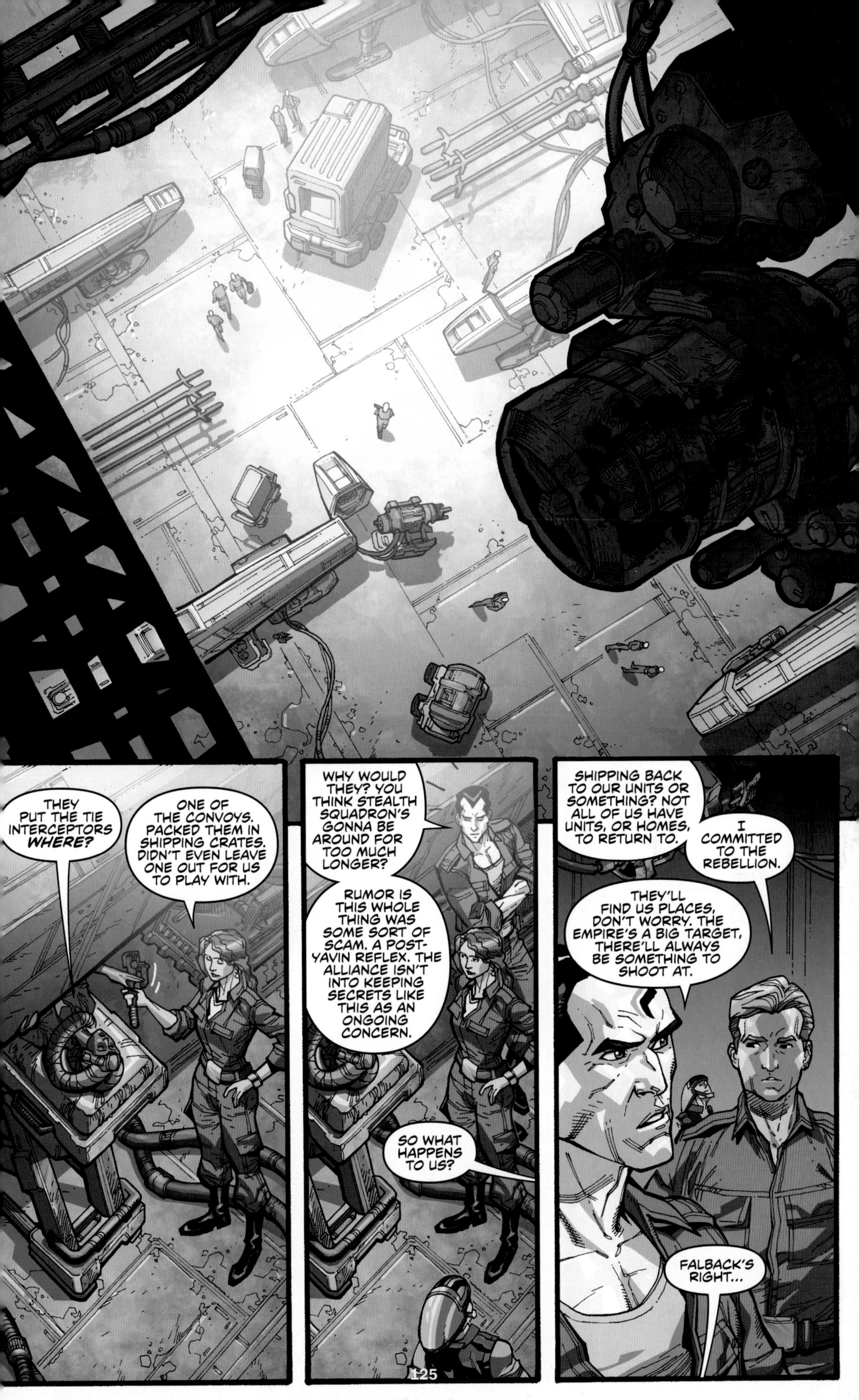
THEY PUT THE TIE INTERCEPTORS *WHERE?*
ONE OF THE CONVOYS. PACKED THEM IN SHIPPING CRATES. DIDN'T EVEN LEAVE ONE OUT FOR US TO PLAY WITH.
WHY WOULD THEY? YOU THINK STEALTH SQUADRON'S GONNA BE AROUND FOR TOO MUCH LONGER?
RUMOR IS THIS WHOLE THING WAS SOME SORT OF SCAM. A POST-YAVIN REFLEX. THE ALLIANCE ISN'T INTO KEEPING SECRETS LIKE THIS AS AN ONGOING CONCERN.
SO WHAT HAPPENS TO US?
SHIPPING BACK TO OUR UNITS OR SOMETHING? NOT ALL OF US HAVE UNITS, OR HOMES, TO RETURN TO.
I COMMITTED TO THE REBELLION.
THEY'LL FIND US PLACES, DON'T WORRY. THE EMPIRE'S A BIG TARGET, THERE'LL ALWAYS BE SOMETHING TO SHOOT AT.
FALBACK'S RIGHT...

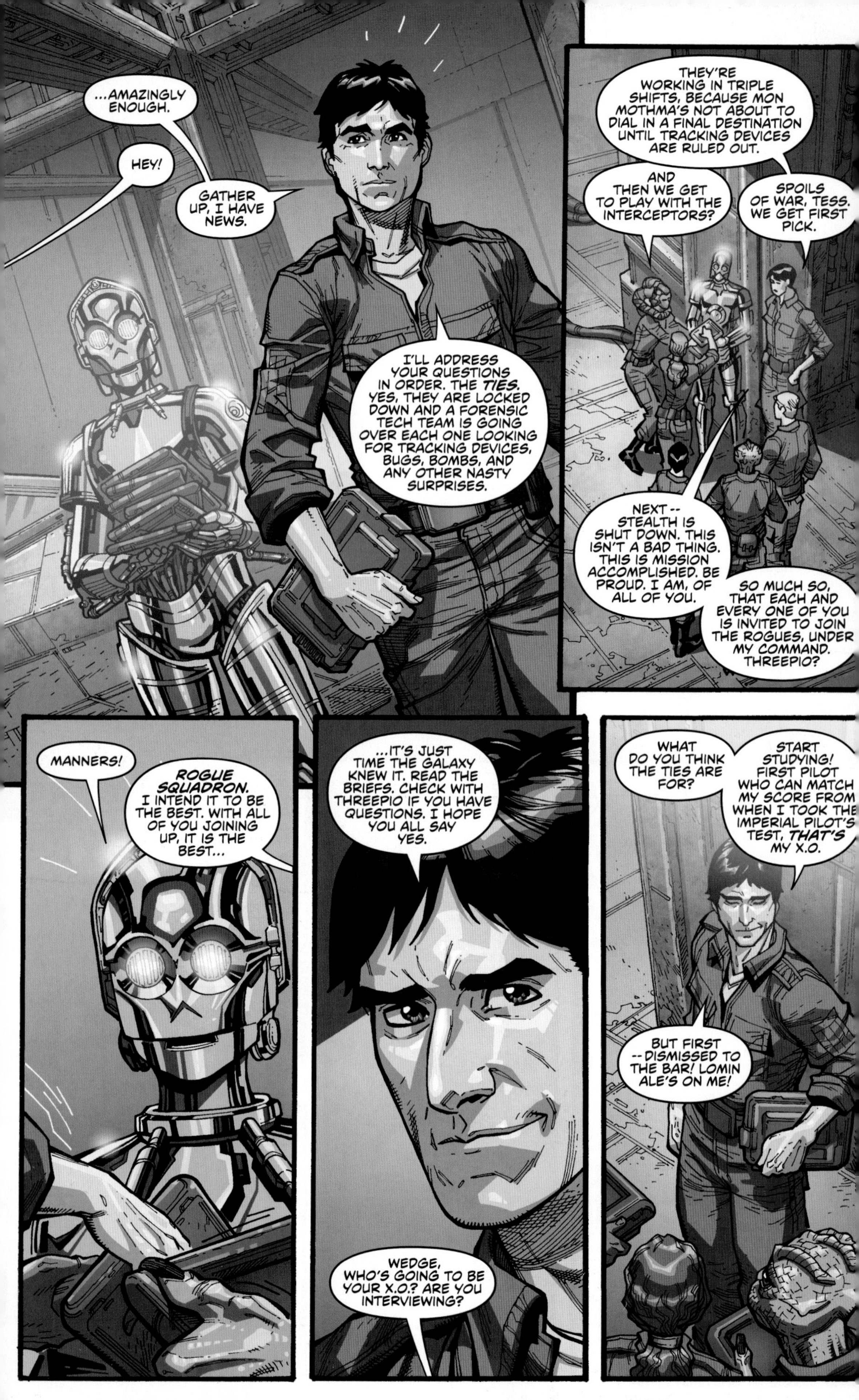

...AMAZINGLY ENOUGH.
HEY!
GATHER UP, I HAVE NEWS.
I'LL ADDRESS YOUR QUESTIONS IN ORDER. THE *TIES.* YES, THEY ARE LOCKED DOWN AND A FORENSIC TECH TEAM IS GOING OVER EACH ONE LOOKING FOR TRACKING DEVICES, BUGS, BOMBS, AND ANY OTHER NASTY SURPRISES.
THEY'RE WORKING IN TRIPLE SHIFTS, BECAUSE MON MOTHMA'S NOT ABOUT TO DIAL IN A FINAL DESTINATION UNTIL TRACKING DEVICES ARE RULED OUT.
AND THEN WE GET TO PLAY WITH THE INTERCEPTORS?
SPOILS OF WAR, TESS. WE GET FIRST PICK.
NEXT -- STEALTH IS SHUT DOWN. THIS ISN'T A BAD THING. THIS IS MISSION ACCOMPLISHED. BE PROUD. I AM, OF ALL OF YOU.
SO MUCH SO, THAT EACH AND EVERY ONE OF YOU IS INVITED TO JOIN THE ROGUES, UNDER MY COMMAND. THREEPIO?
MANNERS!
ROGUE SQUADRON. I INTEND IT TO BE THE BEST. WITH ALL OF YOU JOINING UP, IT IS THE BEST...
...IT'S JUST TIME THE GALAXY KNEW IT. READ THE BRIEFS. CHECK WITH THREEPIO IF YOU HAVE QUESTIONS. I HOPE YOU ALL SAY YES.
WEDGE, WHO'S GOING TO BE YOUR X.O.? ARE YOU INTERVIEWING?
WHAT DO YOU THINK THE TIES ARE FOR?
START STUDYING! FIRST PILOT WHO CAN MATCH MY SCORE FROM WHEN I TOOK THE IMPERIAL PILOT'S TEST, *THAT'S* MY X.O.
BUT FIRST -- DISMISSED TO THE BAR! LOMIN ALE'S ON ME!

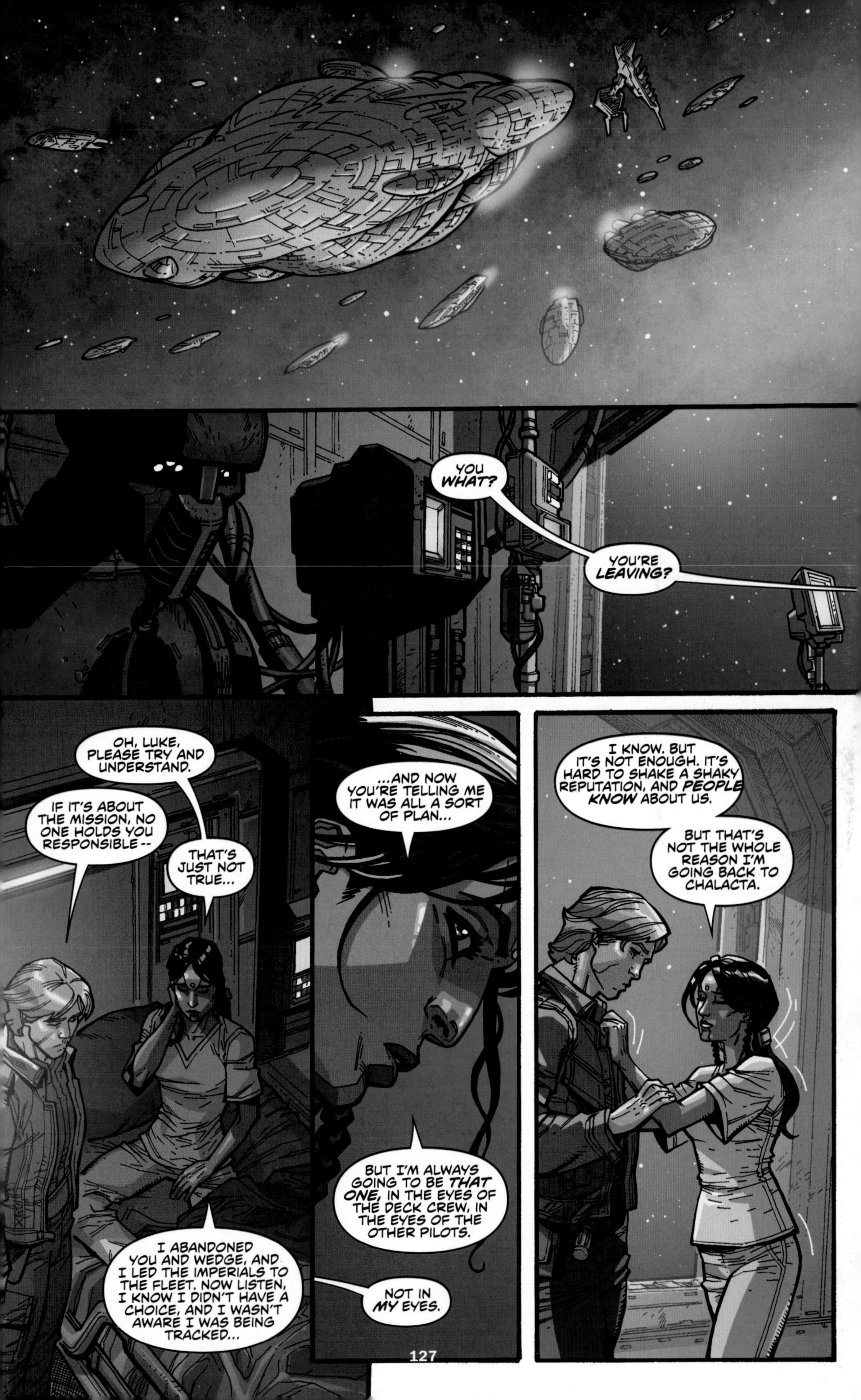
YOU WHAT?
YOU'RE LEAVING?
OH, LUKE, PLEASE TRY AND UNDERSTAND.
IF IT'S ABOUT THE MISSION, NO ONE HOLDS YOU RESPONSIBLE --
THAT'S JUST NOT TRUE...
I ABANDONED YOU AND WEDGE, AND I LED THE IMPERIALS TO THE FLEET. NOW LISTEN, I KNOW I DIDN'T HAVE A CHOICE, AND I WASN'T AWARE I WAS BEING TRACKED...
...AND NOW YOU'RE TELLING ME IT WAS ALL A SORT OF PLAN...
BUT I'M ALWAYS GOING TO BE THAT ONE, IN THE EYES OF THE DECK CREW, IN THE EYES OF THE OTHER PILOTS.
NOT IN MY EYES.
I KNOW. BUT IT'S NOT ENOUGH. IT'S HARD TO SHAKE A SHAKY REPUTATION, AND PEOPLE KNOW ABOUT US.
BUT THAT'S NOT THE WHOLE REASON I'M GOING BACK TO CHALACTA.

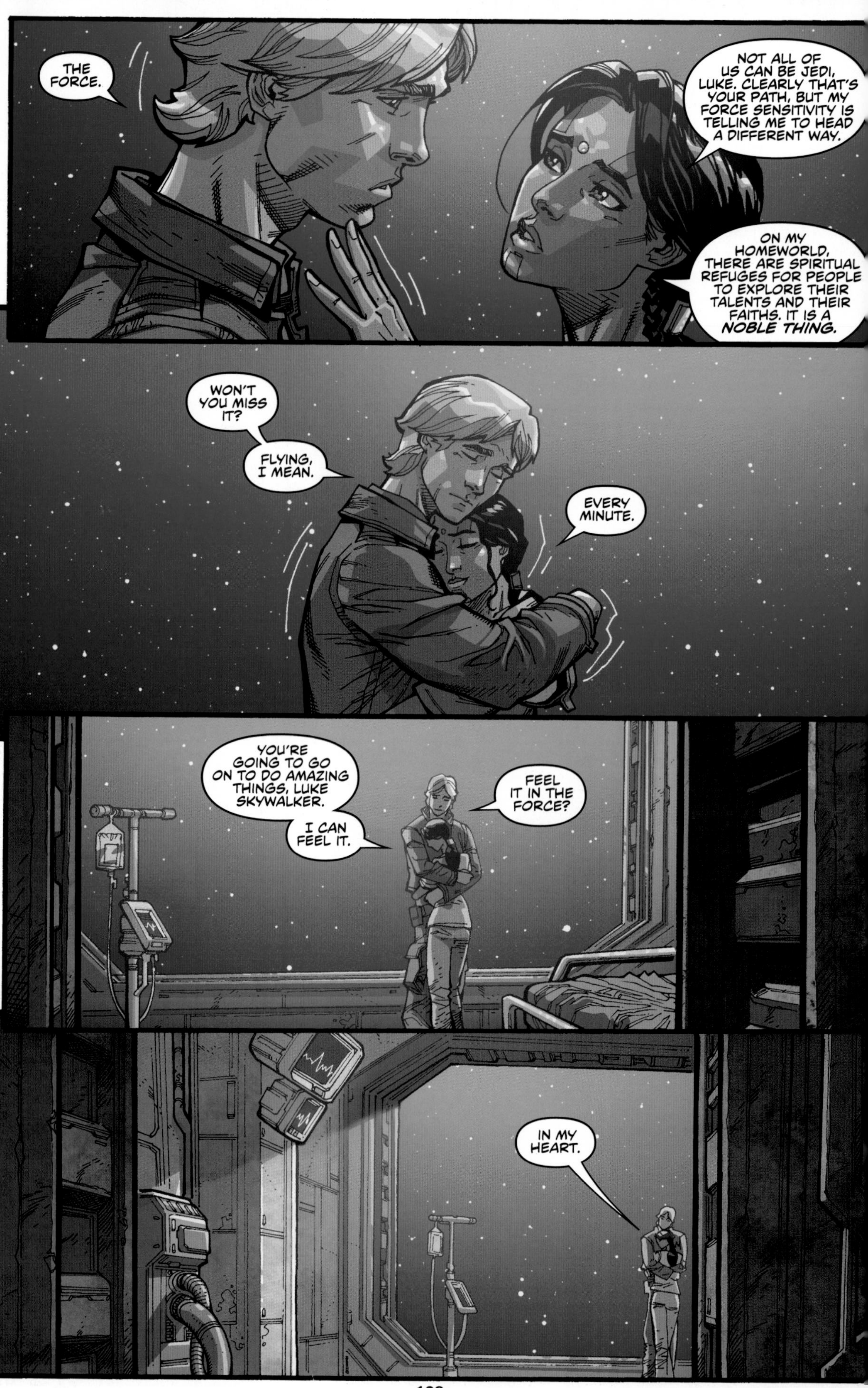
THE FORCE.
NOT ALL OF US CAN BE JEDI, LUKE. CLEARLY THAT'S YOUR PATH, BUT MY FORCE SENSITIVITY IS TELLING ME TO HEAD A DIFFERENT WAY.
ON MY HOMEWORLD, THERE ARE SPIRITUAL REFUGES FOR PEOPLE TO EXPLORE THEIR TALENTS AND THEIR FAITHS. IT IS A *NOBLE THING.*
WON'T YOU MISS IT?
FLYING, I MEAN.
EVERY MINUTE.
YOU'RE GOING TO GO ON TO DO AMAZING THINGS, LUKE SKYWALKER.
I CAN FEEL IT.
FEEL IT IN THE FORCE?
IN MY HEART.

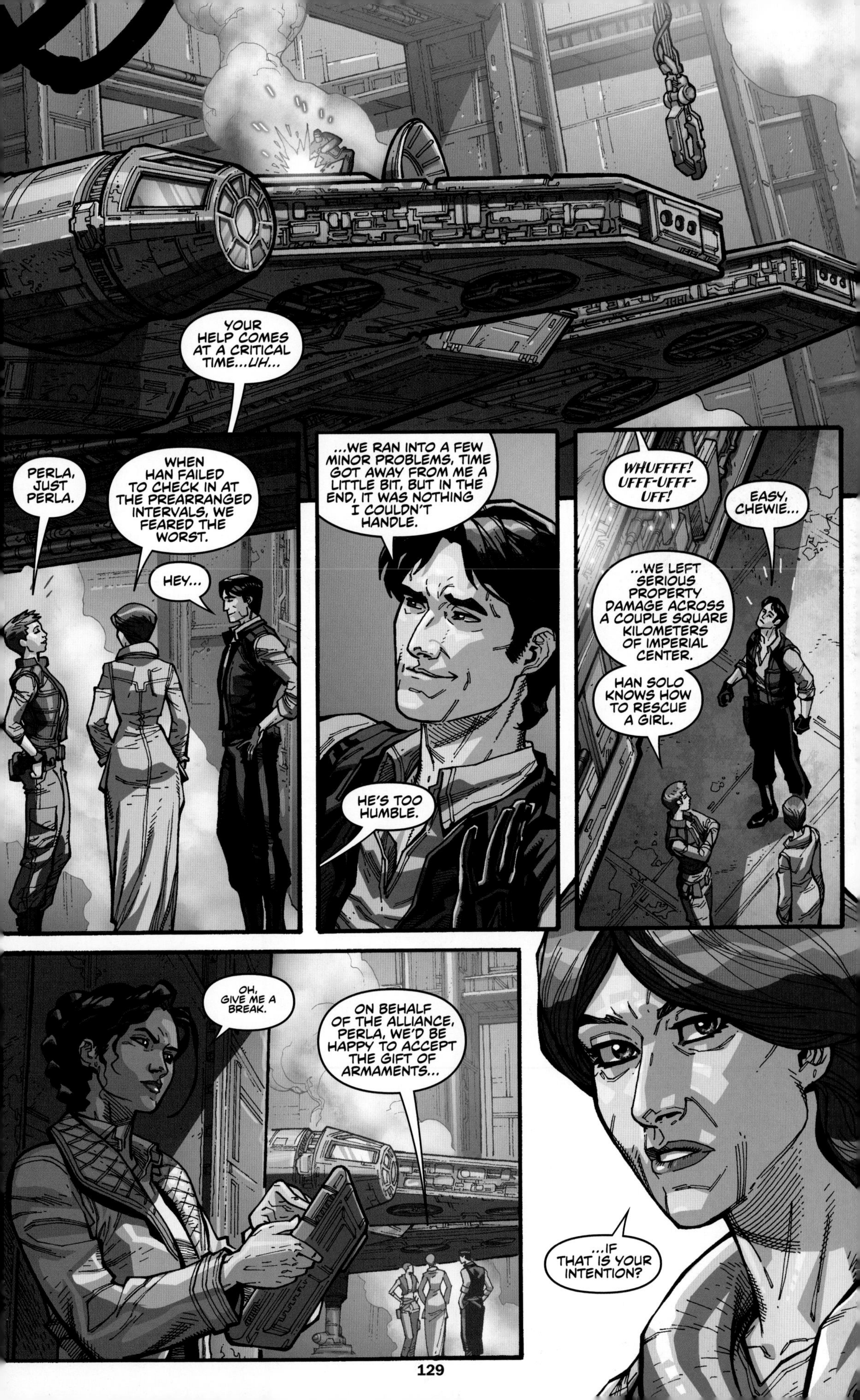
YOUR HELP COMES AT A CRITICAL TIME...UH...
PERLA, JUST PERLA.
WHEN HAN FAILED TO CHECK IN AT THE PREARRANGED INTERVALS, WE FEARED THE WORST.
HEY...
...WE RAN INTO A FEW MINOR PROBLEMS, TIME GOT AWAY FROM ME A LITTLE BIT, BUT IN THE END, IT WAS NOTHING I COULDN'T HANDLE.
HE'S TOO HUMBLE.
WHUFFFF! UFFF-UFFF-UFF!
EASY, CHEWIE...
...WE LEFT SERIOUS PROPERTY DAMAGE ACROSS A COUPLE SQUARE KILOMETERS OF IMPERIAL CENTER.
HAN SOLO KNOWS HOW TO RESCUE A GIRL.
OH, GIVE ME A BREAK.
ON BEHALF OF THE ALLIANCE, PERLA, WE'D BE HAPPY TO ACCEPT THE GIFT OF ARMAMENTS...
...IF THAT IS YOUR INTENTION?

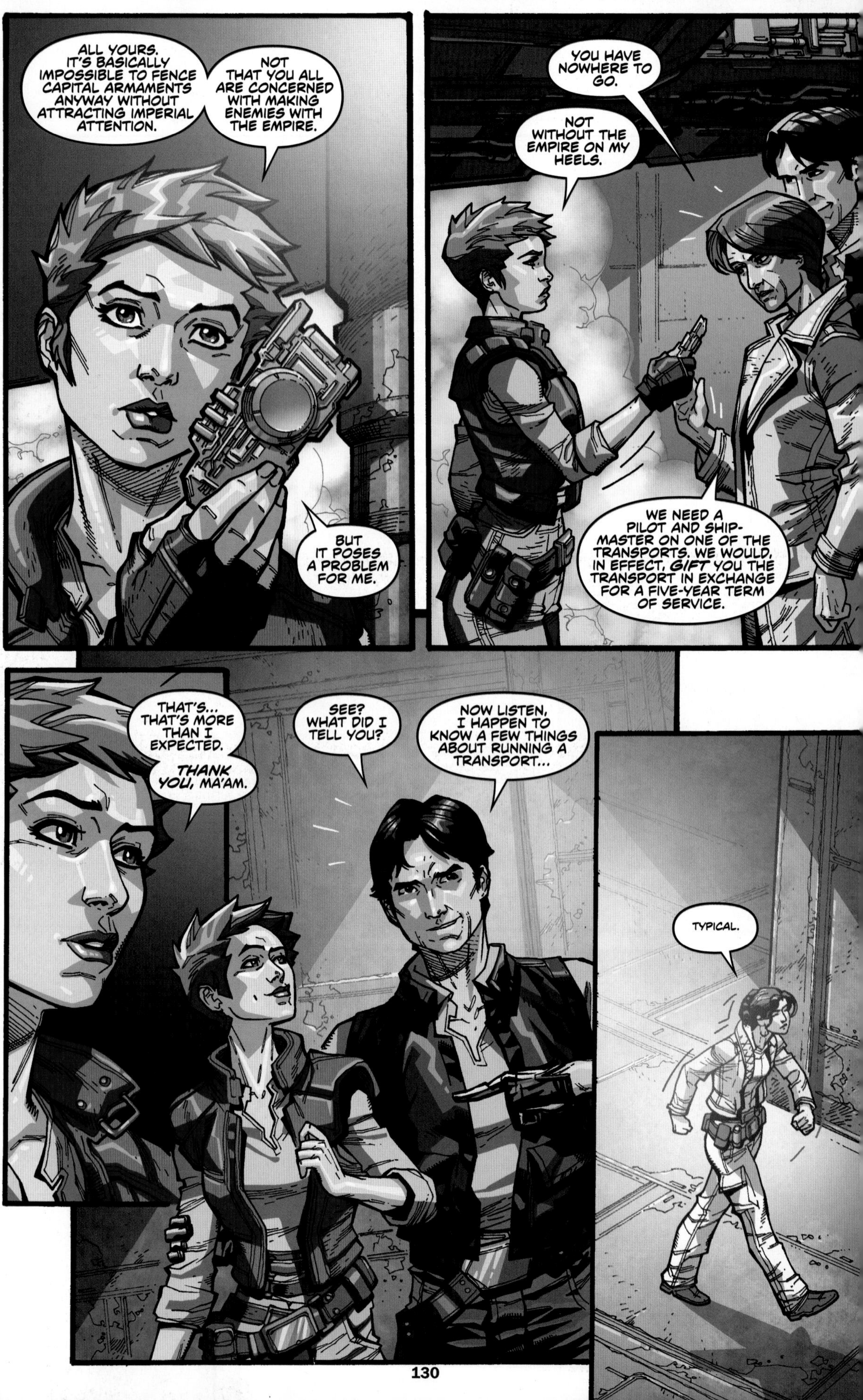
ALL YOURS. IT'S BASICALLY IMPOSSIBLE TO FENCE CAPITAL ARMAMENTS ANYWAY WITHOUT ATTRACTING IMPERIAL ATTENTION.
NOT THAT YOU ALL ARE CONCERNED WITH MAKING ENEMIES WITH THE EMPIRE.
BUT IT POSES A PROBLEM FOR ME.
YOU HAVE NOWHERE TO GO.
NOT WITHOUT THE EMPIRE ON MY HEELS.
WE NEED A PILOT AND SHIP-MASTER ON ONE OF THE TRANSPORTS. WE WOULD, IN EFFECT, *GIFT* YOU THE TRANSPORT IN EXCHANGE FOR A FIVE-YEAR TERM OF SERVICE.
THAT'S... THAT'S MORE THAN I EXPECTED. *THANK YOU,* MA'AM.
SEE? WHAT DID I TELL YOU?
NOW LISTEN, I HAPPEN TO KNOW A FEW THINGS ABOUT RUNNING A TRANSPORT...
TYPICAL.

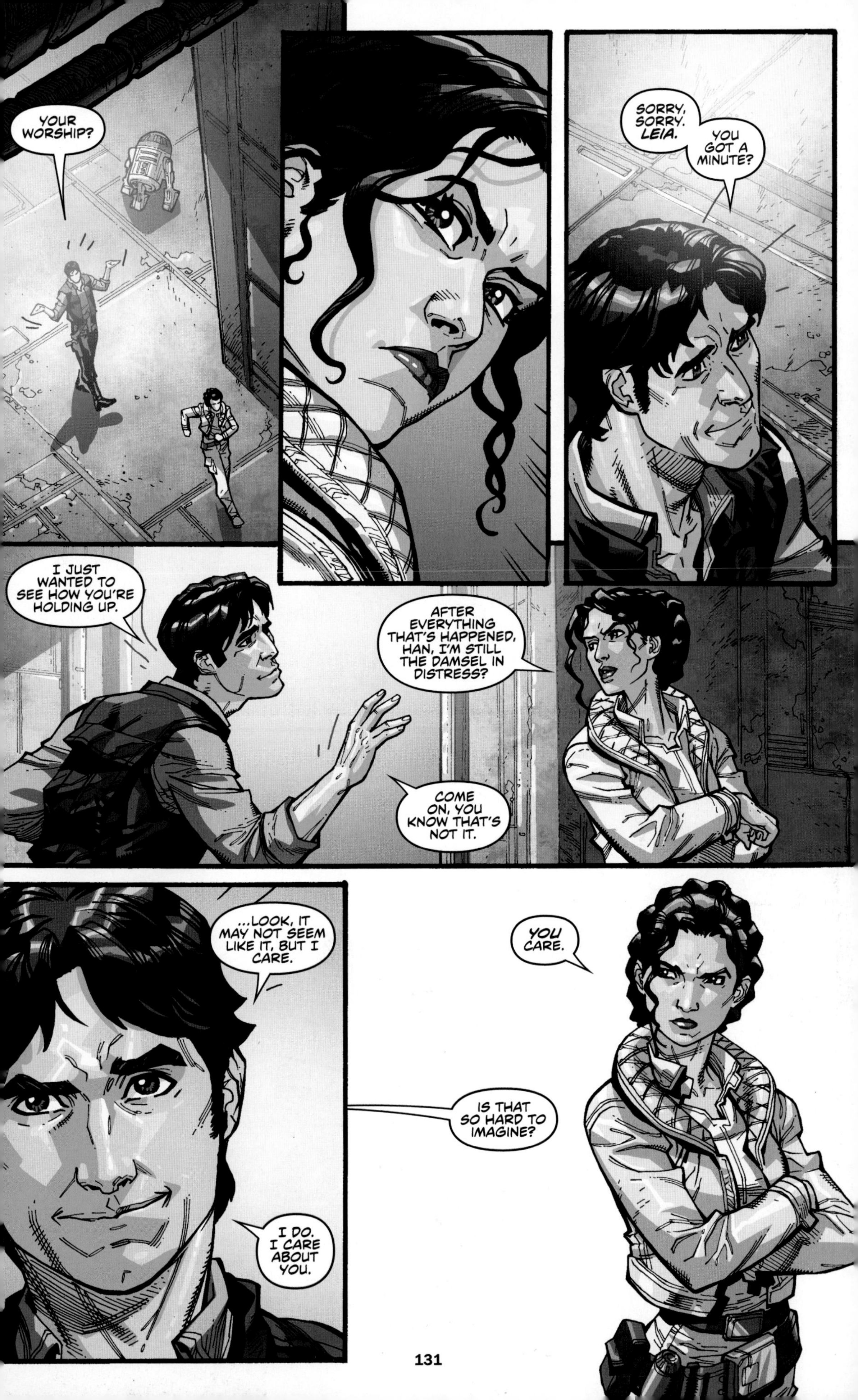
YOUR WORSHIP?
SORRY, SORRY. *LEIA.*
YOU GOT A MINUTE?
I JUST WANTED TO SEE HOW YOU'RE HOLDING UP.
AFTER EVERYTHING THAT'S HAPPENED, HAN, I'M STILL THE DAMSEL IN DISTRESS?
COME ON, YOU KNOW THAT'S NOT IT.
...LOOK, IT MAY NOT SEEM LIKE IT, BUT I CARE.
YOU CARE.
IS THAT SO HARD TO IMAGINE?
I DO. I CARE ABOUT YOU.

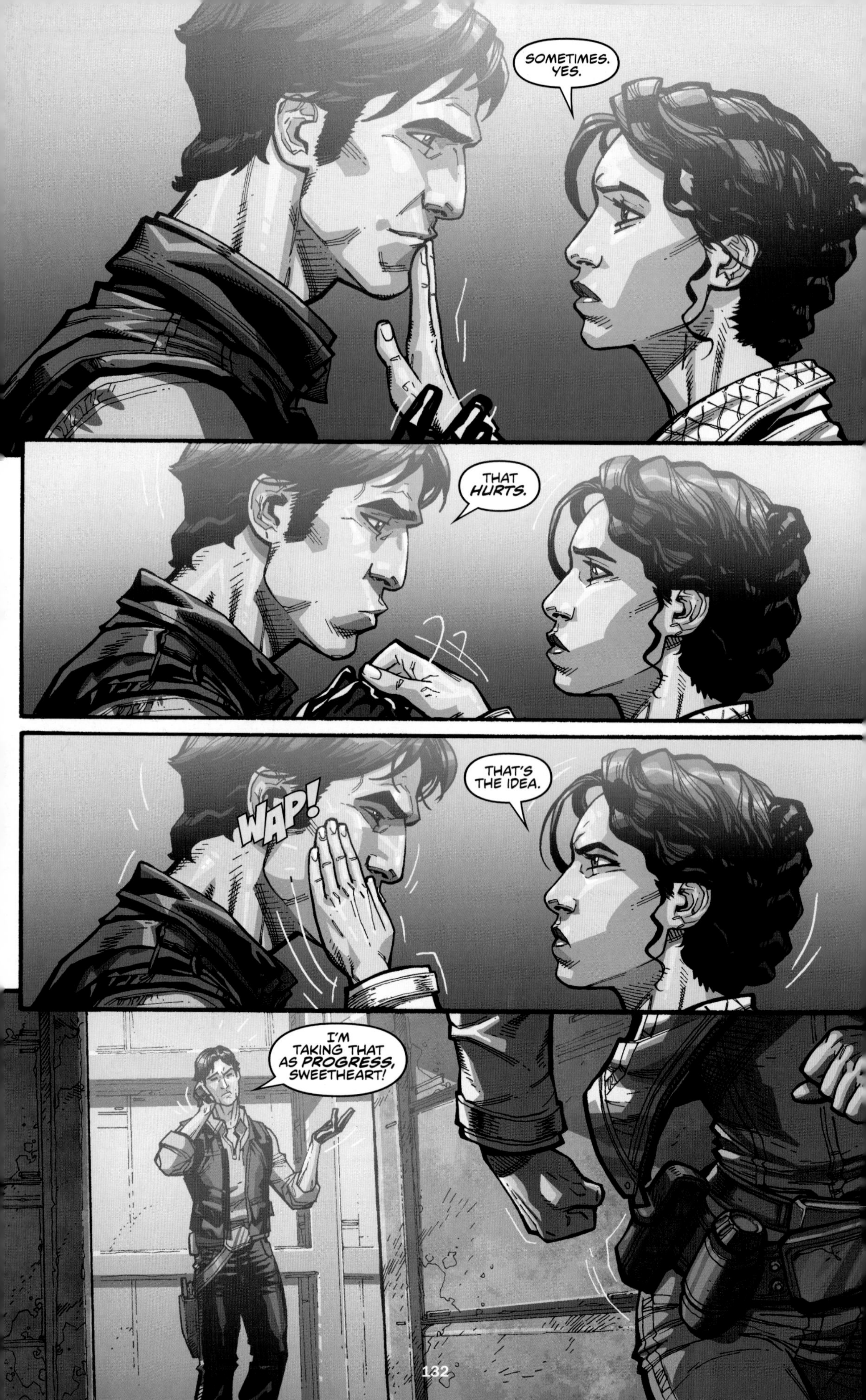
SOMETIMES. YES.
THAT HURTS.
THAT'S THE IDEA.
WAP!
I'M TAKING THAT AS PROGRESS, SWEETHEART!

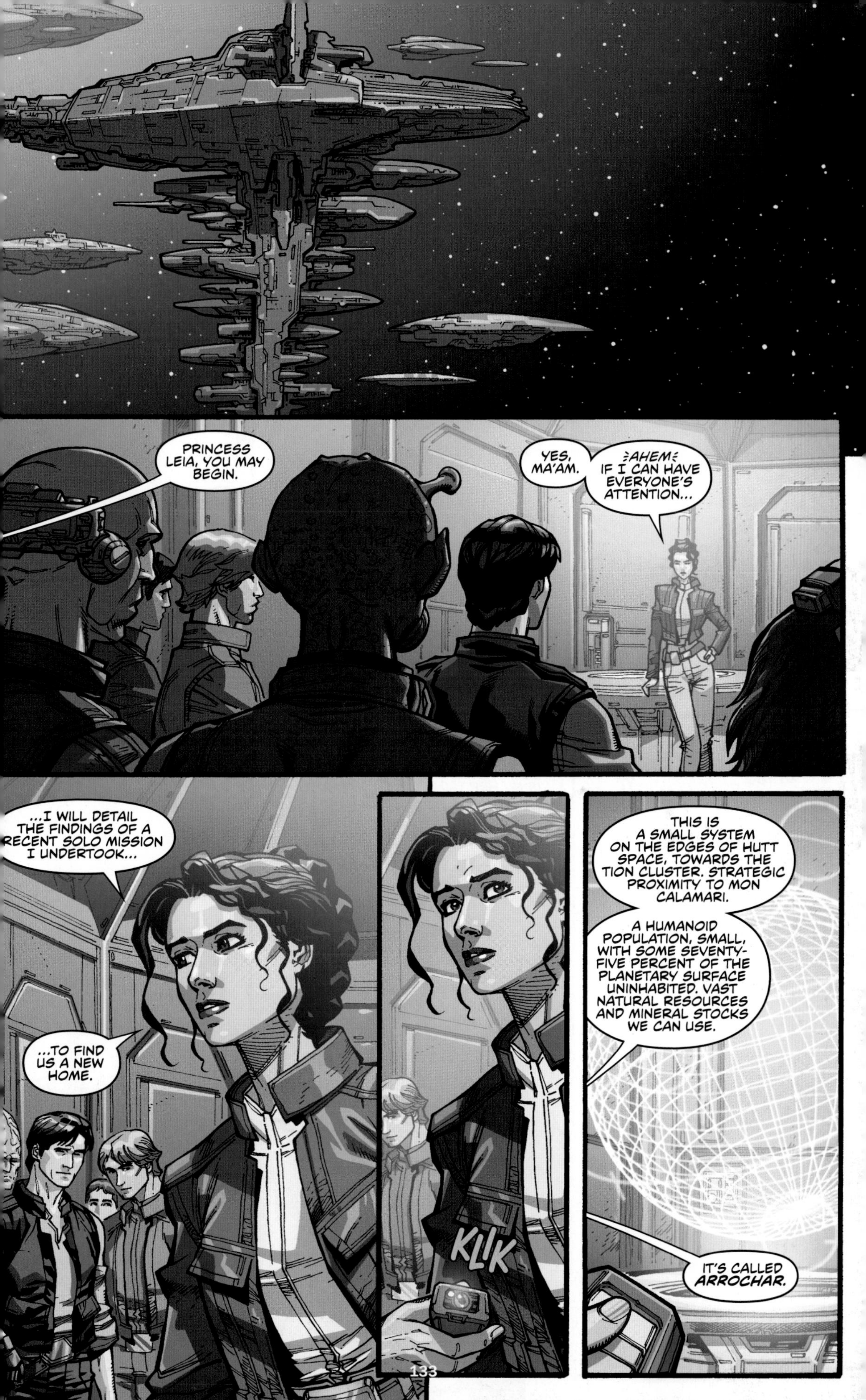
PRINCESS LEIA, YOU MAY BEGIN.
YES, MA'AM.
AHEM IF I CAN HAVE EVERYONE'S ATTENTION...
...I WILL DETAIL THE FINDINGS OF A RECENT SOLO MISSION I UNDERTOOK...
...TO FIND US A NEW HOME.
KLIK
THIS IS A SMALL SYSTEM ON THE EDGES OF HUTT SPACE, TOWARDS THE TION CLUSTER. STRATEGIC PROXIMITY TO MON CALAMARI.
A HUMANOID POPULATION, SMALL, WITH SOME SEVENTY-FIVE PERCENT OF THE PLANETARY SURFACE UNINHABITED. VAST NATURAL RESOURCES AND MINERAL STOCKS WE CAN USE.
IT'S CALLED *ARROCHAR.*

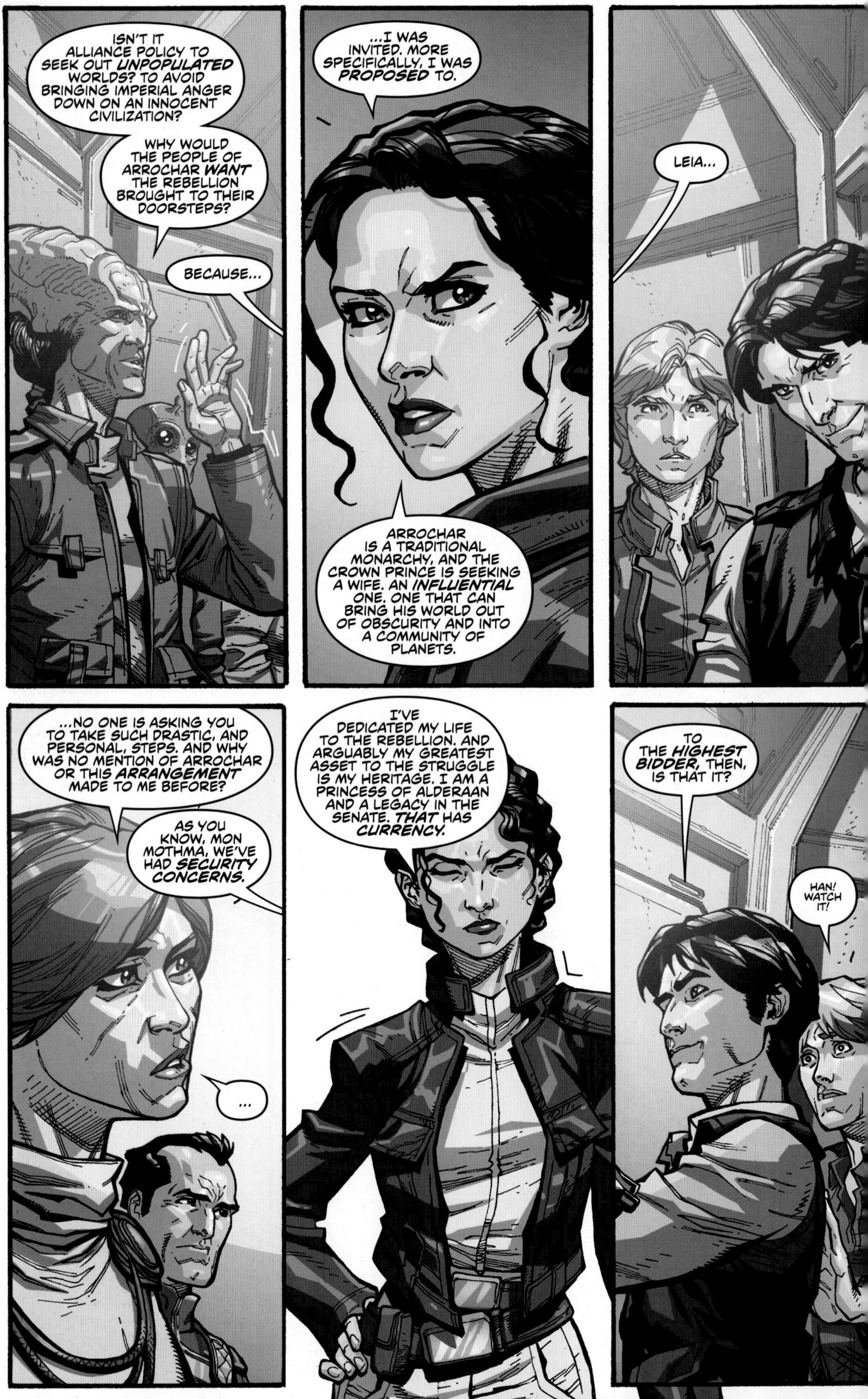
ISN'T IT ALLIANCE POLICY TO SEEK OUT UNPOPULATED WORLDS? TO AVOID BRINGING IMPERIAL ANGER DOWN ON AN INNOCENT CIVILIZATION?
WHY WOULD THE PEOPLE OF ARROCHAR WANT THE REBELLION BROUGHT TO THEIR DOORSTEPS?
BECAUSE...
...I WAS INVITED. MORE SPECIFICALLY, I WAS PROPOSED TO.
ARROCHAR IS A TRADITIONAL MONARCHY, AND THE CROWN PRINCE IS SEEKING A WIFE. AN INFLUENTIAL ONE. ONE THAT CAN BRING HIS WORLD OUT OF OBSCURITY AND INTO A COMMUNITY OF PLANETS.
LEIA...
...NO ONE IS ASKING YOU TO TAKE SUCH DRASTIC, AND PERSONAL, STEPS. AND WHY WAS NO MENTION OF ARROCHAR OR THIS ARRANGEMENT MADE TO ME BEFORE?
AS YOU KNOW, MON MOTHMA, WE'VE HAD SECURITY CONCERNS.
...
I'VE DEDICATED MY LIFE TO THE REBELLION. AND ARGUABLY MY GREATEST ASSET TO THE STRUGGLE IS MY HERITAGE. I AM A PRINCESS OF ALDERAAN AND A LEGACY IN THE SENATE. THAT HAS CURRENCY.
TO THE HIGHEST BIDDER, THEN, IS THAT IT?
HAN! WATCH IT!

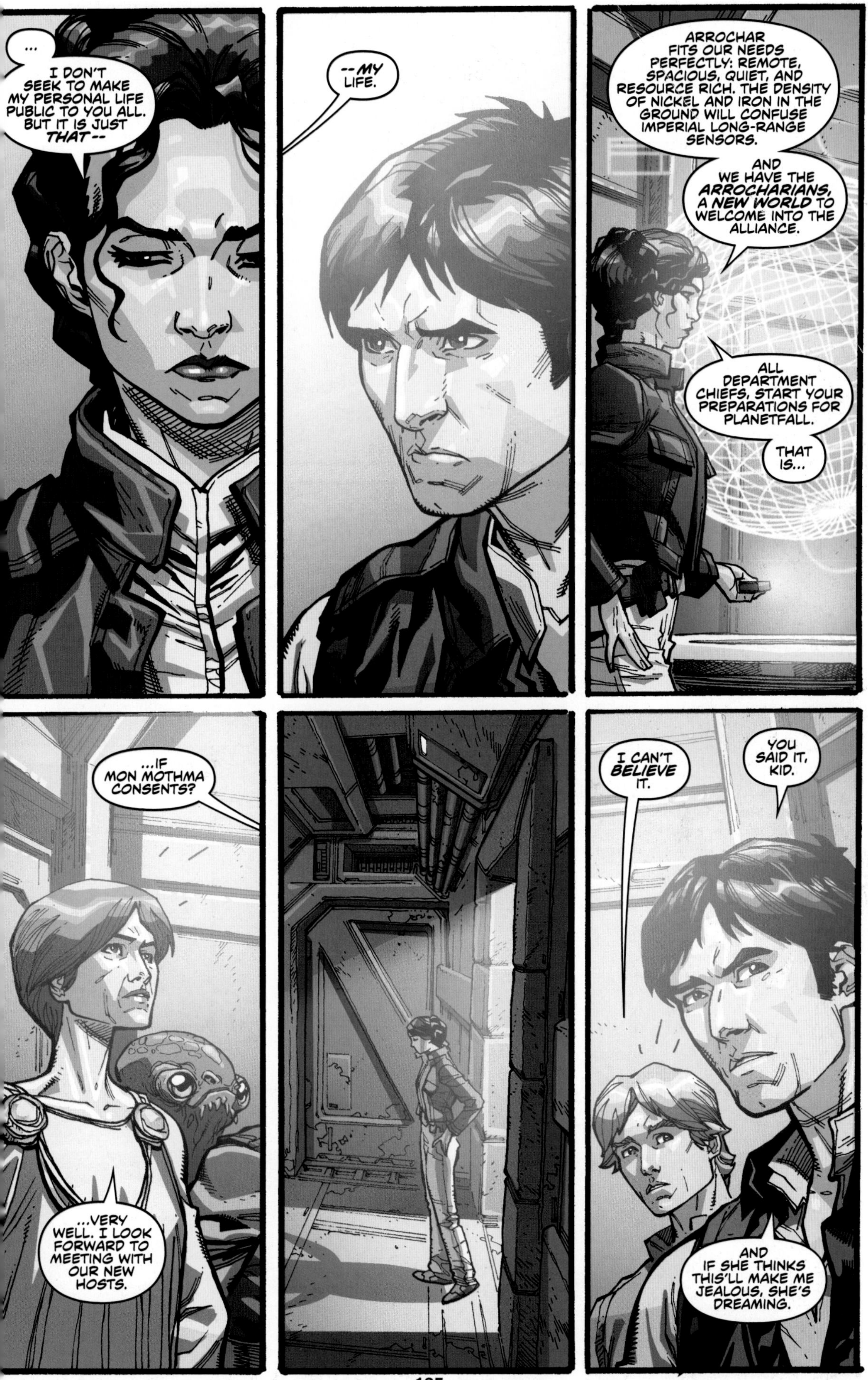
...
I DON'T SEEK TO MAKE MY PERSONAL LIFE PUBLIC TO YOU ALL. BUT IT IS JUST *THAT*--
--*MY* LIFE.
ARROCHAR FITS OUR NEEDS PERFECTLY: REMOTE, SPACIOUS, QUIET, AND RESOURCE RICH. THE DENSITY OF NICKEL AND IRON IN THE GROUND WILL CONFUSE IMPERIAL LONG-RANGE SENSORS.
AND WE HAVE THE *ARROCHARIANS*, A *NEW WORLD* TO WELCOME INTO THE ALLIANCE.
ALL DEPARTMENT CHIEFS, START YOUR PREPARATIONS FOR PLANETFALL.
THAT IS...
...IF MON MOTHMA CONSENTS?
...VERY WELL. I LOOK FORWARD TO MEETING WITH OUR NEW HOSTS.
I CAN'T *BELIEVE* IT.
YOU SAID IT, KID.
AND IF SHE THINKS THIS'LL MAKE ME JEALOUS, SHE'S DREAMING.

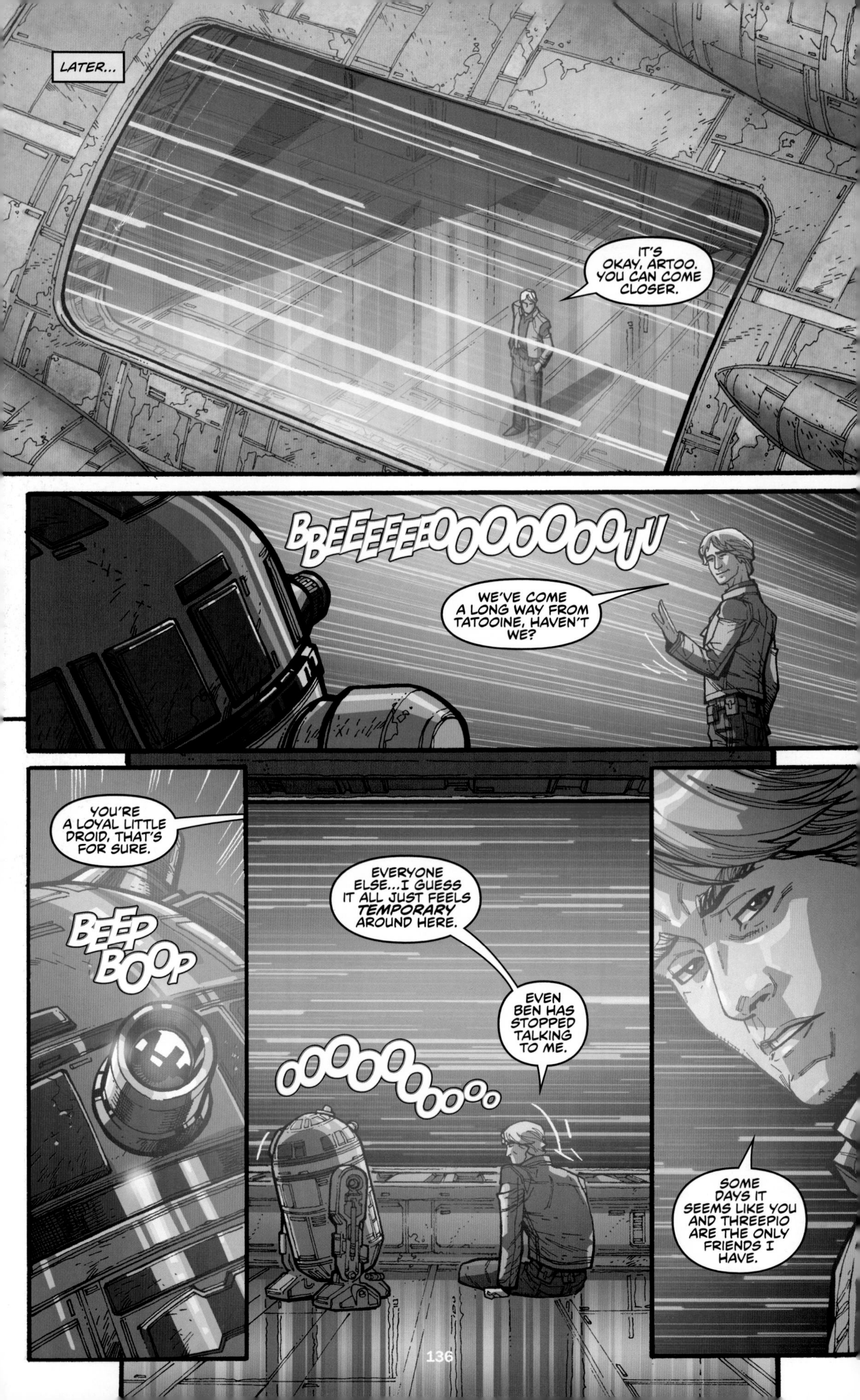
LATER...
IT'S OKAY, ARTOO. YOU CAN COME CLOSER.
BBEEEEEEOOOOOOOOUU
WE'VE COME A LONG WAY FROM TATOOINE, HAVEN'T WE?
YOU'RE A LOYAL LITTLE DROID, THAT'S FOR SURE.
BEEP BOOP
EVERYONE ELSE...I GUESS IT ALL JUST FEELS *TEMPORARY* AROUND HERE.
EVEN BEN HAS STOPPED TALKING TO ME.
OOOOOOOOOOOOOO
SOME DAYS IT SEEMS LIKE YOU AND THREEPIO ARE THE ONLY FRIENDS I HAVE.

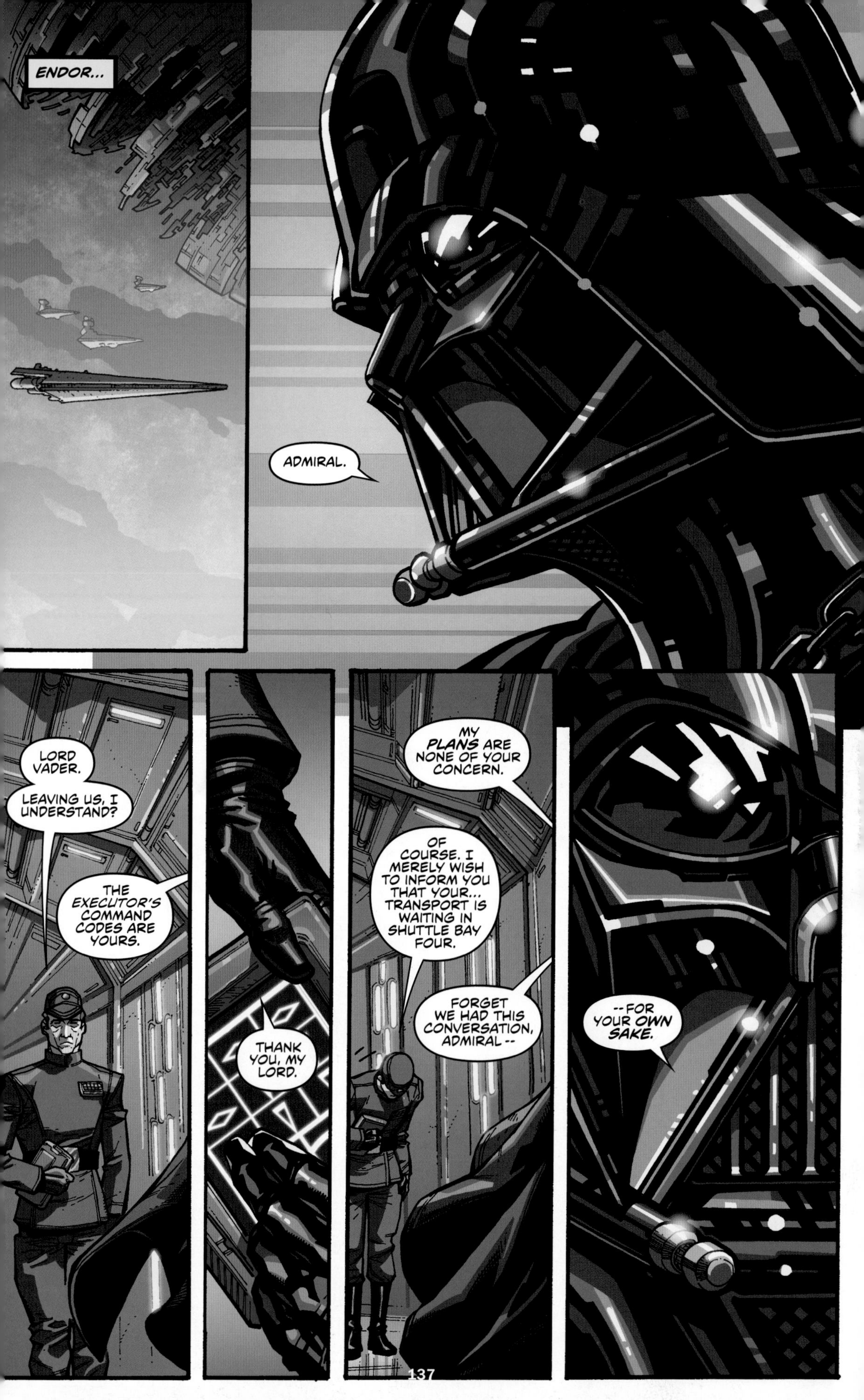
ENDOR...
ADMIRAL.
LORD VADER.
LEAVING US, I UNDERSTAND?
THE EXECUTOR'S COMMAND CODES ARE YOURS.
THANK YOU, MY LORD.
MY PLANS ARE NONE OF YOUR CONCERN.
OF COURSE. I MERELY WISH TO INFORM YOU THAT YOUR... TRANSPORT IS WAITING IN SHUTTLE BAY FOUR.
FORGET WE HAD THIS CONVERSATION, ADMIRAL--
--FOR YOUR OWN SAKE.

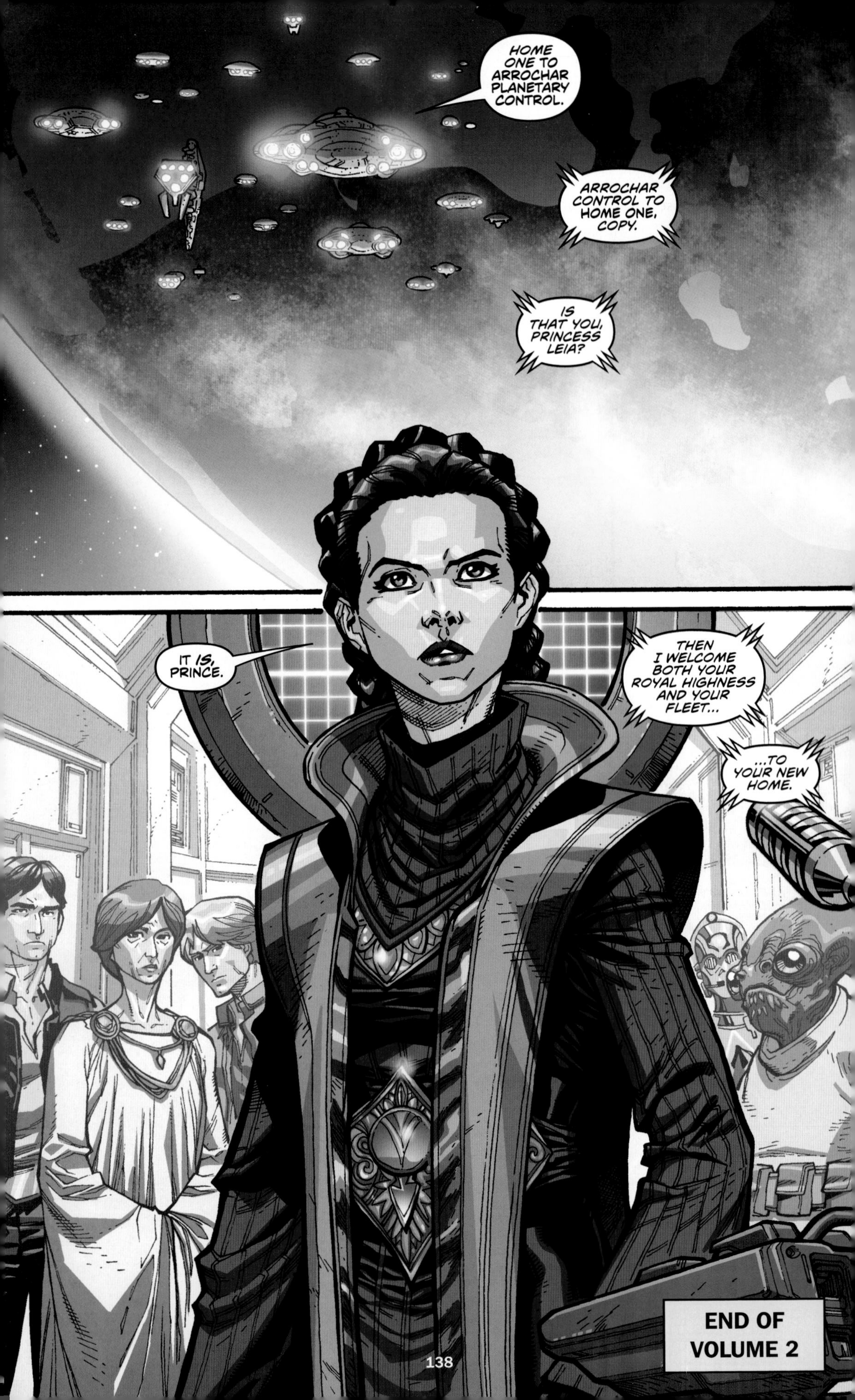
HOME ONE TO ARROCHAR PLANETARY CONTROL.
ARROCHAR CONTROL TO HOME ONE, COPY.
IS THAT YOU, PRINCESS LEIA?
IT IS, PRINCE.
THEN I WELCOME BOTH YOUR ROYAL HIGHNESS AND YOUR FLEET...
...TO YOUR NEW HOME.
END OF VOLUME 2

STAR WARS GRAPHIC NOVEL TIMELINE (IN YEARS)

Dawn of the Jedi—36,000 BSW4

Omnibus: Tales of the Jedi—5,000–3,986 BSW4

Knights of the Old Republic—3,964–3,963 BSW4

The Old Republic—3678, 3653, 3600 BSW4

Lost Tribe of the Sith—2974 BSW4

Knight Errant—1,032 BSW4

Jedi vs. Sith—1,000 BSW4

Jedi: The Dark Side—53 BSW4

Omnibus: Rise of the Sith—33 BSW4

Episode I: The Phantom Menace—32 BSW4

Omnibus: Emissaries and Assassins—32 BSW4

Omnibus: Quinlan Vos—Jedi in Darkness—31–30 BSW4

Omnibus: Menace Revealed—31–22 BSW4

Honor and Duty—22 BSW4

Blood Ties—22 BSW4

Episode II: Attack of the Clones—22 BSW4

Clone Wars—22–19 BSW4

Omnibus: Clone Wars—22–19 BSW4

Clone Wars Adventures—22–19 BSW4

Darth Maul: Death Sentence—20 BSW4

Episode III: Revenge of the Sith—19 BSW4

Purge—19 BSW4

Dark Times—19 BSW4

Omnibus: Droids—5.5 BSW4

Omnibus: Boba Fett—3 BSW4–10 ASW4

Agent of the Empire—3 BSW4

The Force Unleashed—2 BSW4

Omnibus: At War with the Empire—1 BSW4

Episode IV: A New Hope—SW4

Star Wars—0 ASW4

Classic Star Wars—0–3 ASW4

Omnibus: A Long Time Ago. . . .—0–4 ASW4

Empire—0 ASW4

Omnibus: The Other Sons of Tatooine—0 ASW4

Omnibus: Early Victories—0–3 ASW4

Jabba the Hutt: The Art of the Deal—1 ASW4

Episode V: The Empire Strikes Back—3 ASW4

Omnibus: Shadows of the Empire—3.5–4.5 ASW4

Episode VI: Return of the Jedi—4 ASW4

Omnibus: X-Wing Rogue Squadron—4–5 ASW4

The Thrawn Trilogy—9 ASW4

Dark Empire—10 ASW4

Crimson Empire—11 ASW4

Jedi Academy: Leviathan—12 ASW4

Union—19 ASW4

Chewbacca—25 ASW4

Invasion—25 ASW4

Legacy—130–138 ASW4

Dawn of the Jedi
36,000 years before
Star Wars: A New Hope

Old Republic Era
25,000–1000 years before
Star Wars: A New Hope

Rise of the Empire Era
1000–0 years before Star
Wars: A New Hope

Rebellion Era
0–5 years after
Star Wars: A New Hope

New Republic Era
5–25 years after
Star Wars: A New Hope

New Jedi Order Era
25+ years after
Star Wars: A New Hope

Legacy Era
130+ years after
Star Wars: A New Hope

Vector
Crosses four eras in timeline

Volume 1 contains:
Knights of the Old Republic Volume 5
Dark Times Volume 3
Volume 2 contains:
Rebellion Volume 4
Legacy Volume 6

Infinities
Does not apply to timeline

Sergio Aragones Stomps Star Wars
Star Wars Tales
Omnibus: Infinities
Tag and Bink
Star Wars Visionaries

BSW4 = before *Episode IV: A New Hope*. ASW4 = after *Episode IV: A New Hope*.

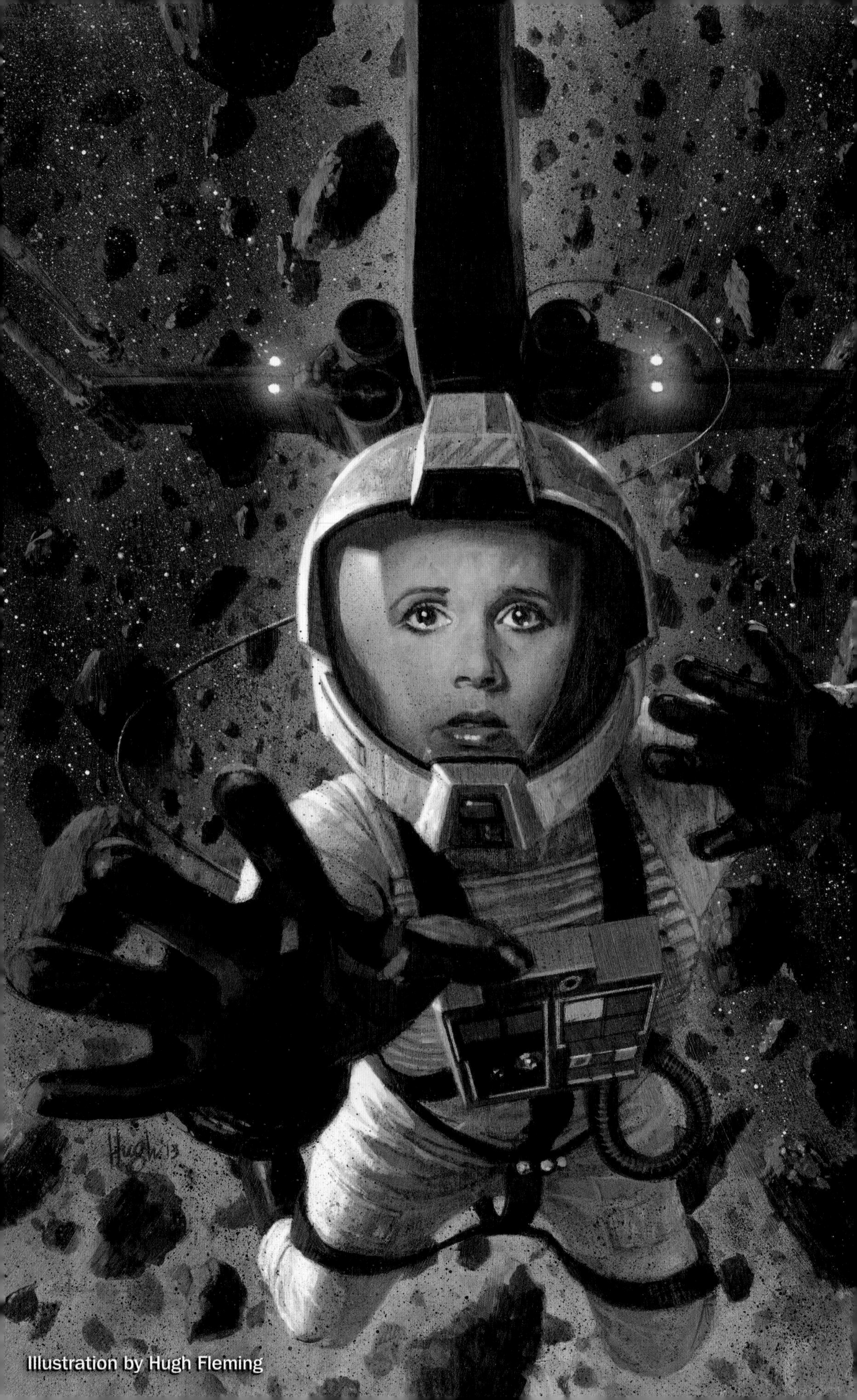

Illustration by Hugh Fleming

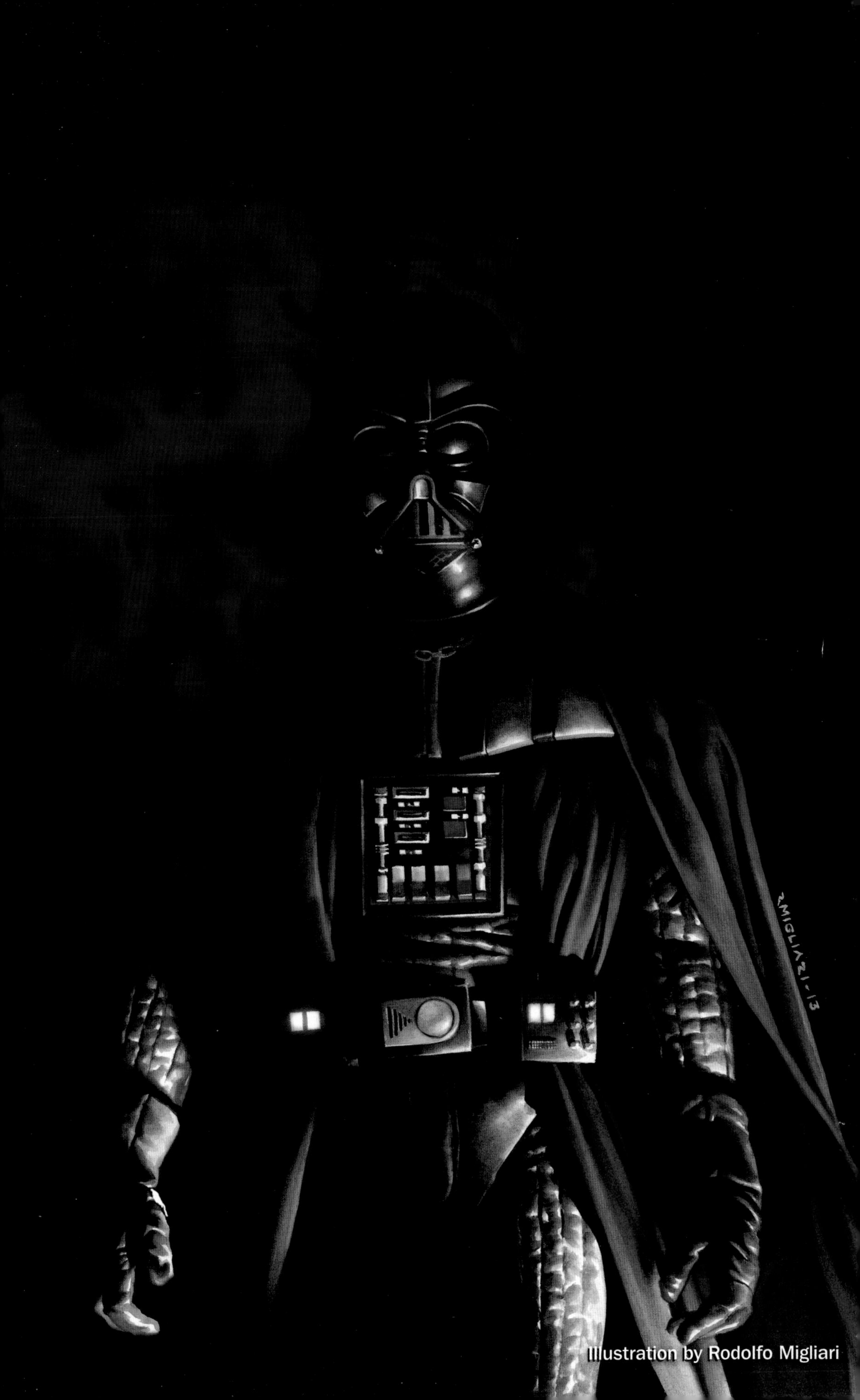
RMIGLIARI-13

Illustration by Rodolfo Migliari

STAR WARS HARDCOVER VOLUMES

STAR WARS
THE THRAWN TRILOGY
TIMOTHY ZAHN

STAR WARS: THE THRAWN TRILOGY

Collects the comics adaptations of Timothy Zahn's best-selling novels *Heir to the Empire*, *Dark Force Rising*, and *The Last Command*. Years after the fall of the Empire, the last of the Emperor's warlords, Admiral Thrawn, is ready to destroy the New Republic—and the odds are stacked against Luke, Leia, and Han!

ISBN 978-1-59582-417-2 | $34.99

STAR WARS
DARK EMPIRE TRILOGY

STAR WARS: DARK EMPIRE TRILOGY

Six years after the fall of the Empire in *Return of the Jedi*, the battle for the galaxy's freedom rages on. The Empire has been mysteriously reborn . . . Princess Leia and Han Solo struggle to hold together the New Republic while Luke Skywalker fights an inner battle as he is drawn to the dark side . . .

ISBN 978-1-59582-612-1 | $29.99

STAR WARS
THE CRIMSON EMPIRE SAGA

STAR WARS: THE CRIMSON EMPIRE SAGA

The blood-soaked tale of the last surviving member of Emperor Palpatine's Royal Guard is now complete! From revenge to redemption, the story of Kir Kanos takes him from the deserts of Yinchorr, to the halls of Imperial power, and to the inner circle of the New Republic.

ISBN 978-1-59582-947-4 | $34.99

STAR WARS

STAR WARS: LEGACY

The future of Star Wars and the future of the Skywalkers is told in John Ostrander and Jan Duursema's acclaimed *Star Wars: Legacy*. A Sith legion has conquered the Empire, the Jedi have been scattered, and the galaxy is divided. Into this comes Cade Skywalker, heir to the Skywalker legacy . . .

Book 1: ISBN 978-1-61655-178-0 | $34.99
Book 2: ISBN 978-1-61655-209-1 | $34.99
Book 3: ISBN 978-1-61655-260-2 | $34.99

STAR WARS
DARTH VADER AND THE LOST COMMAND

STAR WARS: DARTH VADER AND THE LOST COMMAND

Still haunted by the death of Anakin Skywalker's beloved Padmé, Darth Vader is tasked with a mission to locate a lost Imperial expeditionary force—led by the son of Vader's rising nemesis, Moff Tarkin. Vader's journey is compounded by traitors among his crew and the presence of the mysterious Lady Saro.

ISBN 978-1-59582-778-4 | $24.99

STAR WARS
DARTH VADER AND THE GHOST PRISON

STAR WARS: DARTH VADER AND THE GHOST PRISON

A traitorous uprising against the Galactic Empire leaves Emperor Palpatine close to death. Saving the Emperor—and the Empire—appears to be a lost cause . . . unless Darth Vader and a young lieutenant can uncover the secrets of the Jedi Council and locate the mysterious "Ghost Prison."

ISBN 978-1-61655-059-2 | $24.99

STAR WARS: DARTH VADER AND THE NINTH ASSASSIN

Eight assassins hired to murder Darth Vader—eight assassins dead. Now the man who enlisted them seeks a ninth assassin. When it comes to avenging his son, no sacrifice is too great to acquire the one man who can kill the Dark Lord of the Sith . . . The hunt for Darth Vader is on!

ISBN 978-1-61655-207-7 | $24.99

DARK HORSE BOOKS

AVAILABLE AT YOUR LOCAL COMICS SHOP OR BOOKSTORE!

To find a comics shop in your area, call 1-888-266-4226
For more information or to order direct: • On the web: DarkHorse.com • E-mail: mailorder@darkhorse.com • Phone: 1-800-862-0052 Mon.–Fri. 9 AM to 5 PM Pacific Time

STAR WARS OMNIBUS COLLECTIONS

STAR WARS: TALES OF THE JEDI

Including the *Tales of the Jedi* stories "The Golden Age of the Sith," "The Freedon Nadd Uprising," and "Knights of the Old Republic," these huge omnibus editions are the ultimate introduction to the ancient history of the *Star Wars* universe!

Volume 1: ISBN 978-1-59307-830-0 | $24.99   **Volume 2: ISBN 978-1-59307-911-6 | $24.99**

STAR WARS: KNIGHTS OF THE OLD REPUBLIC

Padawan Zayne Carrick is suddenly a fugitive framed for the murder of his fellow Jedi-in-training. Little does the galaxy know, Zayne's own Masters are behind the massacre and dead set on recovering him before he can reveal the truth.

Volume 1: ISBN 978-1-61655-206-0 | $24.99   **Volume 3: ISBN 978-1-61655-227-5 | $24.99**
Volume 2: ISBN 978-1-61655-213-8 | $24.99

STAR WARS: RISE OF THE SITH

These thrilling tales illustrate the events leading up to *Episode I: The Phantom Menace*, when the Jedi Knights preserved peace and justice . . . as well as prevented the return of the Sith.

ISBN 978-1-59582-228-4 | $24.99

STAR WARS: EMISSARIES AND ASSASSINS

Discover more stories featuring Anakin Skywalker, Amidala, Obi-Wan, and Qui-Gon set during the time of *Episode I: The Phantom Menace*!

ISBN 978-1-59582-229-1 | $24.99

STAR WARS: MENACE REVEALED

Included here are one-shot adventures, short story arcs, specialty issues, and early *Dark Horse Extra* comic strips! All of these tales take place after *Episode I: The Phantom Menace*, and lead up to *Episode II: Attack of the Clones*.

ISBN 978-1-59582-273-4 | $24.99

STAR WARS: QUINLAN VOS—JEDI IN DARKNESS

From his first appearance as a mind-wiped amnesiac to his triumphant passage to the rank of Jedi Master, few Jedi had more brushes with the powers of the dark side and the evil of the underworld than Quinlan Vos.

ISBN 978-1-59582-555-1 | $24.99

STAR WARS: THE COMPLETE SAGA—EPISODES I THROUGH VI

The comics adaptations of the complete *Star Wars* film saga—in one volume! From the first fateful encounter with Darth Maul to Luke Skywalker's victory over the Sith and Darth Vader's redemption, it's all here.

ISBN 978-1-59582-832-3 | $24.99

STAR WARS: CLONE WARS

The Jedi Knights who were once protectors of the peace must become generals, leading the clone armies of the Republic to war! These stories follow *Attack of the Clones* and feature Jedi heroes Obi-Wan Kenobi, Anakin Skywalker, Mace Windu, and Quinlan Vos.

Volume 1: The Republic Goes to War ISBN 978-1-59582-927-6 | $24.99
Volume 2: The Enemy on All Sides ISBN 978-1-59582-958-0 | $24.99
Volume 3: The Republic Falls ISBN 978-1-59582-980-1 | $24.99

STAR WARS: DARK TIMES

The struggles of the Jedi intertwine with those of others now living in fear, including the diverse crew of a smuggling ship, the *Uhumele*, and a Nosaurian whose troubles begin when the Clone Wars end.

Volume 1: ISBN 978-1-61655-251-0 | $24.99   **Volume 2: ISBN 978-1-61655-252-7 | $24.99**

AVAILABLE AT YOUR LOCAL COMICS SHOP OR BOOKSTORE!

To find a comics shop in your area, call 1-888-266-4226
For more information or to order direct: • On the web: DarkHorse.com • E-mail: mailorder@darkhorse.com
• Phone: 1-800-862-0052 Mon.–Fri. 9 AM to 5 PM Pacific Time

STAR WARS © Lucasfilm Ltd. & ™ (BL 8000)

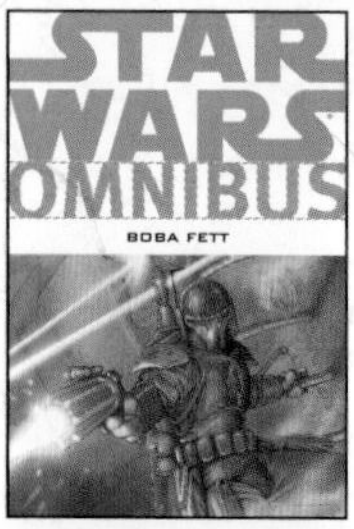
STAR WARS
OMNIBUS
BOBA FETT

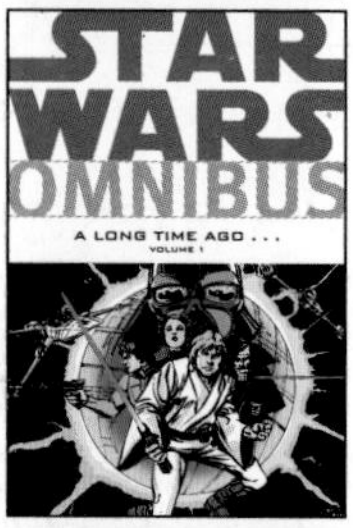
STAR WARS
OMNIBUS
A LONG TIME AGO . . .

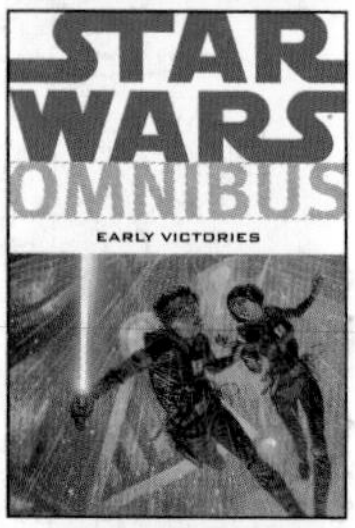
STAR WARS
OMNIBUS
EARLY VICTORIES

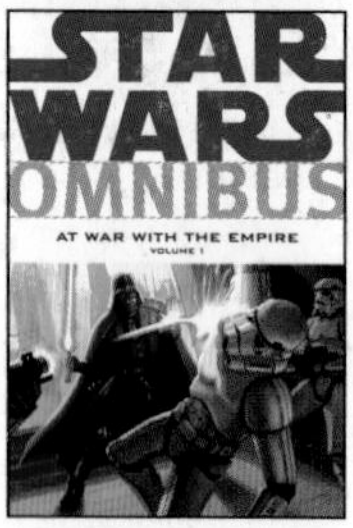
STAR WARS
OMNIBUS
AT WAR WITH THE EMPIRE

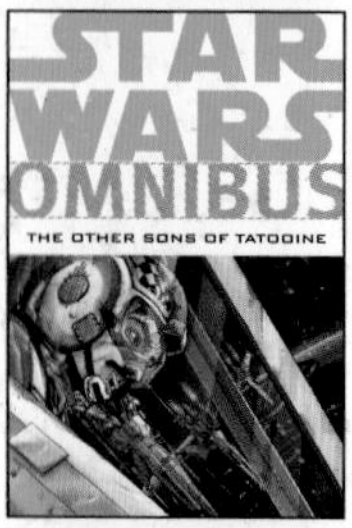
STAR WARS
OMNIBUS
THE OTHER SONS OF TATOOINE

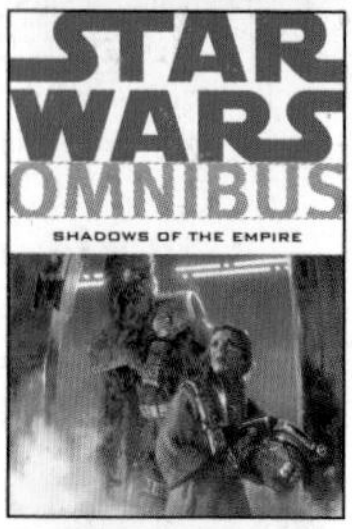
STAR WARS
OMNIBUS
SHADOWS OF THE EMPIRE

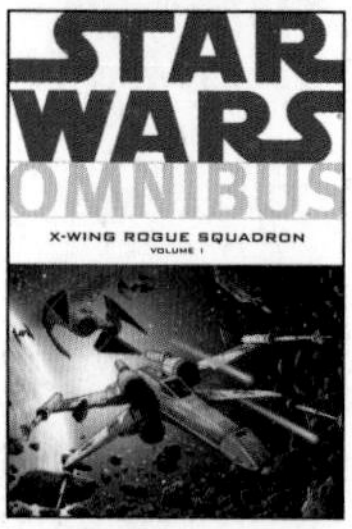
STAR WARS
OMNIBUS
X-WING ROGUE SQUADRON

STAR WARS OMNIBUS COLLECTIONS

STAR WARS: BOBA FETT

Boba Fett, the most feared, most respected, and most loved bounty hunter in the galaxy, now has all of his comics stories collected into one massive volume!

ISBN 978-1-59582-418-9 | $24.99

STAR WARS: INFINITIES

Three different tales where *one thing* happens differently than it did in the original trilogy of *Star Wars* films. Luke Skywalker, Princess Leia, Han Solo, and Darth Vader are launched onto new trajectories!

ISBN 978-1-61655-078-3 | $24.99

STAR WARS: A LONG TIME AGO. . . .

Star Wars: A Long Time Ago. . . . omnibus volumes feature classic *Star Wars* stories not seen in over twenty years! Originally printed by Marvel Comics, these recolored stories are sure to please Star Wars fans both new and old.

Volume 1: ISBN 978-1-59582-486-8 | $24.99
Volume 2: ISBN 978-1-59582-554-4 | $24.99
Volume 3: ISBN 978-1-59582-639-8 | $24.99
Volume 4: ISBN 978-1-59582-640-4 | $24.99
Volume 5: ISBN 978-1-59582-801-9 | $24.99

STAR WARS: WILD SPACE

Rare and previously uncollected stories! Contains work from some of comics' most famous writers and artists (including Alan Moore, Chris Claremont, Archie Goodwin, Walt Simonson, and Alan Davis), plus stories featuring the greatest heroes and villains of *Star Wars*!

Volume 1: ISBN 978-1-61655-146-9 | $24.99
Volume 2: ISBN 978-1-61655-147-6 | $24.99

STAR WARS: EARLY VICTORIES

Following the destruction of the first Death Star, Luke Skywalker and Princess Leia find there are many more battles to be fought against the Empire and Darth Vader!

ISBN 978-1-59582-172-0 | $24.99

STAR WARS: AT WAR WITH THE EMPIRE

Stories of the early days of the Rebel Alliance and the beginnings of its war with the Empire—tales of the *Star Wars* galaxy set before, during, and after the events in *Star Wars: A New Hope!*

Volume 1: ISBN 978-1-59582-699-2 | $24.99
Volume 2: ISBN 978-1-59582-777-7 | $24.99

STAR WARS: THE OTHER SONS OF TATOOINE

Luke's story has been told time and again, but what about the journeys of his boyhood friends, Biggs Darklighter and Janek "Tank" Sunber? Both are led to be heroes in their own right: one of the Rebellion, the other of the Empire . . .

ISBN 978-1-59582-866-8 | $24.99

STAR WARS: SHADOWS OF THE EMPIRE

Featuring all your favorite characters from the *Star Wars* trilogy—Luke Skywalker, Princess Leia, and Han Solo—this volume includes stories written by acclaimed novelists Timothy Zahn and Steve Perry!

ISBN 978-1-59582-434-9 | $24.99

STAR WARS: X-WING ROGUE SQUADRON

The starfighters of the Rebel Alliance become the defenders of a new Republic in these stories featuring Wedge Antilles and his team of ace pilots known throughout the galaxy as Rogue Squadron.

Volume 1: ISBN 978-1-59307-572-9 | $24.99
Volume 2: ISBN 978-1-59307-619-1 | $24.99
Volume 3: ISBN 978-1-59307-776-1 | $24.99

AVAILABLE AT YOUR LOCAL COMICS SHOP OR BOOKSTORE!

To find a comics shop in your area, call 1-888-266-4226

For more information or to order direct: • On the web: DarkHorse.com • E-mail: mailorder@darkhorse.com • Phone: 1-800-862-0052 Mon.–Fri. 9 AM to 5 PM Pacific Time • STAR WARS © Lucasfilm Ltd. & ™ (BL 8001)